EXPLORATIONS IN AMERICAN HISTORY

A SKILLS APPROACH

MARK A. STOLER

University of Vermont

MARSHALL TRUE

University of Vermont

EXPLORATIONS IN AMERICAN HISTORY

A SKILLS APPROACH

VOLUME II
Since 1865

ALFRED A. KNOPF
NEW YORK

First Edition

9876543

Copyright © 1987 by Newbery Award Records, Inc.

Library of Congress Cataloging-in-Publication Data

Stoler, Mark A.
Explorations in American History.

Contents: v. 1. To 1865 -- v. 2. Since 1865.
1. United States--Historiography.   2. United States--
History--Sources.   I. True, Marshall.   II. Title.
E175.S76   1986   973'.032   86-10458
                   ISBN 0-394-35281-5 (v. 1)
                   ISBN 0-394-35471-0 (v. 2)
        ISBN 0-394-36567-4 (Teacher's Edition, v. 1)
        ISBN 0-394-36568-2 (Teacher's Edition, v. 2)

Text design by Susan Phillips

Manufactured in the United States of America

For Charon

MT

For Those Who Helped Me Walk Again

MAS

AND TO OUR STUDENTS AT THE UNIVERSITY OF VERMONT

PREFACE

What is history? Usually, it is defined simply as the study of the past. Actually, it is much more.

History is, first of all, the study of humankind's *entire* past, the study of *all* events—political, social, economic, cultural, scientific, intellectual, material, or abstract—that have taken place over the thousands of years of recorded time. History is also a way of thinking and a way of interpreting the present as well as the past. As such, it is not only one of the oldest disciplines to which men and women have turned their minds and efforts but also an extremely rich, complex, and exciting one. It demands a high level of knowledge, thought, creativity, and skill. In return, it offers much.

History can help you rediscover past ideas with continued relevance for the present. These ideas range from the technological (as evidenced by our new interest in the ancient windmill and wind power as an alternate energy source) to the ideological (as shown by our continued belief in the concepts articulated in the centuries-old Declaration of Independence and Constitution). History can also help you see parallels between past and present and the interconnectedness of human beings over time as well as space. It is interesting to note, for example, that our generation is by no means the first in American history to be faced with numerous political, economic, social, and international problems. Corruption and abuses of power, unemployment and high interest rates, racism and sexism, the Cold War and the nuclear arms race with the Soviet Union are indeed "current events." Yet they are also symptomatic of broader problems that were as evident and important in 1886, or 1786, or 1686 as they are in 1986.

Perhaps most important, the study of history can explain the processes by which our society has reached its present state and even the processes by which you as an individual have become what you are. The importance of such knowledge cannot be overemphasized, for it is impossible to know where you are, or where you are going, unless you are first aware of where you have been and how you got from that point to the present. The continuing popularity of genealogy, or tracing one's "roots," is impressive testimony to public awareness of this truth. In the broadest sense, then, history is a way of learning about the present as well as the past.

Finally, history is inevitable. We are all forced to live in it and relate to it. Consciously or not, each individual is both an actor on the historical stage and a historian. We all interpret the past in light of our own present and we all act on the basis of our knowledge, or lack thereof, regarding that past. The only questions are how we accomplish these processes and how aware we are of them. To be ignorant of history is not to avoid it but to become its victim.

This does not mean that historical knowledge is the universal panacea. The study of history has not solved—nor can it solve—the world's problems. Neither can it predict the future. But as this preface attempts to show, history is much more than simple storytelling and the presentation of irrelevant facts from the past, and it involves much more than mere rote memorization. It is not something simple, linear, one-dimensional, or completely objective.

A survey course is designed to introduce you to these numerous facets of history and to provide you with a useful, basic overview of the historical process (in this case as it has applied to the United States). It can also enable you to develop a series of skills that are of basic importance to the study not only of history but also of other aspects of the humanities and social sciences; that are, in fact, vital to a successful undergraduate education and, we believe, to life itself.

This particular volume is unique in its emphasis on the acquisition of those skills. It is primarily devoted to learning and applying them, and it has been designed to mesh with your textbook readings, lectures, and class discussions.

The most important skills for historical study are those of clear and critical reading, thinking, and writing. Each chapter in this book contains both explanations and exercises designed to develop your abilities in these areas, and your instructor may ask you to complete some or all of these exercises. You should realize in this regard that reading and thinking clearly are inseparable from writing clearly, that poor writing is often a reflection of incomplete reading and illogical thinking, and that efforts to clarify your writing will often help to improve your reading and clarify your thoughts. You should also realize that the value of historical knowledge depends on the ability to *communicate* that knowledge to others, and that such communication requires the ability to compose prose that others can follow.

Along with such general skills, this volume will introduce you to a series of more specific skills, the mastery of which is essential to the study of history. These include the ability to understand and use a university library; to identify, question and analyze different types of secondary and primary sources; to cite historical material correctly; to present historical data using maps, charts, and graphs; to work with a range of nontraditional sources, from architectural drawings to films; to form intelligent hypotheses; to deal with cause-and-effect relationships over time; and to understand and use conflicting historical interpretations of the past. The acquisition of these skills will give you a deeper understanding of the material studied in this course and will show you the breadth of the discipline of history. It should also teach you a great deal about gathering and using the information you need to live in a complex world.

We originally wrote this volume in 1978 as part of a general revision of our U.S. history survey courses at the University of Vermont. Since then we have consistently revised it in response to student and faculty suggestions as well as our own experiences in the courses. This edition incorporates our most recent revisions. Many of them have been added so as to make the volume usable in any U.S. history survey course, rather than simply our own.

From the inception of this project we have been indebted to the University of Vermont's Instructional Development Center. In 1978, it provided both encouragement for this new project and financial assistance through an Instructional Incentive Grant. In 1980, the Center's newly established Curriculum Publication Series produced our first formal edition of this volume, and in 1983–1984 the Center provided financial assistance for additional revisions. We would like to express our thanks to John Clarke, Barbara Collins, David Holmes, Alton Roberts, and Lynn Tarbutton of the Center for all their help and support.

Numerous colleagues on the University of Vermont campus provided invaluable assistance, comments, and criticisms in the preparation of this volume. Within our own department, we are particularly indebted to Connie McGovern, Jerry Felt, Sam Hand, Susan Jackson, and Neil Stout for team-teaching the courses with us, suffering through some of our early experiments and mistakes, making contributions to individual chapters, and offering numerous suggestions. We would also like to thank our chairpersons past and present, Wolfe Schmokel and Bill Metcalfe, for their encouragement and support. In other departments, Mary Jane Dickerson, Karen LeFevre, and Frank Manchel (of English), Ted Miles and Hal Meeks (of Geography), and the entire reference staff at Bailey-Howe Library offered important insights and suggestions in the preparation of individual chapters. Our deepest appreciation goes to all of them, as well as to Stuart Johnson of Addison-Wesley for his interest and support in the early preparation of these volumes, and to Fred H. Burns of Alfred A. Knopf, Inc., who guided them through the final stages of publication.

Finally, we would like to thank the students in our U.S. history survey courses between 1978 and 1986 who participated in, and sometimes suffered from, our numerous experiments with the skills approach. Their comments, criticisms, and detailed suggestions proved invaluable in preparing these volumes. These volumes are thus not only *for* our students, but also partly and genuinely *by* them. Encouraging student participation in their own learning is in large measure the reason we wrote *Explorations in American History* in the first place, and it is therefore appropriate that this volume be dedicated to them.

MARSHALL TRUE
MARK A. STOLER

CONTENTS

INTRODUCTION
HOW TO USE THIS VOLUME

This volume is designed to help you learn a series of important skills associated with the study of history in general, and United States history in particular. It consists of ten chapters. Each chapter is divided into three basic sections and is linked by title, introductory material, and examples to specific time periods examined within any introductory course surveying the history of the United States.

The first section of each chapter introduces and explains the skills being discussed within the context of historical events and issues that took place during one of those time periods. Often, this section is accompanied by supplementary material (such as documents, maps, excerpts, or essays) provided either within or at the end of the chapter. This supplementary material offers you examples of the types of historical evidence being analyzed in the chapter. It also forms the basis for the two other sections of the chapter (the written assignments and the additional questions to consider), and it should be read carefully.

The second section of each chapter contains numbered instructions for written assignments. Your professor will tell you which of the numbered assignments to complete, and he or she may very well change some of them and provide you with more specific guidance. If you do not receive instructions, we advise you to complete the written assignments on your own as a way of practicing and mastering the skills under discussion. Since most of these assignments are essays, you can also improve your writing skills. Where specific short answers are required, your professor should be able to provide you with a list of the correct ones. At all times you should make sure you understand any specific instructions given by your professor before you proceed with a written assignment.

The third section of each chapter contains numbered additional questions for you to consider regarding the skills and written assignments you have just completed studying. As in the previous section, your professor may give you directions about how to handle these questions. In large lecture courses, you may be asked simply to think about them on your own, or to be prepared to talk about them in weekly discussion groups. In smaller courses, your instructor may lead a discussion of some or all of them in class, or ask you to lead such a discussion. As in the previous section, you should make sure you understand any instructions given by your professor before proceeding.

We hope that you will be interested in examining some of the historical problems and skills presented in this volume in greater depth. Just as the course you are taking is an introduction to historical study, so is this volume. The hope shared by your instructors and by us is that your experiences with both this volume and this course will encourage you to pursue your studies in greater depth on your own.

EXPLORATIONS IN AMERICAN HISTORY
A SKILLS APPROACH

1

RECONSTRUCTION AND RACE RELATIONS AFTER THE CIVIL WAR

QUESTIONING, USE OF THE LIBRARY, HISTORICAL REFERENCE, AND FORM

By 1898, black Americans had good reason to be disillusioned. With the military defeat of the Confederacy and the passage of the Thirteenth Amendment to the Constitution in 1865, President Lincoln's 1863 Emancipation Proclamation became a reality; formerly slaves for life, blacks were now free people. Soon thereafter, the passage of the Fourteenth and Fifteenth Amendments to the Constitution granted them citizenship and the right to vote. Congressional legislation and the continued presence of Union troops in the South under the "Radical" Reconstruction program seemed to illustrate a strong determination on the part of the federal government to enforce these amendments and to guarantee the former slaves full equality and participation in the political, economic, and social life of the nation.

During the 1870s and 1880s, however, the federal government gradually reversed itself. Troops were removed from the South, legislation was allowed to lapse, and former Confederates were allowed to regain power. While sharecropping and tenant farming made blacks virtual serfs to their former white masters, a series of state and local laws totally segregated and disenfranchised them. During the 1880s and 1890s, the Supreme Court sanctioned this segregation and disenfranchisement by ruling that Con-

1

gress had no jurisdiction over private discrimination (the *Civil Rights Cases* of 1883), by declaring that "separate but equal" facilities did not violate the Fourteenth Amendment (*Plessy* v. *Ferguson,* 1896), and by stating that neither literacy tests nor poll taxes violated the Fifteenth Amendment (*Williams* v. *Mississippi,* 1898). By the turn of the century, blacks had thus lost most of their hard-won rights and were virtually slaves again.

Your textbook will provide you with a good deal of information on this rather dismal chapter in the nation's past; in the process, it should lead you to question two commonly held "myths" about American history: that Radical Reconstruction was an unmitigated disaster and that American history in general shows a linear development and expansion of democratic rights for all American people. In reality, Radical Reconstruction had many successes as well as failures, and the history of black Americans during this time reveals a series of high and low points in the attainment of equal rights which were anything but linear in their emergence and development.

To question these myths is not merely to correct popular misconceptions about the past. It is also to *revise* previous historical accounts on the basis of both new evidence and new frames of reference. Historians writing during the 1930s, for example, were reinforced in their negative assessment of Radical Reconstruction by the prevailing racist attitudes of the society within which they lived; historians writing today live in a different environment, and this leads them to different conclusions from their predecessors even when they use the same evidence.

This process of historical revision and interpretation is explained in greater detail in Chapter 10 of this volume (your textbook may also explain it in special sections). What is important for you to note here is that such a process exists and that what appears to be fact to one generation is often myth to the next. You should also realize that historical facts do not "speak for themselves"—that they make sense only when placed in a framework of interpretation. Your textbook presents you with the most recent interpretations of the American past, but its conclusions, too, may in time be considered incorrect and subject to revision.

History, in short, is far from being an objective and unchanging study of the past. The conclusions we reach are determined to a large extent by the era in which we live and by the questions that we ask. In this regard, one should never accept what is written about the past as "truth" simply because it appears on a printed page. Any historical conclusions are subject to careful scrutiny and disagreement.

QUESTIONING

In addition to being questioned because it is a product of its era, a textbook also needs to be questioned because it is only a *survey introduction* rather than a definitive work on a topic and is therefore limited in its coverage.

Discussion of the Thirteenth, Fourteenth, and Fifteenth Amendments only within the context of race relations, for example, ignores numerous important aspects of these measures. How many of those aspects does your text explain, and to what extent?

One way to answer these questions is to read the *actual documents* being referred to, as well as the textbook description of them, and to compare what is in the text with what is in the documents themselves. Documents are one type of *primary source,* the basic raw material for all historical writing (which is referred to as *secondary*); they should be consulted whenever possible (see the other chapters of this volume, especially Chapter 6, for additional information on primary sources).

In this case, the relevant documents are readily available, for the entire Constitution is reprinted in the back of your textbook. Turn to it and read the three amendments yourself, particularly the critical Fourteenth Amendment. Note that it makes no mention of race or color, that it has five separate sections, and that these sections go far beyond the issue of citizenship for blacks. Why were these sections included? What were their purposes, and what do they say about this amendment?

Now turn to the relevant pages in your textbook and see if the explanation it gives of the Fourteenth Amendment accounts for the totality of the document. Such an explanation would deal not only with the issue of black rights but also with the struggles between President Johnson and the Congress, between the northern and southern states, between moderate and radical Republicans, and between Democrats and Republicans. It would also deal with the *consequences* of this critical amendment, be they immediate, long-term, expected, or unexpected.

In this regard, you should note that some of the most important consequences of the Fourteenth Amendment had little if anything to do with race relations. In defining U.S. citizenship and making the federal government the protector of citizens' rights against abuses by state governments, the amendment struck a mortal blow at the old states' rights doctrine, reversed previous views regarding the most likely source of tyranny (from the federal to the state governments), drastically altered the Constitution and the nature of the federal system, and thereby laid the essential basis for the emergence of present-day federal power. People living at the time were clearly aware of some of these implications (it is no accident, for example, that after the Civil War and passage of this amendment the country was officially referred to as *this* rather than *these* United States), but could any of them have foreseen that this amendment would be used in the late nineteenth century to declare unconstitutional state laws regulating corporate activity, or that it would be used in the twentieth century to justify enormous extensions of federal power? Historical events, in short, have numerous unplanned consequences over time as well as numerous causes, and a full understanding of these consequences and causes requires both careful reading of the available documents and constant questioning. In and of itself, no textbook can provide you with such an understanding.

Even without examination of an actual document, an inquiring student should be able to see that a textbook usually raises more questions than it answers. In regard to the Fourteenth Amendment, for example, does your text tell you *who* wrote it, *where* and *when* it was written (as opposed to passed), *what* was in the original draft and whether it differed from the final draft, *why* it was written, and *how* it became part of the Constitution? Historians, of course, constantly ask questions of the "who, when, where, and what" variety, but it is important to realize that they also ask how and why events occurred and that the very process of asking these two questions often leads to more questions of the first variety. As a student of history, you should constantly be questioning what you read and in the process become aware of the limitations and biases of all written material.

THE LIBRARY

As you question what you read, you will need to know *where* and *how* to find the answers. Where to find them is clear—the library. This building is the heart of any institution of higher education and should be the focal point of your intellectual endeavors. In and of itself, however, the library is only a building. By learning to use it intelligently you will increase dramatically the benefits to be derived from your work as a student. And intelligent use requires knowledge of what the library contains, how it is organized, and how to find what you want.

The first area to explore is the *public* or *card catalogue,* a compilation of thousands of index cards listing all the books and periodicals in your library along with their location by *call number.* The drawers holding these cards are usually located in a prominent and easily accessible section of the library; they may be arranged in two alphabetized sections, one by author and title and one by subject. The author/title section is used when you know the author and/or title of a book and need merely to discover its library location; the subject section is used when you want to explore the library's holdings on a particular topic. When using the author/title catalogue to find the location of a book, you will be wise to double-check under the author's name if you do not find a title entry, and vice versa. When using the subject catalogue, you should first consult the large red volumes nearby, the *Library of Congress Subject Headings,* to discover the terms used in the catalogue for the area you are studying. (Many University libraries are replacing their card catalogues with computers, which should increase the speed and efficiency with which you can use the library's holdings.)

While the subject catalogue appears to be the most appropriate place to find materials capable of answering questions, you can usually obtain more relevant information in a shorter period of time by using the author/title catalogue to find the location of specialized *reference* works. In most libraries, these works are located in a special *reference section* containing a large number of noncirculating volumes of exceptional value to you. You can often find specific data far more quickly by using reference encyclopedias and dictionaries than by starting with the subject catalogue. Reference bibliographies and indexes can give you a full listing of scholarly articles and books published in your area of interest as well as valuable information about the contents of these works. We therefore recommend consulting the appropriate reference works *first,* using the card catalogue only to find their location, and then, after you have completed your reference research, to discover whether and where your library has the specific books and articles that the reference volumes have shown to be relevant to your topic. If your library does not have a work you desire, the reference section can often be used to order specific materials via interlibrary loan. The librarian can help you with this and with finding specific reference works of value; you should consult this individual whenever you need assistance.

For the study of history, there are literally thousands of reference works available. Many of these are listed and explained in Helen J. Poulton, *The Historian's Handbook: A Descriptive Guide to Reference Works* (Norman, Okla.: University of Oklahoma Press, 1972), and in the history sections of Eugene Sheehy's *Guide to Reference Works,* rev. 8th ed., by C. M. Winchell, ed. (Chicago: American Library Association, 1976) and Carl M. White's *Sources of Information in the Social Sciences,* 2nd ed. (Chicago: American Library Association, 1973). For the study of American history on a survey level, however, the number of pivotal works is substantially smaller and quite manageable. These works are explained directly below.

If you want to check or obtain specific facts about events in U.S. history you should consult Thomas H. Johnson, *The Oxford Companion to American History* (New York: Oxford University Press, 1966) or Louise B. Ketz, ed., *Dictionary of American History,* rev. ed., 8 vols. (New York: Scribner's, 1976). For a listing and explanation of facts in chronological as opposed to alphabetical order, see Gordon Carruth, ed., *The Encyclopedia of American Facts and Dates,* 7th ed. (New York: Crowell, 1979), or Richard B. Morris, ed., *Encyclopedia of American History,* 6th ed. (New York: Harper & Row, 1982).

For biographical research, Allen Johnson and Dumas Malone, eds., *Dictionary of American Biography,* 20 vols., supplements 1–7, and complete index guide (New York: Scribner's, 1944–1981), commonly known as the *DAB,* is indispensable. It provides biographical sketches of thousands of prominent figures in American history, and each sketch closes with a discussion of the best sources for additional research on that person's life. A newer work, edited by Edward T. James, Barbara Sicherman, and Carol Hurd Green, is *Notable American Women,* 4 vols. (Cambridge: Harvard University Press, 1971, 1980); it fills some notable gaps in the *DAB* and should be the first work you consult if your subject is a woman.

If you need to research a topic or individual in depth, the information provided in these works will not be adequate. Instead, you should consult specific bibliographies and indexes of works in U.S. history so that you can compose a preliminary list of appropriate sources to look up in the card catalogue and read. The *first* such bibliography to consult for books and articles in U.S. history is Frank Freidel, ed., *The Harvard Guide to American History,* 2nd rev. ed., 2 vols. (Cambridge: Belknap Press of Harvard University Press, 1974). If you need more extensive coverage, use the New York Public Library's *Dictionary Catalogue of the History of the Americas,* 28 vols. and 9-vol. supplement (Boston: G. K. Hall, 1961, 1973), and the U.S. Library of Congress's *A Guide to the Study of the United States of America* (Washington, D.C.: U.S. Government Printing Office, 1960, 1976). Special bibliographies on specific subjects in U.S. history are also available and are described in the previously cited works by Poulton, Sheehy, and White.

One of the most important but commonly ignored sources of detailed information consists of *articles* published in *scholarly journals.* These articles are particularly useful because they deal with very specific subjects in depth and often summarize in twenty to fifty pages an analysis also published in a book-length study. They are commonly ignored because individual articles are not listed in the card catalogue; therefore many students do not know how to find them. Here specific reference works can be exceptionally valuable.

One common mistake that many students make is to confuse a *scholarly* with a *popular* article and to consult a key index for popular articles, the *Reader's Guide to Periodical Literature,* when they really need a guide to scholarly journals. The *Reader's Guide* lists only articles in mass-circulation magazines; while these magazines are often valuable as primary sources (see Chapter 6), their articles are in no way valid historical analyses and should not be used as such.

Numerous indexes list and comment on scholarly articles published in historical journals. For the study of U.S. history, the most valuable index is *America: History and Life.* In addition to being limited to American history, this annual index provides summaries, or *abstracts,* of individual articles. These abstracts enable you to tell, before reading it, whether a specific article is truly relevant to your topic. One section of *America: History and Life* also lists book reviews that will help you tell whether a particular book is relevant. Abstracts of some of these reviews can be found in the annual *Book Review Digest.*

To make full and proper use of these or any article index, you should read in their introductory sections how they are organized and the meaning of their abbreviations. Since the card catalogue lists only periodicals, not specific articles within them, you will also need to copy from the index the article author and title, the name of the journal, and the volume number, date, and page numbers for the specific article you wish to consult. You can then use the card catalogue to find the call number of the journal you need, locate the appropriate volume, and look up the article. Many libraries have separate periodical sections and most libraries maintain listings of journals that will enable you to bypass the card catalogue. These listings are designed to make use of the periodicals collection easier and less time-consuming. Ask a librarian to explain the easiest approach to locating journals in the library you are using. Keep in mind, however, that *only* the periodical index can provide you with information on the article itself.

Other important reference works provide detailed information on specific types of historical material. *The New York Times Index* is invaluable for finding information in America's "newspaper of record." For geographic information, consult Charles Oscar Paullin's *Atlas of the Historical Geography of the United States* (Washington, D.C., and New York: Carnegie Institute and American Geographical Society, 1932); W. Kirk Reynolds, ed., *Atlas of American History*, 2nd rev. ed. (New York: Scribner's, 1984); or Clifford L. and Elizabeth H. Lord, *Historical Atlas of the United States*, rev. ed. (New York: Holt, 1953). Statistical information can be found in the U.S. Census Bureau's *Historical Statistics of the United States* (Washington, D.C.: U.S. Government Printing Office, 1975), a two-volume work with updates entitled *Statistical Abstracts of the United States*. For a one-volume overview of government documents, consult Laurence F. Schmeckebier, *Government Publications and Their Use* (Washington, D.C.: Brookings Institute, 1969). The most comprehensive guide to congressional documents is the massive *U.S. Serial Set Index* published by the Congressional Information Service. Additional guides are available on specific time periods, subjects, and types of government documents. Many libraries have special sections and librarians for government documents that you should consult prior to undertaking any document research.

Many college and university libraries have additional sections for special manuscript collections, maps, microfilm, new books, and photocopying. Most also have a *reserve* section, an area set aside for books and articles placed there by professors because they will be used by large numbers of students. Works on reserve can usually be taken out only for a few hours or days; you should check on the specific rules and procedures used by your library. In most libraries, reference works, periodicals, and documents must be read in the library; only books can be checked out.

FORM: BIBLIOGRAPHIES, FOOTNOTES, AND STYLE MANUALS

In addition to knowing how to use the library, you need to know the correct form to use when presenting the results of your research. In this regard, you should realize that the finest research in the world is worthless if it cannot be clearly communicated to others. The ability to do this rests not only on correct grammar and organization but also on proper citation form for footnotes and bibliographies.

There ought to be no mystery about footnotes and bibliographies. They are part of all research papers and serve to guide your reader to your sources of information and interpretation. It is very important that your *citations,* as footnotes and bibliographies are called, be clear and uniform and that they follow the specific rules that govern their use.

A *footnote* or *end note* is used to credit the source of every quotation, paraphrase, fact, or idea you use in a paper and to give the reader the exact location of each item. A *bibliography* simply lists all the sources used in the preparation of a given work.

The primary purposes of footnotes and bibliographies are to provide your readers with information regarding your sources, should they wish to consult them for additional information, and to give proper credit to authors and sources you have used. Not to give such credit is falsely to claim it for yourself, a very serious and punishable academic offense known as *plagiarism.* Bluntly stated, plagiarism is a form of theft. If you do not provide a bibliography and footnotes (as well as quote marks whenever direct quotes are used), you are falsely claiming by this omission that the words and ideas you use are your own. Unless otherwise instructed by your professor, you should therefore include proper footnotes and bibliographies with *all* written assignments, with footnotes being placed either at the bottom of the page or the end of your paper. They can be single-spaced with double spacing between entries or double-spaced with triple spacing between entries; ask your professor which form to use.

Footnotes *must* be used for all direct quotations *or* paraphrases; for charts, diagrams, graphs, and statistics taken from another work; and for interpretations made by others. They should also be used to cite sources for little-known facts and can on occasion be used to discuss a tangential issue (this is known as a "discursive" footnote). If you have numerous citations to the same source in one paragraph, you can usually simplify matters by placing a single footnote at the end of the paragraph.

Footnotes and bibliographies are governed by a set of very specific but evolving rules regarding the information to be provided and the order in which it is to be presented. The purpose of these rules is to ensure that your reader will be able to find the work or works you cite. It is thus essential for you to provide all the information required, and in the proper order. Should you omit some of the information or decide to change the order of presentation, you will only confuse your readers and make it impossible for them to go back to your sources. In citing scholarly articles, for example, standard form requires you to put the title of the article in quote marks, to underline the title of the journal, and then to provide the volume number of the journal, the date (in parentheses), and the page number or numbers. Suppose you choose instead to underline the article title and put the journal title in quote marks, or to put the page number before the volume number, or not to include the date. Could your reader possibly find the information you cite? Could *you* find that information again?

Proper form for books and articles is fairly straightforward. Footnotes are indicated in the text by raised, consecutive arabic numerals half a space above the line and immediately after a reference to another source, as is shown at the end of this sentence.[1] The footnote is then presented at the bottom of the page or the end of your paper. The first line of the note is indented and preceded by the raised arabic numeral. Information is then provided according to the following forms. (In type written materials, titles of books and journals; italicized below, would be underlined.) For books:

> Author's first and last name, *Title of Book* (Place of Publication: Publisher, year), p. and page number.

For articles in journals:

> Author's first and last name, "Title of Article," *Title of Journal,* volume number (date), page number.

Proper footnotes for a book and a scholarly article that could answer the questions previously raised in this chapter regarding the Fourteenth Amendment and Reconstruction would thus be presented as follows:

> Joseph B. James, *The Framing of the Fourteenth Amendment* (Urbana: University of Illinois Press, 1956), pp. 90-93.

> Charles O. Lerche, "Congressional Interpretations of the Guarantee of a Republican Form of Government During Reconstruction," *Journal of Southern History,* 15 (1949), 192-211.

These so-called "full" citations need be given only once for each source. For later references, you should use a shortened form, which includes only the author's last name and the page number (i.e.,[3]James, p. 95). If you are using more than one book or article by the same author, however, include a shortened version of the title of the work (i.e.,[3]James, *Fourteenth Amendment,* p. 95). Please note that ibid. ("the same") and op. cit. ("cited elsewhere") are no longer used, though you will see them in older works.

In a bibliography, basically the same information is given as in a footnote, but with different ordering and punctuation. Bibliographies should include all works consulted for your paper, not merely those cited in the footnotes. The citations are arranged alphabetically by author's last name, and the last name is therefore given first. The second and following lines, instead of the first, are indented to make the author's last name stand out, and periods replace commas. In book citations, parentheses and page numbers are deleted. For the works previously cited as footnotes, proper bibliographic form would look like this:

> James, Joseph B. *The Framing of the Fourteenth Amendment.* Urbana: University of Illinois Press, 1956.
> Lerche, Charles O. "Congressional Interpretations of the Guarantee of a Republican Form of Government

During Reconstruction." *Journal of Southern History.* 15 (1949), 192–211.

While proper form is thus fairly simple, it is important to realize that variations exist; that different forms are used for other types of sources such as government documents, newspapers, and so on; and that form occasionally varies with the discipline involved. Because of these variations and complexities and because of the importance of clear and correct citations, you should have a detailed guide to consult for proper footnote and bibliographical forms. All *style manuals* contain such guides in the form of special chapters on citation. They also contain important information on preparing and writing papers, and many provide more detailed information on use of the library. You should therefore plan to purchase one of these manuals as a key reference work and to consult it whenever you are preparing a paper.

The most commonly used and cited student manual is Joseph Gibaldi and Walter S. Achtert, *MLA Handbook for Writers of Research Papers,* 2nd ed., (New York: Modern Language Association, 1984). Also very popular are *The Chicago Manual of Style,* 13th ed. (Chicago: University of Chicago Press, 1982) and its student complement by Kate L. Turabian, *Student's Guide for Writing College Papers,* 3rd ed. (Chicago: University of Chicago Press, 1976). Joan H. Garrett-Goodyear et al., *Writing Papers: A Handbook for Students at Smith College,* a very concise and inexpensive manual, is now available to students at other colleges. Of the numerous manuals available from commercial publishers, the most comprehensive and up to date are Robert V. Daniels, *Studying History: How and Why,* 3rd ed. (Englewood Cliffs, N.J.: Prentice-Hall, 1981); James D. Lester, *Writing Research Papers: A Complete Guide,* 4th ed. (Glenview, Ill.: Scott, Foresman, 1984); and Melissa Walker, *Writing Research Papers: A Norton Guide* (New York: Norton, 1984).

Since these manuals vary in content and recommended form and since many others are available, you should consult your professor before purchasing one to find out if he or she has any preference or recommendation.

ASSIGNMENTS

1. Compose six questions on a Reconstruction and/or race relations topic that are not answered in your textbook. Each question should begin with a different word of inquiry ("what," "when," "where," "who," "how," "why"), and all should deal with the same general topic.
2. Take your list of questions to the library. If a librarian or self-guided tour is available, take it. If not, examine the library areas and reference works discussed in this chapter. Your instructor may give you a special exercise to complete on these works.

3. How many of your questions could be answered by consulting only reference works? Which ones would you use?

4. Using the appropriate reference bibliographies and indexes, find at least two books and two scholarly articles that would provide detailed answers to the questions you have asked. Then, make use of the abstracts and book reviews (or summaries) available to choose the one book and one scholarly article that would be most appropriate for answering your questions.

5. Use the card catalogue, the stacks, the periodicals section and/or the periodicals list to find the book and the article chosen. Cite each in correct footnote *and* bibliographic form and place the appropriate call number in the left-hand margin. If your library does not have the book or article, choose another.

6. As an alternative assignment, if you have already completed the version of this assignment in volume 1 and/or if so instructed by your professor, compose a preliminary bibliography for a paper to answer the questions you have raised. Comment in *annotations* on the content and value of each work cited.

ADDITIONAL QUESTIONS TO CONSIDER

1. What shortcomings in the textbook are revealed by the questions you have raised? How do you account for these shortcomings? Does your textbook appear to have particular strengths and weaknesses in terms of coverage or particular biases in terms of interpretation?

2. What documents would you wish to consult in answering your questions? Where and how would you find these documents?

3. On what specific occasions would you use footnotes in a paper? When are they not necessary?

4. Exactly how would you, or did you if you chose assignment 6, go about preparing a preliminary bibliography for a research paper on Reconstruction or race relations history? How should the card catalogue be used? What circumstances should lead you to add or delete specific works?

2

INDUSTRIALIZATION AND URBANIZATION
USING MAPS, TABLES, AND GRAPHS
FOR HYPOTHESIS FORMATION

Industrialization, as your text and lectures make clear, transformed America. By 1900 the electric light, the bicycle, the streetcar, the skyscraper, the elevator, canned foods, and gas kitchen ranges were commonplace conveniences of everyday life. Forty years earlier these items had been either rarities or dreams.

The commonplace nature of these items points to a dramatic transformation that had taken place in American life, a transformation whose nature and rapidity may be illustrated in a number of ways. Bernard A. Weisberger, for example, points out that in 1846 the railroad was a novelty, by 1876 it was an achievement, and by 1900 it was an indispensable necessity to the functioning of the U.S. economy. The rise of the railroad was paralleled by American use of energy—the horsepower produced from all sources for doing industrial work increased more than *seventeen-fold* from 1860 to 1900. New means of transportation, and new sources and uses of power, combined with new methods of organizing work to produce a "revolutionary transformation" in the United States "from a homemade to a store-bought society."

Obviously, millions of Americans found their lives transformed in this industrial era. New jobs, new living arrangements, new problems, new opportunities abounded. Industrialization left no aspect of American life untouched.

One of the most dramatic and certainly most visible effects of the industrial revolution on the United States was the rise of cities; the shift from homemade to storebought was also a shift from rural to urban. In 1860 the United States had a total population of 31,443,321; in 1900 almost that many Americans (30,160,000) lived in cities. Much of this rise in the importance of the city in American life is directly attributable to industrialization. This can be illustrated by another statistic; by 1890, although the nation's ten largest urban centers had only 8 percent of the population, they produced just about 40 percent of U.S. manufactured goods.

Cities attracted industry for a variety of reasons, which can only be briefly summarized here. The development of the railroad and the advent of first steam and then electric power offered easier access to raw materials and water power, two components of industrial concentration. Moreover, in every branch of American manufacturing, new inventions expanded productivity and invited larger-scale manufacturing enterprises. These large-scale enterprises required large concentrations of workers, who were increasingly to be found in urban areas. New factory jobs, of course, invited new migrants; new migrants invited additional industry. Thus industrial expansion and urban population growth were linked and reinforcing.

This process, of course, worked to increase the population of established commercial centers like New York, Philadelphia, Baltimore, and Boston. Industrialization also produced entirely new cities. Chicago may be the most spectacular example here; it grew from a small city of just over 100,000 in 1860 to the nation's "second city" with a population of more than 2 million in 1910. But other cities—Detroit, Pittsburgh, Milwaukee, and Cleveland—likewise grew thanks to a thriving industrial expansion. Smaller and middle-sized cities also grew rapidly in this period. In Table 2.1 below, for example, note that the number of small cities in the 10,000 to 25,000 range increased from 58 in 1860 to 280 in 1900. The number of mid-sized cities (those in the 50,000 to 99,000 range) also increased rapidly, from 7 in 1860 to 40 in 1900. This would lead to the *hypothesis* that some of the urban growth in the United States was due to the establishment of new commercial centers in recently settled farming areas.

A hypothesis is a tentative theory or supposition that can be tested by the available evidence and can serve as a guide in the search for additional evidence. Whenever you examine historical evidence, you formulate hypotheses (the question-asking exercise in Chapter 1 is a simple kind of hypothesis formation); additional research generally leads you to refine or reformulate your hypothesis. For example, Maps 2.1 and 2.2 provide evidence about the hypothesis that urban growth reflected the establishment of new commercial centers. The existence of a number of dots west of the Mississippi River would tend to confirm this hypothesis. Yet an examina-

TABLE 2.1 Urban Territories, 1860–1900

Class and Population Size	1860	1870	1880	1890	1900
Urban territory	392	663	939	1348	1737
Places of 1,000,000 or more			1	3	3
500,000–999,999	2	2	3	1	3
250,000–499,999	1	5	4	7	9
100,000–249,999	6	7	12	17	23
50,000–99,999	7	11	15	30	40
25,000–49,999	19	27	42	66	82
10,000–24,999	58	116	146	230	280
5,000–9,999	136	186	249	340	465
2,500–4,999	163	309	467	654	832

tion of these maps also suggests that this hypothesis is extremely limited in explaining urban growth in the last four decades of the nineteenth century. Look, for example, at the increase in the number of cities in long-settled regions of the United States. A better hypothesis would therefore be that urban growth reflected the expansion of old commercial centers as well as the establishment of new ones. This suggests another point about hypotheses: the more explanatory power they have, the more valuable they are, and you can increase the value of a hypothesis by refining it as much as the evidence permits. Good hypotheses about industrialization and urbanization will, then, be fairly complicated because they have to account for a number of factors.

When you are dealing with complicated historical evidence, maps and tables can be valuable tools for both explanation and illustration. Quite often, historians place the information provided by these sources on a *time-series graph* to examine and highlight its significance and to show relationships or trends in simple form. This type of graph has measurements of time on one axis and measurements of the factor being analyzed on the other. Each set of coordinates is properly marked with a dot, and the dots are then connected to form a continuous line. That line will clearly illustrate whatever trends exist. Relationships can be illustrated by creating more than one line of coordinates on the same graph. This is shown by Figure 2.1, a graph from a standard U.S. history text.

Raw data from maps and tables can, of course, be placed directly on a graph. Quite often, however, historians find that these data are more meaningful when some trends have been determined beforehand. In the first paragraph of this chapter, for example, we cited not the actual numbers for the increase in energy used from 1860 to 1900 but a percentage increase of seventeenfold, or 1,700 percent. We arrived at this figure by subtracting the energy used in 1860 from the energy used in 1900, dividing the resulting figure by the 1860 figure, and multiplying this last figure by 100. The actual numbers involved and calculations are reproduced directly below.

MAP 2.1

STATES, TERRITORIES, AND CITIES
1860

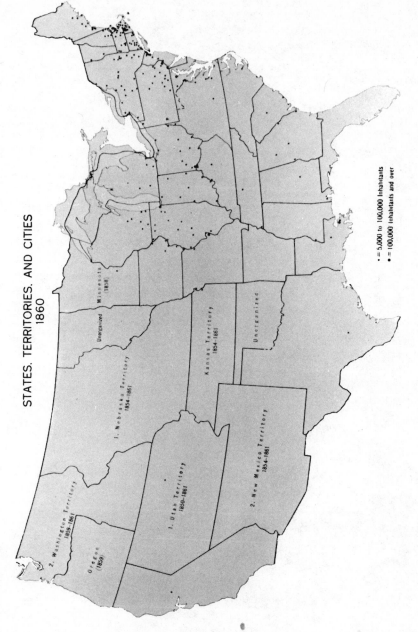

• = 5,000 to 100,000 Inhabitants
● = 100,000 Inhabitants and over

Maps 2.1 and 2.2 from Charles O. Paullin, *Atlas of the Historical Geography of the United States* (Washington, D.C., and New York: Carnegie Institute and American Geographical Society, 1932), plates 64 and 65. Reprinted by permission.

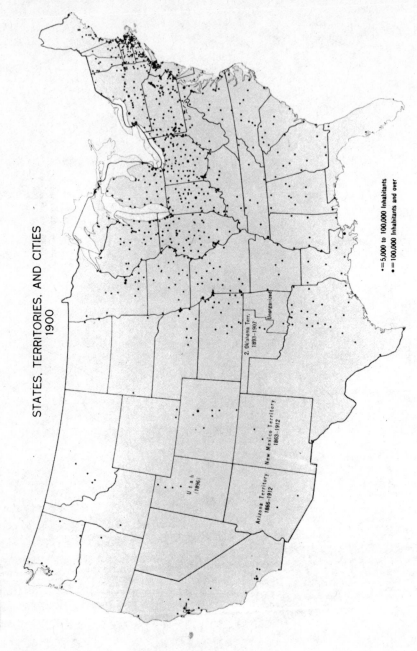

MAP 2.2

STATES, TERRITORIES, AND CITIES
1900

• = 5,000 to 100,000 Inhabitants
● = 100,000 Inhabitants and over

2. Oklahoma Terr.
1893–1907

Unorganized

New Mexico Territory
1863–1912

Arizona Territory
1865–1912

Utah
(1896)

FIGURE 2.1 Total Population, 1860–1930

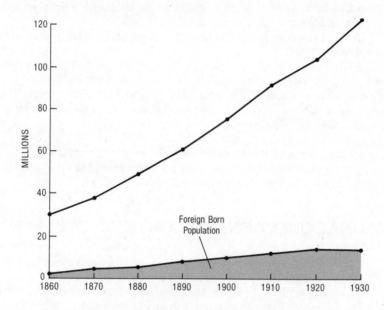

From Rebecca Brooks Gruver, *An American History,* 3rd ed. (Reading, Mass.: Addison-Wesley, 1981), p. 653. Reprinted by permission of Alfred A. Knopf, Inc.

All energy used in 1860 = 2,535,000
All energy used in 1900 = 46,215,000

First subtract   46,215,000
            − 2,535,000
            _____
            43,680,000

Then divide and multiply $\dfrac{43,680,000}{2,535,000} \times 100 = 1723\%$

In this particular case, the percentage increase is much more meaningful than the raw numbers; the historian might therefore wish to make a graph of percentage increases over time rather than simply numerical increases. To do this, he or she would simply put percentage increases instead of raw numbers on one axis of the graph, calculate those increases for each year on the other axis (the base shifts each time to the preceding year), and mark and connect the resulting dots. The calculations required for the following assignment(s) are equally simple and straightforward and can be done either by hand or with the aid of a pocket calculator.

ASSIGNMENTS

1. Examine the tables and maps reproduced on the following pages. Briefly summarize the kinds of evidence they contain.

2. Perform one of the analytical tasks listed below.

   a. Prepare a time-series graph that illustrates the relationship between urban growth and the rise of manufacturing.
   b. Prepare a time-series graph that illustrates the increase in immigration into the United States.
   c. Calculate a selected series of percentage increases or decreases to reflect the changing nature of immigration into the United States.
   d. Compare the city distribution maps (Maps 2.1 and 2.2) with either railroad expansion maps or rise of manufacturing maps (available in the historical atlases discussed in Chapter 1 or in your textbook).

3. On the basis of one of these analytical tasks or one of your own devising, develop a hypothesis that seeks to explain some aspect of the relationship of industrial growth to urbanization in the United States.

ADDITIONAL QUESTIONS TO CONSIDER

1. To test and further refine your hypothesis, what additional evidence would you wish to examine?
2. What additional hypotheses do the maps and tables provided suggest to you?
3. The maps, tables, and graphs referred to in this chapter all deal with industrialization and urbanization of the nation as a whole. Similar information is available in many libraries for state and local history. See if your library has such information. If so, examine it and develop some hypotheses. Do the state and local data, patterns, and hypotheses match the national ones? If not, how can you explain the differences?
4. According to some historians, Populism represented an organized, rural protest against the urbanization of America. Examine statistics from the elections of 1892 and 1896 and use them to confirm, refine, or alter this hypothesis.

TABLE 2.2 European Immigrants by Country, 1866–1900

Year	All countries	Northwestern Europe					Central Europe			Eastern Europe		Southern Europe	
		Total	Great Britain	Ireland	Scandinavia	Other North-western	Germany	Poland*	Other Central	U.S.S.R. and Baltic States	Other Eastern	Italy	Other Southern
	88	89	90	91	92	93	94	95	96	97	98	99	100
1900	448,572	424,700	12,509	35,730	31,151	5,822	18,507	—	114,847	90,787	6,852	100,135	8,360
1899	311,715	297,349	13,456	31,673	22,192	5,150	17,476	—	62,491	60,982	1,738	77,419	4,772
1898	229,299	217,786	12,894	25,128	19,282	4,698	17,111	4,726	39,797	29,828	1,076	58,613	4,633
1897	230,832	216,397	12,752	28,421	21,089	5,323	22,533	4,165	33,031	25,816	943	59,431	2,893
1896	343,267	329,067	24,565	40,262	33,199	7,611	31,885	691	65,103	51,445	954	68,060	5,292
1895	258,536	250,342	28,833	46,304	26,852	7,313	32,173	790	33,401	35,907	768	35,427	2,574
1894	285,631	277,052	22,520	30,231	32,400	9,514	53,989	1,941	38,638	39,278	1,027	42,977	4,537
1893	439,730	429,324	35,189	43,578	58,945	17,888	78,756	16,374	57,420	42,310	625	72,145	6,094
1892	579,663	570,876	42,215	51,383	66,295	21,731	119,168	40,536	76,937	81,511	1,331	61,631	8,188
1891	560,319	546,085	66,605	55,706	60,107	21,824	113,554	27,497	71,042	47,426	1,222	76,055	5,047
1890	455,302	445,680	69,730	53,024	50,368	20,575	92,427	11,073	56,199	35,598	723	52,003	3,960
1889	444,427	434,790	87,992	65,557	57,504	22,010	99,538	4,922	34,174	33,916	1,145	25,307	2,725
1888	546,889	538,131	108,692	73,513	81,924	23,251	109,717	5,826	45,811	33,487	1,393	51,558	2,959
1887	490,109	482,829	93,378	68,370	67,629	17,307	106,865	6,128	40,265	30,766	2,251	47,622	2,248
1886	334,203	329,529	62,929	49,619	46,735	11,737	84,403	3,939	28,680	17,800	670	21,315	1,702
1885	395,346	353,083	57,713	51,795	40,704	13,732	124,443	3,085	27,309	17,158	941	13,642	2,561
1884	518,592	453,686	65,950	63,344	52,728	18,768	179,676	4,536	36,571	12,689	388	16,510	2,526
1883	603,322	522,587	76,606	81,486	71,994	24,271	194,786	2,011	27,625	9,909	163	31,792	1,944
1882	788,992	648,186	102,991	76,432	105,326	27,796	250,630	4,672	29,150	16,918	134	32,159	1,978
1881	669,431	528,545	81,376	72,342	81,582	26,883	210,485	5,614	27,935	5,041	102	15,401	1,784
1880	457,257	348,691	73,273	71,603	65,657	15,042	84,638	2,177	17,267	5,014	35	12,354	1,631
1879	177,826	134,259	29,955	20,013	21,820	9,081	34,602	489	5,963	4,453	29	5,791	2,063
1878	138,469	101,612	22,150	15,932	12,254	6,929	29,313	547	5,150	3,048	29	4,344	1,916
1877	141,857	106,195	23,581	14,569	11,274	8,621	29,298	533	5,396	6,599	32	3,195	3,097
1876	169,986	120,920	29,291	19,575	12,323	10,923	31,937	925	6,276	4,775	38	3,015	1,842
1875	227,498	182,961	47,905	37,957	14,322	11,987	47,769	984	7,658	7,997	27	3,631	2,724
1874	313,839	262,783	62,021	53,707	19,178	15,998	87,291	1,795	8,850	4,073	62	7,666	2,142
1873	459,803	397,541	89,500	77,344	35,481	22,892	149,671	3,338	7,112	1,634	53	8,757	1,759
1872	404,806	352,155	84,912	68,732	28,575	15,614	141,109	1,647	4,410	1,018	20	4,190	1,928
1871	321,350	265,145	85,455	57,439	22,132	7,174	82,554	535	4,887	673	23	2,816	1,457
1870	387,203	328,626	103,677	56,996	30,742	9,152	118,225	223	4,425	907	6	2,891	1,382
1869	352,768	315,963	84,438	40,786	43,941	10,585	131,042	184	1,499	343	18	1,489	1,638
1868	138,840	130,090	24,127	32,068	11,985	4,293	55,831	—	192	141	4	891	558
1867	315,722	283,751	52,641	72,879	8,491	12,417	133,426	310	692	205	26	1,624	1,040
1866	318,568	278,916	94,924	36,690	14,495	13,648	115,892	412	93	287	18	1,382	1,075

*Between 1899 and 1900, included with Austria-Hungary, Germany, and Russia.

TABLE 2.3 Manufactures Summary, 1849–1899: Factories and Hand and Neighborhood Industries

Year	Total Number of Establishments	Production Workers (1,000)	Wages (millions of dollars)	Value Added by Manufacture (millions of dollars)
1849	123,025	857	237	464
1859	140,433	1,311	379	854
1869	252,148	2,054	621	1,395
1879	253,852	2,733	948	1,973
1889	353,864	4,129	1,821	4,102
1899	509,490	5,098	2,207	5,475

3

RESPONSES TO INDUSTRIALIZATION
LITERATURE IN HISTORY AND WRITING

By the end of the nineteenth century, Americans were well aware that the dizzying "coming of age" of the United States as an industrial and technological society had created a new world of dramatic growth and change. Many of them embraced this growth and change as highly beneficial. Andrew Carnegie, to name one, hailed the United States as an example of "triumphant democracy" and propounded a progressive view of history, arguing that America would inevitably, through modern technology, create a new world civilization of reduced labor and enriched health and leisure. Such optimism was by no means limited to great industrialists. In a lecture delivered at Hull House in 1890, architect Frank Lloyd Wright urged his fellow artists to discover "the poetry of the machine age." Industrialization, he maintained, had degraded old art forms and left "a pandemonium of tin masks, huddled deformities and decayed methods," but it had also provided the materials and technology for a new and better art. Wright was convinced that the artist could and should use these materials and technology to forge an ideal artistic and humanistic expression of American society.

Other Americans were less optimistic, for industrialization clearly produced at least as many problems as benefits. Most visibly, the stark contrast in the new industrial society between the ornate, palatial homes of the wealthy and the rat-infested tenements of the poor seemed to illustrate the creation of a fundamental, permanent, and dangerous division in American society.

This inequitable distribution of the new wealth in America did not escape the notice of a number of critics and reformers. In *Progress and Poverty* (1870), for example, Henry George warned his fellow Americans in vivid language of the essential paradox of their industrial revolution:

> The present century . . . has been marked by a prodigious increase in wealth-producing power. . . . It was natural to expect, and it was expected, that . . . the enormous increase in the power of producing wealth would make real poverty a thing of the past. . . . [But] disappointment has followed disappointment. . . . We plow new fields, we open new mines, we found new cities; we drive back the Indian and exterminate the buffalo; we girdle the land with iron roads and lace the air with telegraph wires; we add knowledge to knowledge, and utilize invention after invention. . . . Yet it becomes no easier for the masses of our people to make a living. On the contrary, it becomes harder. . . . The gulf between the employed and the employer is growing wider; social contrasts are becoming sharper; as liveried carriages appear, so do barefooted children.

George was not alone in believing that the "association of poverty with progress" was the "great enigma" of his era. Henry Demarest Lloyd, a lawyer and financial editor for the *Chicago Tribune,* wrote a scathing indictment of monopolists like John D. Rockefeller of Standard Oil, who would enslave the public in their ruthless quest for profit. As an alternative, Lloyd called for the establishment of a cooperative commonwealth in which the public would own monopolies. In his enormously popular novel *Looking Backward 2000–1887* (1888), Edward Bellamy also urged Americans to embrace a socialist "fraternal cooperation" in order to establish a technological utopia free from the greed of lawyers, bankers, and politicians.

LITERATURE IN HISTORY

However radical such a proposal may have appeared, it was by no means a rejection of industrialization per se. Rather, Lloyd and Bellamy embraced technology in much the same way Carnegie and Wright had and argued simply for a different industrial and political organization to remove its bad side effects. Numerous American authors were less sanguine. Henry James and Edith Wharton, for example, rejected industrialized America and turned either to the past or to Europe for their creative sustenance. Sarah Orne Jewett responded by praising the virtues of old-fashioned rural life in her writings. And some authors exhibited a duality toward industrialization and its problems that confused their readers as well as later generations. Mark Twain, for example, seemed to embrace the industrial revolution wholeheartedly in both his major works and his life. His later writings, however, reveal severe disillusionment with American life and the consequences of industrialization. Writing about the urban poor with the innovative "realist" style in *Maggie*, Stephen Crane appeared to be joining George, Lloyd, and Bellamy in calling for major change; his work probably helped convert many Americans to the need for reform. In letters to friends and admirers, however, he made brutally clear that he had little sympathy for such efforts and that he was merely showing the impact of environment on human beings, painting "pictures of his time as they appear[ed] to him," and showing people "as they seem to me."

These examples illustrate both the value and the difficulty of using literature to study history. Literature constitutes an extraordinarily rich source for historical study, for literary artists are trained observers who often see and express problems more clearly than the average citizen can. It is a complex source, however, and one that cannot be used in the same way as public documents or private correspondence. Literary works are often shaped by an author's esthetic or financial considerations as well as by social concerns, and each piece of literature must be dealt with as an entity in itself. Moreover, an individual piece of literature can simultaneously reflect and criticize society's values. Unfortunately, estimating the extent to which the public shares the views of the author is by no means as simple as counting sales.

The tasks of the historian examining literature involve answering the questions associated with these issues. Is an individual piece of literature an example of how many people viewed their age, or is it merely one individual's view? Does it reflect the values of its society, criticize and attempt to change those values, or bear little relationship to them? What were the historical consequences of a literary work, and were those consequences planned or unplanned? Just what is the author's relationship to society, and what can an author's work tell you about its creator and about the era in which it was created?

Obviously, the answers to these questions depend upon the author and the specific work in question; one cannot generalize from one individual or book. At the end of this chapter, you will find excerpts from the writings of three authors from this era: Stephen Crane, Mark Twain, and Sarah Orne Jewett. In reading these excerpts, keep in mind the questions just raised as well as what each excerpt is saying about industrialization and its consequences. Be prepared to discuss your conclusions as requested in the "Additional Questions" section of the chapter.

WRITING

Since this chapter deals with literary sources, it is appropriate that the assignment involve some essay writing on your part. In addition to being able to read critically and ask appropriate questions, the historian must be able to express conclusions in effective prose so that they can be clearly communicated to others. Good writing is one of the trademarks of the historian and of the educated person in general; it is mandatory for effective communication.

Good writing is hard work. George Orwell acknowledged this in his essay "Politics and the English Language" (1946). Orwell suggested that good writers asked four questions about *every sentence* they wrote: "What am I trying to say? What words will express it? What image or idiom will make it clearer? Is this image fresh enough to have an effect?" Orwell was writing to protest the stale language of postwar politics, but his advice still applies in a world where television, politics, and much else provide us with ready-made phrases and slogans that we can employ as a substitute for our own words or ideas.

One of the most important goals of this volume is to encourage you to work on your writing skills—to use your own words and ideas in writing history. Since good writing is largely the product of practice and effort, we urge you to regard the written assignments in this book, essay exams in this and other courses, and indeed all your written work as opportunities to practice effective writing.

What is effective writing? Books have been written to answer this question, but—sadly—the magic formula has not been found. Yet at the simplest level, good writing is characterized by clarity, coherence, and liveliness. You must make your meaning clear; you cannot expect your reader to guess at your meaning. Your ideas must be well organized. Coherence requires that your argument should be logical and proceed in an orderly way from beginning to end. Liveliness is vital. No writer wants readers to fall asleep or to lose track of the argument. Liveliness also demands that the writer include vivid, concrete details. These are essential to good historical writing because they are the evidence that supports generalizations.

As you begin to work on the assignments in this book, you should discover the necessity of revising your written work. Since we often write to find out what we think, rewriting is an integral part of our thinking process. You should be aware that this revising process is complex and difficult; nobody likes to change the words that seemed so appropriate when they were first written. Revision is worthwhile, however, since only by discovering what you think can you communicate your ideas and convictions to others (see Chapter 4 for additional comments on revising).

We would advise that you take the task of communicating *your* ideas to others seriously. Too much student writing is marred by students' successful efforts to imitate bad academic writing. If you are trying—as you should—to discover your own ideas, you handicap yourself inordinately if you attempt to imitate someone else's prose style.

If there are no magic formulas, there *are* some solid rules and guideposts. In his essay, George Orwell offered the following six rules to effective writing:

1. Never use a metaphor, simile or other figure of speech which you are used to seeing in print [or hearing on television].
2. Never use a long word where a short one will do.
3. If it is possible to cut a word out, always cut it out.
4. Never use the passive [voice] when you can use the active [voice].
5. Never use a foreign phrase, a scientific word, or a jargon word if you can think of an everyday English equivalent.
6. Break any of these rules sooner than say anything outright barbarous.

We think Orwell offered good advice. You will find these rules valuable as you work on your writing skills.

The style manuals discussed in Chapter 1 present detailed guidelines for effective writing; we therefore once again recommend that you purchase and use one of them. If you desire further advice beyond what is offered in these manuals, there are a number of good books about writing that you might consult. We would recommend two books by Peter Elbow, *Writing Without Teachers* (New York: Oxford University Press, 1973) and *Writing With Power* (New York: Oxford University Press, 1981). Elbow is particularly good at suggesting solutions to writers' problems. William Zinsser's *On Writing Well* (New York: Harper & Row, 1966) is a masterful commentary on the ingredients of good prose. Finally, William Strunk and E. B. White, in *Elements of Style,* 3rd ed. (New York: Macmillan, 1978), provide a witty and wise guide to the rules of effective writing.

In addition to a style manual, the library of every student writer should include a good dictionary. Webster's *New Collegiate Dictionary,* 9th ed. (Springfield, Mass.: Merriam-Webster, 1983) is still the standard desk dictionary, but there are also reasonably good soft-cover dictionaries, including those published by American Heritage and Oxford. As with the style manuals, you should see if your professor has any advice or preferences in this regard.

ASSIGNMENTS

1. Read the introductions and excerpts at the end of this chapter from the works of Stephen Crane, Mark Twain, and Sarah Orne Jewett.
2. Select a passage from *one* of these excerpts that illustrates the impact of industrialization on some aspect of American life.
3. Write a one-page essay (250 to 300 words) that explains *how* the passage selected illustrates both this impact *and* the author's reaction to it.
4. As an alternative assignment, write a brief essay comparing and contrasting the reactions of Crane, Twain, and Jewett to industrialization as revealed in the excerpts reproduced.

ADDITIONAL QUESTIONS TO CONSIDER

1. Do you believe the excerpt you chose is an accurate reflection of the impact of industrialization on some aspect of American society? Why?
2. If you did not do the alternative assignment, be prepared to compare and contrast the reactions of Crane, Twain, and Jewett to industrialization as revealed in the excerpts reproduced. How would you categorize these reactions? What additional information would you wish to have if you were asked to explain why they reacted as they did?
3. As noted below, Stephen Crane's *Maggie* did not sell until after *The Red Badge of Courage* had made him famous. Does this affect an assessment of the impact of *Maggie* on its audience and/or the degree to which society was willing to accept what Crane was saying? Why? If the answer is yes, how?
4. In light of Mark Twain's previous reputation, how do you think the public interpreted *A Connecticut Yankee in King Arthur's Court* when it was first published? How does the public interpret it today, and how do you account for discrepancies between that interpretation and the one provided in the introductory notes for Twain?
5. What does the excerpt from Sarah Orne Jewett's *Country of Pointed Firs* suggest about the limits and/or advantages of regional writing?
6. In general, what are the strengths and weaknesses of literature as a source for historical study?

STEPHEN CRANE

The Red Badge of Courage, Stephen Crane's well-known Civil War story, appeared as a newspaper serial in 1894 and as a book in 1895. The tale became a best-seller and firmly established Crane's reputation as a writer. Its popularity was widely attributed to its novelty: a war story told from the point of view of a private, Henry Fleming. Using this technique, Crane was able to capture a sense of "what it really had been like" for the ordinary soldier as well as explore the conflict between tradition and reality, which troubled both its author and much of nineteenth-century America. Henry went to war expecting heroism, fanfare, and glory; instead, he experienced filth, confusion, boredom, and death. Ironically, Crane was able to capture the reality of a war of which he had no experience.

Maggie: A Girl of the Streets was published before *The Red Badge of Courage* and reflected some of Crane's own experience living on the edge of the Bowery and eking out a precarious existence. Although *Maggie* attracted little acclaim and no sales when it was first published, it has demonstrated strong staying power and critics agree that it is an important work in the development of modern American fiction. The section reproduced below describes Maggie's attitude toward her work in a Bowery tenement sweatshop and the temptations of urban life.

VIII

As thoughts of Pete came to Maggie's mind, she began to have an intense dislike for all of her dresses.

"What ails yeh? What makes ye be allus fixin' and fussin'?" her mother would frequently roar at her.

She began to note with more interest the well-dressed women she met on the avenues. She envied elegance and soft palms. She craved those adornments of person which she saw every day on the street, conceiving them to be allies of vast importance to women.

Studying faces, she thought many of the women and girls she chanced to meet smiled with serenity as though for ever cherished and watched over by those they loved.

The air in the collar-and-cuff establishment strangled her. She knew she was gradually and surely shrivelling in the hot, stuffy room. The begrimed windows rattled incessantly from the passing of elevated trains. The place was filled with a whirl of noises and odors.

She became lost in thought as she looked at some of the grizzled women in the room, mere mechanical contrivances sewing seams and grinding out, with heads bent over their work, tales of imagined or real girlhood happiness, or of past drunks, or the baby at home, and unpaid wages. She wondered how long her youth would endure. She began to see the bloom upon her cheeks as something of value.

She imagined herself, in an exasperating future, as a scrawny woman with an eternal grievance. She thought Pete to be a very fastidious person concerning the appearance of women.

She felt that she should love to see somebody entangle their fingers in the oily beard of the fat foreigner who owned the establishment. He was a detestable creature. He wore white socks with low shoes. He sat all day delivering orations in the depths of a cushioned chair. His pocket-book deprived them of the power of retort.

"What do you sink I pie fife dolla a week for? Play? No, py tamn!"

Maggie was anxious for a friend to whom she could talk about Pete. She would have liked to discuss his admirable mannerisms with a reliable mutual friend. At home, she found her mother often drunk and always raving. It seemed that the world had treated this woman very badly, and she took a deep revenge upon such portions of it as came within her reach. She broke furniture as if she were at last getting her rights. She swelled with virtuous indignation as she carried the lighter articles of household use, one by one, under the shadows of the three gilt balls. . . .

Jimmie came when he was obliged to by circumstances over which he had no control. His well-trained legs brought him staggering home and put him to bed some nights when he would rather have gone elsewhere.

Swaggering Pete loomed like a golden sun to Maggie. He took her to a dime museum, where rows of meek freaks astonished her. She contemplated their deformities with awe and thought them a sort of chosen tribe.

Pete, racking his brains for amusement, discovered the Central Park Menagerie and the Museum of Arts. Sunday afternoons would sometimes find them at these places. Pete did not appear to be particularly interested in what he saw. He stood around looking heavy, while Maggie giggled in glee.

Once at the menagerie he went into a trance of admiration before the spectacle of a very small monkey threatening to thrash a cageful because one of them had pulled his tail and he had not wheeled about quickly enough to discover who did it. Ever after Pete knew that monkey by sight, and winked at him, trying to induce him to fight with other and larger monkeys.

At the museum, Maggie said, "Dis is outa sight!"

"Aw, rats!" said Pete; "wait till next summer an' I'll take yehs to a picnic."

While the girl wandered in the vaulted rooms, Pete occupied himself in returning, stony stare for stony stare, the appalling scrutiny of the watchdogs of the treasures. Occasionally he would remark in loud tones. "Dat jay has got glass eyes," and sentences of the sort. When he tired of this amusement he would go to the mummies and moralize over them.

Usually he submitted with silent dignity to all that he had to go through, but at times he was goaded into comment.

"Aw!" he demanded once. "Look at all dese little jugs! Hundred jugs in a row! Ten rows in a case, an' 'bout a t'ousand cases! What d' blazes use is dem?"

In the evenings of week days he often took her to see plays in which the dazzling heroine was rescued from the palatial home of her treacherous guardian by the hero with the beautiful sentiments. The latter spent most of his time out at soak in pale-green snow-storms, busy with a nickel-plated revolver rescuing aged strangers from villains.

Maggie lost herself in sympathy with the wanderers swooning in snowstorms beneath happy-hued church windows, while a choir within sang "Joy to the World." To Maggie and the rest of the audience this was transcendental realism. Joy always within, and they, like the actor, inevitably without. Viewing it, they hugged themselves in ecstatic pity of their imagined or real condition.

The girl thought the arrogance and granite-heartedness of the magnate of the play were very accurately drawn. She echoed the maledictions that the occupants of the gallery showered on this individual when his lines compelled him to expose his extreme selfishness.

Shady persons in the audience revolted from the pictured villainy of the drama. With untiring zeal they hissed vice and applauded virtue. Unmistakably bad men evinced an apparently sincere admiration for virtue. The loud gallery was overwhelmingly with the unfortunate and the oppressed. They encouraged the struggling hero with cries, and jeered the villain, hooting and calling attention to his whiskers. When anybody died in the pale-green snowstorms, the gallery mourned. They sought out the painted misery and hugged it as akin.

In the hero's erratic march from poverty in the first act to wealth and triumph in the final one, in which he forgives all the enemies that he has left, he was assisted by the gallery, which applauded his generous and noble sentiments and confounded the speeches of his opponents by making irrelevant but very sharp remarks. Those actors who were cursed with the parts of villains were confronted at every turn by the gallery. If one of them rendered lines containing the most subtle distinctions between right and wrong, the gallery was immediately aware that the actor meant wickedness, and denounced him accordingly.

The last act was a triumph for the hero, poor and of the masses, the representative of the audience, over the villain and the rich man, his pockets stuffed with bonds, his heart packed with tyrannical purposes, imperturbable amid suffering.

Maggie always departed with raised spirits from these melodramas. She rejoiced at the way in which the poor and virtuous eventually overcame the wealthy and wicked. The theatre made her think. She wondered if the culture and refinement she had seen imitated, perhaps grotesquely, by the heroine on the stage, could be acquired by a girl who lived in a tenement house and worked in a shirt factory.

IX

A group of urchins were intent upon the side door of a saloon. Expectancy gleamed from their eyes. They were twisting their fingers in excitement.

"Here she comes!" yelled one of them suddenly.

The group of urchins burst instantly asunder and its individual fragments were spread in a wide, respectable half-circle about the point of interest. The saloon door opened with a crash, and the figure of a woman appeared upon the threshold. Her gray hair fell in knotted masses about her shoulders. Her face was crimsoned and wet with perspiration. Her eyes had a rolling glare.

"Not a cent more of me money will yehs ever get—not a red! I spent me money here for t'ree years, an' now yehs tells me yeh'll sell me no more stuff! Go fall on yerself, Johnnie Murckre! 'Disturbance?' Disturbance be blowed! Go fall on yerself, Johnnie—"

The door received a kick of exasperation from within, and the woman lurched heavily out on the sidewalk.

The gamins in the half-circle became violently agitated. They began to dance about and hoot and yell and jeer. A wide dirty grin spread over each face.

The woman made a furious dash at a particularly outrageous cluster of little boys. They laughed delightedly, and scampered off a short distance, calling out to her over their shoulders. She stood tottering on the curbstone and thundered at them.

"Yeh devil's kids!" she howled, shaking her fists. The little boys whooped in glee. As she started up the street they fell in behind and marched uproariously. Occasionally she wheeled about and made charges on them. They ran nimbly out of reach and taunted her.

In the frame of a gruesome doorway she stood for a moment cursing them. Her hair straggled, giving her red features a look of insanity. Her great fists quivered as she shook them madly in the air.

The urchins made terrific noises until she turned and disappeared. Then they filed off quietly in the way they had come.

The woman floundered about in the lower hall of the tenement house, and finally stumbled up the stairs. On an upper hall a door was opened and a collection of heads peered curiously out, watching her. With a wrathful snort the woman confronted the door, but it was slammed hastily in her face and the key was turned.

She stood for a few minutes, delivering a frenzied challenge at the panels. "Come out in deh hall, Mary Murphy, if yehs want a scrap! Come ahn! yeh overgrown terrier, come ahn!"

She began to kick the door. She shrilly defied the universe to appear and do battle. Her cursing trebles brought heads from all doors save the one she threatened. Her eyes glared in every direction. The air was full of her tossing fists.

"Come ahn! deh hull gang of yehs, come ahn!" she roared at the spectators. An oath or two, catcalls, jeers, and bits of facetious advice were given in reply. Missiles clattered about her feet.

"What's wrong wi'che?" said a voice in the gathered gloom, and Jimmie came forward. He carried a tin dinner pail in his hand and under his arm a truckman's brown apron done in a bundle. "What's wrong?" he demanded.

"Come out! all of yehs, come out," his mother was howling. "Come ahn an' I'll stamp yer faces tru d' floor."

"Shet yer face, an' come home, yeh old fool!" roared Jimmie at her. She strode up to him and twirled her fingers in his face. Her eyes were darting flames of unreasoning rage, and her frame trembled with eagerness for a fight.

"An' who are youse? I ain't givin' a snap of me fingers fer youse!" she bawled at him. She turned her huge back in tremendous disdain and climbed the stairs to the next floor.

Jimmie followed, and at the top of the flight he seized his mother's arm and started to drag her toward the door of their room.

"Come home!" he gritted between his teeth.

"Take yer hands off me! Take yer hands off me!" shrieked his mother.

She raised her arm and whirled her great fist at her son's face. Jimmie dodged his head, and the blow struck him in the back of the neck. "Come home!" he gritted again. He threw out his left hand and writhed his fingers about her middle arm. The mother and the son began to sway and struggle like gladiators.

"Whoop!" said the Rum Alley tenement house. The hall filled with interested spectators.

"Hi, ol' lady, dat was a dandy!"

"T'ree t' one on d' red!"

"Ah, quit yer scrappin'!"

The door of the Johnson home opened and Maggie looked out. Jimmie made a supreme cursing effort and hurled his mother into the room. He quickly followed and closed the door. The Rum Alley tenement swore disappointedly and retired.

The mother slowly gathered herself up from the floor. Her eyes glittered menacingly upon her children.

"Here now," said Jimmie, "we've had enough of dis. Sit down, an' don' make no trouble."

He grasped her arm and, twisting it, forced her into a creaking chair.

"Keep yer hands off me!" roared his mother again.

"Say, yeh ol' bat! Quit dat!" yelled Jimmie, madly. Maggie shrieked and ran into the other room. To her there came the sound of a storm of crashes and curses. There was a great final thump and Jimmie's voice cried: "Dere, now! Stay still." Maggie opened the door now, and went warily out. "Oh, Jimmie!"

He was leaning against the wall and swearing. Blood stood upon bruises on his knotty forearms where they had scraped against the floor or the wall in the scuffle. The mother lay screeching on the floor, the tears running down her furrowed face.

Maggie, standing in the middle of the room, gazed about her. The usual upheaval of the tables and chairs had taken place. Crockery was strewn broadcast in fragments. The stove had been disturbed on its legs, and now leaned idiotically to one side. A pail had been upset and water spread in all directions.

The door opened and Pete appeared. He shrugged his shoulders. "Oh, gee!" he observed.

He walked over to Maggie and whispered in her ear: "Ah, what d' hell, Mag? Come ahn and we'll have a outa-sight time."

The mother in the corner upreared her head and shook her tangled locks.

"Aw, yer bote no good, needer of yehs," she said, glowering at her daughter in the gloom. Her eyes seemed to burn balefully. "Yeh've gone t' d' devil, Mag Johnson, yehs knows yehs have gone t' d' devil. Yer a disgrace t' yer people. An' now, git out an' go ahn wid dat doe-faced jude of yours. Go wid him, curse yeh, an' a good riddance. Go, an' see how yeh likes it."

Maggie gazed long at her mother.

"Go now, an' see how yeh likes it. Git out. I won't have sech as youse in me house! Git out, d' yer hear! Damn yeh, git out!"

The girl began to tremble.

At this instant Pete came forward. "Oh, what d' hell, Mag, see?" whispered he softly in her ear. "Dis all blows over. See? D' ol' woman 'ill be all right in d' mornin'. Come ahn out wid me! We'll have a outa-sight time."

The woman on the floor cursed. Jimmie was intent upon his bruised forearms. The girl cast a glance about the room filled with a chaotic mass of *débris,* and at the writhing body of her mother.

"Git th' devil outa here."

Maggie went.

X

Jimmie had an idea it wasn't common courtesy for a friend to come to one's home and ruin one's sister. But he was not sure how much Pete knew about the rules of politeness.

The following night he returned home from work at a rather late hour in the evening. In passing through the halls he came upon the gnarled and leathery old woman who possessed the music box. She was grinning in the dim light that drifted through dust-stained panes. She beckoned to him with a smudged forefinger.

"Ah, Jimmie, what do yehs tink I tumbled to, las' night! It was deh funnies' t'ing I ever saw," she cried, coming close to him and leering. She was trembling with eagerness to tell her tale. "I was by me door las' night when yer sister and her jude feller came in late, oh, very late. An' she, the dear, she was a-cryin' as if her heart would break, she was. It was deh funnies' t'ing I ever saw. An' right out here by me door she asked him did he love her, did he. An' she was a-crying as if her heart would break, poor t'ing. An' him, I could see be deh way what he said it dat she had been askin' orften; he says, 'Oh, gee, yes,' he says, says he. 'Oh, gee, yes.' "

Storm-clouds swept over Jimmie's face, but he turned from the leathery old woman and plodded on upstairs.

" 'Oh, gee, yes,' " she called after him. She laughed a laugh that was like a prophetic croak.

There was no one in at home. The rooms showed that attempts had been made at tidying them. Parts of the wreckage of the day before had been repaired by an unskillful hand. A chair or two and the table stood uncertainly upon legs. The floor had been newly swept. The blue ribbons had been restored to the curtains, and the lambrequin, with its immense sheaves of yellow wheat and red roses of equal size, had been returned, in a worn and sorry state, to its place at the mantel. Maggie's jacket and hat were gone from the nail behind the door.

Jimmie walked to the window and began to look through the blurred glass. It occurred to him to wonder vaguely, for an instant, if some of the women of his acquaintance had brothers.

Suddenly, however, he began to swear.

"But he was me frien'! I brought 'im here! Dat's d' devil of it!"

He fumed about the room, his anger gradually rising to the furious pitch.

"I'll kill deh jay! Dat's what I'll do! I'll kill deh jay!"

He clutched his hat and sprang toward the door. But it opened, and his mother's great form blocked the passage.

"What's d' matter wid yeh?" exclaimed she, coming into the room.

Jimmie gave vent to a sardonic curse and then laughed heavily.

"Well, Maggie's gone teh d' devil! Dat's what! See?"

"Eh?" said his mother.

"Maggie's gone teh d' devil! Are yehs deaf?" roared Jimmie, impatiently.

"Aw, git out!" murmured the mother, astounded.

Jimmie grunted, and then began to stare out the window. His mother sat down in a chair, but a moment later sprang erect and delivered a maddened whirl of oaths. Her son turned to look at her as she reeled and swayed in the middle of the room, her fierce face convulsed with passion, her blotched arms raised high in imprecation.

"May she be cursed for ever!" she shrieked. "May she eat nothin' but stones and deh dirt in deh street. May she sleep in deh gutter an' never see deh sun shine again. D' bloomin'—"

"Here now," said her son. "Go fall on yerself, an' quit dat."

The mother raised lamenting eyes to the ceiling.

"She's d' devil's own chil', Jimmie," she whispered. "Ah, who would t'ink such a bad girl could grow up in our fambly, Jimmie, me son. Many d' hour I've spent in talk wid dat girl an' tol' her if she ever went on d' streets I'd see her damned. An' after all her bringin' up, an' what I tol' her and talked wid her, she goes teh d' bad, like a duck teh water."

The tears rolled down her furrowed face. Her hands trembled.

"An' den when dat Sadie MacMallister next door to us was sent teh d' devil by dat feller what worked in d' soap factory, didn't I tell our Mag dat if she—"

"Ah, dat's anudder story," interrupted the brother. "Of course, dat Sadie was nice an' all dat—but—see—it ain't dessame if—well, Maggie was diff'ent —see—she was diff'ent."

He was trying to formulate a theory that he had always unconsciously held, that all sisters excepting his own could, advisedly, be ruined.

He suddenly broke out again. "I'll go t'ump d' mug what done her d' harm. I'll kill 'im! He t'inks he kin scrap, but when he gits me a-chasin' 'im he'll fin' out where he's wrong, d' big stiff! I'll wipe up d' street wid 'im."

In a fury he plunged out the doorway. As he vanished the mother raised her head and lifted both hands, entreating.

"May she be cursed for ever!" she cried.

In the darkness of the hallway Jimmie discerned a knot of women talking volubly. When he strode by they paid no attention to him.

"She allus was a bold thing," he heard one of them cry in an eager voice. "Dere wasn't a feller come teh deh house but she'd try teh mash 'im. My Annie says deh shameless t'ing tried teh ketch her feller, her own feller, what we useter know his fader."

"I could 'a tol' yehs dis two years ago," said a woman, in a key of triumph. "Yes, sir, it was over two years ago dat I says teh my ol' man, I says, 'Dat Johnson girl ain't straight,' I says, 'Oh, rats!' he says, 'Oh, hell!' 'Dat's all right, I says, 'but I know what I knows,' I says, 'an' it'll come out later. You wait an' see,' I says, 'you see.'"

"Anybody what had eyes could see dat dere was somethin' wrong wid dat girl. I didn't like her actions."

On the street Jimmie met a friend. "What's wrong?" asked the latter. Jimmie explained. "An' I'll t'ump 'im till he can't stand."

"Oh, go ahn!" said the friend. "What's deh use! Yeh'll git pulled in! Everybody'ill be on to it! An' ten plunks! Gee!"

Jimmie was determined. "He t'inks he kin scrap, but he'll fin' out diff'ent."

"Gee," remonstrated the friend, "what's d' use?"

MARK TWAIN

Samuel Clemens, better known by his pen name of Mark Twain, was one of the nation's best-known and best-loved writers. His novel *Huckleberry Finn,* which is deservedly considered a classic of American literature and is a staple of literary survey courses, is rich with tall talk, humorous episodes, and keen insights into life on the Mississippi frontier. Twain also contributed to the history of his era by collaborating with Charles Dudley Warner in a satirical portrait, entitled *The Gilded Age,* of America in the years just after the Civil War.

Superficially, Twain's response to the industrial revolution was wholeheartedly positive. His manuscript for *Tom Sawyer,* published in 1876, was the first submitted to an American publisher in typescript. The Twain household had the first private telephone in Hartford, Connecticut, and Twain himself was an inveterate investor in technological schemes to get rich quick—he spent thousands of dollars, for example, on a mechanical typesetter that never did work properly.

Yet, as the passage reproduced below suggests, Twain's response to industrialization was far more ambivalent than details from his biography indicate. *A Connecticut Yankee in King Arthur's Court* begins with a wonderful parody in praise of technology and invention as Hank Morgan, a nineteenth-century factory foreman, arrives in King Arthur's England with all the benefits of modern civilization. The book ends, however, with a grim essay on the technological atrocities "modern" man can impose on "primitive" societies. The excerpts reproduced below begin with Clarence, Morgan's loyal subordinate, explaining to his master the plans for those atrocities. They are then described in vivid detail, along with their ironic repercussions.

. . . . As a next move, I paid a private visit to that old cave of Merlin's—not the small one—the big one—"

"Yes, the one where we secretly established our first great electric plant when I was projecting a miracle."

"Just so. And as that miracle hadn't become necessary then, I thought it might be a good idea to utilize the plant now. I've provisioned the cave for a siege—"

"A good idea, a first rate idea."

"I think so. I placed four of my boys there, as a guard—inside, and out of sight. Nobody was to be hurt—while outside; but any attempt to enter—well, we said just let anybody try it! Then I went out into the hills and uncovered and cut the secret wires which connected your bedroom with the wires that go to the dynamite deposits under all our vast factories, mills, workshops, magazines, etc., and about midnight I and my boys turned out and connected that wire with the cave, and nobody but you and I suspects where the other end of it goes to. We laid it under ground, of course, and it was all finished in a couple of hours or so. We shan't have to leave our fortress, now, when we want to blow up our civilization."

"It was the right move—and the natural one; a military necessity, in the changed condition of things. Well, what changes *have* come! We expected to be besieged in the palace some time or other, but—however, go on."

"Next, we built a wire fence."

"Wire fence?"

"Yes. You dropped the hint of it yourself, two or three years ago."

"Oh, I remember—the time the Church tried her strength against us the first time, and presently thought it wise to wait for a hopefuler season. Well, how have you arranged the fence?"

"I start twelve immensely strong wires—naked, not insulated—from a big dynamo in the cave—dynamo with no brushes except a positive and a negative one—"

"Yes, that's right."

"The wires go out from the cave and fence-in a circle of level ground a hundred yards in diameter; they make twelve independent fences, ten feet apart—that is to say, twelve circles within circles—and their ends come into the cave again."

"Right; go on."

"The fences are fastened to heavy oaken posts only three feet apart, and these posts are sunk five feet in the ground."

"That is good and strong."

"Yes. The wires have no ground connection outside of the cave. They go out from the positive brush of the dynamo; there is a ground connection through the negative brush; the other ends of the wire return to the cave, and each is grounded independently."

"No-no, that won't do!"

"Why?"

"It's too expensive—uses up force for nothing. You don't want any ground connection except the one through the negative brush. The other end of every wire must be brought back into the cave and fastened independently, and *without* any ground connection. Now, then, observe the economy of it. A cavalry charge hurls itself against the fence; you are using no power, you are spending no money, for there is only one ground connection till those horses come against the wire; the moment they touch it they form a connection with the negative brush *through the ground,* and drop dead. Don't you see—you are using no energy until it is needed; your lightning is there, and ready, like the load in a gun; but it isn't costing you a cent till you touch it off. Oh, yes, the single ground connection—"

"Of course! I don't know how I overlooked that. It's not only cheaper, but it's more effectual than the other way, for if wires break or get tangled, no harm is done."

"No, especially if we have a telltale in the cave and disconnect the broken wire. Well, go on. The gatlings?"

"Yes—that's arranged. In the center of the inner circle, on a spacious platform six feet high, I've grouped a battery of thirteen gatling guns, and provided plenty of ammunition."

"That's it. They command every approach, and when the Church's knights arrive, there's going to be music. The brow of the precipice over the cave—"

"I've got a wire fence there, and a gatling. They won't drop any rocks down on us."

"Well, and the glass-cylinder dynamite torpedoes?"

"That's attended to. It's the prettiest garden that was ever planted. It's a belt forty feet wide, and goes around the outer fence—distance between it and the fence one hundred yards—kind of neutral ground, that space is. There isn't a single square yard of that whole belt but is equipped with a torpedo.

We laid them on the surface of the ground, and sprinkled a layer of sand over them. It's an innocent looking garden, but you let a man start in to hoe it once, and you'll see."

"You tested the torpedoes?"

"Well, I was going to, but—"

"But what? Why, it's an immense oversight not to apply a—"

"Test? Yes, I know; but they're all right; I laid a few in the public road beyond our lines and they've been tested."

"Oh, that alters the case. Who did it?"

"A Church committee."

"How kind!"

"Yes. They came to command us to make submission. You see they didn't really come to test the torpedoes; that was merely an incident."

"Did the committee make a report?"

"Yes, they made one. You could have heard it a mile."

"Unanimous?"

"That was the nature of it. After that I put up some signs, for the protection of future committees, and we have had no intruders since."

"Clarence, you've done a world of work, and done it perfectly."

"We had plenty of time for it; there wasn't any occasion for hurry."

We sat silent awhile, thinking. Then my mind was made up, and I said:

"Yes, everything is ready; everything is shipshape, no detail is wanting. I know what to do, now."

"So do I: sit down and wait."

"No, *sir!* rise up and *strike!*"

"Do you mean it?"

"Yes, indeed! The *de*fensive isn't in my line, and the *off*ensive is. That is, when I hold a fair hand—two-thirds as good a hand as the enemy. Oh, yes, we'll rise up and strike; that's our game."

"A hundred to one, you are right. When does the performance begin?"

"*Now!* We'll proclaim the Republic."

"Well, that *will* precipitate things, sure enough!"

"It will make them buzz, *I* tell you! England will be a hornet's nest before noon tomorrow, if the Church's hand hasn't lost its cunning—and we know it hasn't. Now you write and I'll dictate—thus:

"PROCLAMATION.

"Be It Known Unto All. Whereas the king having died and left no heir, it becomes my duty to continue the executive authority vested in me, until a government shall have been created and set in motion. The monarchy has lapsed, it no longer exists. By consequence, all political power has reverted to its original source, the people of the nation. With the monarchy, its several adjuncts died also; wherefore there is no longer a nobility, no longer a privileged class, no longer an Established Church: all men are become exactly equal, they are upon one common level, and religion is free. *A Republic is hereby proclaimed,* as being the natural estate of a nation when other authority has ceased. It is the duty of the British people to meet together immediately, and by their votes elect representatives and deliver into their hands the government."

I signed it "The Boss," and dated it from Merlin's Cave. Clarence said: "Why, that tells where we are, and invites them to call right away."

"That is the idea. We *strike*—by the Proclamation—then it's their innings. Now have the thing set up and printed and posted, right off; that is, give the order; then, if you've got a couple of bicycles handy at the foot of the hill, ho for Merlin's Cave!"

"I shall be ready in ten minutes. What a cyclone there is going to be tomorrow when this piece of paper gets to work! . . . It's a pleasant old palace, this is; I wonder if we shall ever again—but never mind about that."

CHAPTER XLIII
The Battle of the Sand Belt

IN MERLIN'S CAVE—Clarence and I and fifty-two fresh, bright, well-educated, clean-minded young British boys. At dawn I sent an order to the factories and to all our great works to stop operations and remove all life to a safe distance, as everything was going to be blown up by secret mines, *"and no telling at what moment—therefore, vacate at once."* These people knew me, and had confidence in my word. They would clear out without waiting to part their hair, and I could take my own time about dating the explosion. You couldn't hire one of them to go back during the century, if the explosion was still impending.

We had a week of waiting. It was not dull for me, because I was writing all the time. During the first three days, I finished turning my old diary into this narrative form; it only required a chapter or so to bring it down to date. The rest of the week I took up in writing letters to my wife. It was always my habit to write to Sandy everyday, whenever we were separate, and now I kept up the habit for love of it, and of her, though I couldn't do anything with the letters, of course, after I had written them. But it put in the time, you see, and was almost like talking; it was almost as if I was saying, "Sandy, if you and Hello-Central were here in the cave, instead of only your photographs, what good times we could have!" And then, you know, I could imagine the baby goo-gooing something out in reply, with its fists in its mouth and itself stretched across its mother's lap on its back, and she a-laughing and admiring and worshiping, and now and then tickling under the baby's chin to set it cackling, and then maybe throwing in a word of answer to me herself—and so on and so on—well, don't you know, I could sit there in the cave with my pen, and keep it up, that way, by the hour with them. Why, it was almost like having us all together again.

I had spies out, every night, of course, to get news. Every report made things look more and more impressive. The hosts were gathering, gathering; down all the roads and paths of England the knights were riding, and priests rode with them, to hearten these original Crusaders, this being the Church's war. All the nobilities, big and little, were on their way, and all the gentry. This was all as was expected. We should thin out this sort of folk to such a degree that the people would have nothing to do but just step to the front with their republic and—

Ah, what a donkey I was! Toward the end of the week I began to get this large and disenchanting fact through my head: that the mass of the nation had swung their caps and shouted for the republic for about one day, and there an end! The Church, the nobles, and the gentry then turned one grand, all-disapproving frown upon them and shriveled them into sheep! From that moment the sheep had begun to gather to the fold—that is to say, the camps—and offer their valueless lives and their valuable wool to the "righteous cause." Why, even the very men who had lately been slaves were in the "righteous cause," and glorifying it, praying for it, sentimentally slabbering over it, just like all the other commoners. Imagine such human muck as this; conceive of this folly!

Yes, it was now "Death to the Republic!" everywhere—not a dissenting voice. All England was marching against us! Truly this was more than I had bargained for.

I watched my fifty-two boys narrowly; watched their faces, their walk, their unconscious attitudes: for all these are a language—a language given us purposely that it may betray us in times of emergency, when we have secrets which we want to keep. I knew that that thought would keep saying itself over and over again in their minds and hearts, *All England is marching against us!* and evermore strenuously imploring attention with each repetition, ever more sharply realizing itself to their imaginations, until even in their sleep they would find no rest from it, but hear the vague and flitting creatures of their dreams say, *All England—* ALL ENGLAND—*is marching against you!* I knew all this would happen; I knew that ultimately the pressure would become so great that it would compel utterance; therefore, I must be ready with an answer at that time—an answer well chosen and tranquilizing.

I was right. The time came. They *had* to speak. Poor lads, it was pitiful to see, they were so pale, so worn, so troubled. At first their spokesman could hardly find voice or words; but he presently got both. This is what he said—and he put it in the neat modern English taught him in my schools:

"We have tried to forget what we are—English boys! We have tried to put reason before sentiment, duty before love; our minds approve, but our hearts reproach us. While apparently it was only the nobility, only the gentry, only the twenty-five or thirty thousand knights left alive out of the late wars, we were of one mind, and undisturbed by any troubling doubt; each and every one of these fifty-two lads who stand here before you, said, 'They have chosen —it is their affair.' But think—the matter is altered—*all England is marching against us!* Oh, sir, consider! Reflect! These people are our people, they are bone of our bone, flesh of our flesh, we love them—do not ask us to destroy our nation!"

Well, it shows the value of looking ahead, and being ready for a thing when it happens. If I hadn't foreseen this thing and been fixed, that boy would have had me—I couldn't have said a word. But I *was* fixed. I said:

"My boys, your hearts are in the right place, you have thought the worthy thought, you have done the worthy thing. You are English boys, you will remain English boys, and you will keep that name unsmirched. Give yourselves no further concern, let your minds be at peace. Consider this: while all England *is* marching against us, who is in the van? Who, by the commonest rules of war, will march in the front? Answer me."

"The mounted host of mailed knights."

"True. They are 30,000 strong. Acres deep, they will march. Now, observe: none but *they* will ever strike the sand belt! Then there will be an episode! Immediately after, the civilian multitude in the rear will retire, to meet business engagements elsewhere. None but nobles and gentry are knights, and *none but these* will remain to dance to our music after that episode. It is absolutely true that we shall have to fight nobody but these thirty thousand knights. Now speak, and it shall be as you decide. Shall we avoid the battle, retire from the field?"

"NO!!!"

The shout was unanimous and hearty.

"Are you—are you—well, afraid of these thirty thousand knights?"

That joke brought out a good laugh, the boys' troubles vanished away, and they went gaily to their posts. Ah, they were a darling fifty-two! As pretty as girls, too.

I was ready for the enemy, now. Let the approaching big day come along —it would find us on deck.

The big day arrived on time. At dawn the sentry on watch in the corral came into the cave and reported a moving black mass under the horizon, and a faint sound which he thought to be military music. Breakfast was just ready; we sat down and ate it.

This over, I made the boys a little speech, and then sent out a detail to man the battery, with Clarence in command of it.

The sun rose presently and sent its unobstructed splendors over the land, and we saw a prodigious host moving slowly toward us, with the steady drift and aligned front of a wave of the sea. Nearer and nearer it came, and more and more sublimely imposing became its aspect; yes, all England were there, apparently. Soon we could see the innumerable banners fluttering, and then the sun struck the sea of armor and set it all a-flash. Yes, it was a fine sight; I hadn't ever seen anything to beat it.

At last we could make out details. All the front ranks, no telling how many acres deep, were horsemen—plumed knights in armor. Suddenly we heard the blare of trumpets; the slow walk burst into a gallop, and then— well, it was wonderful to see! Down swept that vast horseshoe wave—it approached the sand belt—my breath stood still; nearer, nearer—the strip of green turf beyond the yellow belt grew narrow—narrower still—became a mere ribbon in front of the horses—then disappeared under their hoofs. Great Scott! Why, the whole front of that host shot into the sky with a thundercrash, and became a whirling tempest of rags and fragments; and along the ground lay a thick wall of smoke that hid what was left of the multitude from our sight.

Time for the second step in the plan of campaign! I touched a button, and shook the bones of England loose from her spine!

In that explosion all our noble civilization-factories went up in the air and disappeared from the earth. It was a pity, but it was necessary. We could not afford to let the enemy turn our own weapons against us.

Now ensued one of the dullest quarter hours I had ever endured. We waited in a silent solitude enclosed by our circles of wire, and by a circle of heavy smoke outside of these. We couldn't see over the wall of smoke, and we couldn't see through it. But at last it began to shred away lazily, and by the end of another quarter hour the land was clear and our curiosity was enabled to satisfy itself. No living creature was in sight! We now perceived that additions had been made to our defenses. The dynamite had dug a ditch more than a hundred feet wide, all around us, and cast up an embankment some twenty-five feet high on both borders of it. As to destruction of life, it was amazing. Moreover, it was beyond estimate. Of course we could not *count* the dead, because they did not exist as individuals, but merely as homogeneous protoplasm, with alloys of iron and buttons.

No life was in sight, but necessarily there must have been some wounded in the rear ranks, who were carried off the field under cover of the wall of smoke; there would be sickness among the others—there always is, after an episode like that. But there would be no reinforcements; this was the last stand of the chivalry of England; it was all that was left of the order, after the recent annihilating wars. So I felt quite safe in believing that the utmost force that could for the future be brought against us would be but small; that is, of knights. I therefore issued a congratulatory proclamation to my army in these words:

SOLDIERS, CHAMPIONS OF HUMAN LIBERTY AND EQUALITY: Your General congratulates you! In the pride of his strength and the vanity of his renown, an arrogant enemy came against you. You were ready. The conflict was brief; on your side, glorious. This mighty victory having been achieved utterly without loss, stands without example in history. So long as the planets shall continue to move in their orbits, the BATTLE OF THE SAND BELT will not perish out of the memories of men.

THE BOSS.

I read it well, and the applause I got was very gratifying to me. I then wound up with these remarks:

"The war with the English nation, as a nation, is at an end. The nation has retired from the field and the war. Before it can be persuaded to return, war will have ceased. This campaign is the only one that is going to be fought. It will be brief—the briefest in history. Also the most destructive to life, considered from the standpoint of proportion of casualties to numbers engaged. We are done with the nation; henceforth we deal only with the knights. English knights can be killed, but they cannot be conquered. We know what is before us. While one of these men remains alive, our task is not finished, the war is not ended. We will kill them all." [Loud and long continued applause.]

I picketed the great embankments thrown up around our lines by the dynamite explosion—merely a lookout of a couple of boys to announce the enemy when he should appear again.

Next, I sent an engineer and forty men to a point just beyond our lines on the south, to turn a mountain brook that was there, and bring it within our lines and under our command, arranging it in such a way that I could make instant use of it in an emergency. The forty men were divided into two shifts of twenty each, and were to relieve each other every two hours. In ten hours the work was accomplished.

It was nightfall, now, and I withdrew my pickets. The one who had had the northern outlook reported a camp in sight, but visible with the glass only. He also reported that a few knights had been feeling their way toward us, and had driven some cattle across our lines, but that the knights themselves had not come very near. That was what I had been expecting. They were feeling us, you see; they wanted to know if we were going to play that red terror on them again. They would grow bolder in the night, perhaps. I believed I knew what project they would attempt, because it was plainly the thing I would attempt myself if I were in their places and as ignorant as they were. I mentioned it to Clarence.

"I think you are right," said he; "it is the obvious thing for them to try."

"Well, then," I said, "if they do it they are doomed."

"Certainly."

"They won't have the slightest show in the world."

"Of course they won't."

"It's dreadful, Clarence. It seems an awful pity."

The thing disturbed me so, that I couldn't get any peace of mind for thinking of it and worrying over it. So, at last, to quiet my conscience, I framed this message to the knights:

To THE HONORABLE THE COMMANDER OF THE INSURGENT CHIVALRY OF ENGLAND: You fight in vain. We know your strength—if one may call it by that name. We know that at the utmost you cannot bring against us above five and twenty thousand knights. Therefore, you have no chance—none whatever. Reflect: we are well equipped, well fortified, we number fifty-four. Fifty-four what? Men? No, *minds*—the capablest in the world; a force against which mere animal might may no more hope to prevail than may the idle waves of the sea hope to prevail against the granite barriers of England. Be advised. We offer you your lives; for the sake of your families, do not reject the gift. We offer you this chance, and it is the last: throw down your arms; surrender unconditionally to the Republic, and all will be forgiven.

(Signed)   THE BOSS.

I read it to Clarence, and said I proposed to send it by a flag of truce. He laughed the sarcastic laugh he was born with, and said:

"Somehow it seems impossible for you to ever fully realize what these nobilities are. Now let us save a little time and trouble. Consider me the commander of the knights yonder. Now then, you are the flag of truce; approach and deliver me your message, and I will give you your answer."

I humored the idea. I came forward under an imaginary guard of the enemy's soldiers, produced my paper, and read it through. For answer, Clarence struck the paper out of my hand, pursed up a scornful lip and said with lofty disdain—

"Dismember me this animal, and return him in a basket to the baseborn knave who sent him; other answer have I none!"

How empty is theory in presence of fact! And this was just fact, and nothing else. It was the thing that would have happened, there was no getting around that. I tore up the paper and granted my mistimed sentimentalities a permanent rest.

Then, to business. I tested the electric signals from the gatling platform to the cave, and made sure that they were all right; I tested and retested those which commanded the fences—these were signals whereby I could break and renew the electric current in each fence independently of the others, at will. I placed the brook connection under the guard and authority of three of my best boys, who would alternate in two-hour watches all night and promptly obey my signal, if I should have occasion to give it—three revolver-shots in quick succession. Sentry duty was discarded for the night, and the corral left empty of life; I ordered that quiet be maintained in the cave, and the electric lights turned down to a glimmer.

As soon as it was good and dark, I shut off the current from all of the fences, and then groped my way out to the embankment bordering our side of the great dynamite ditch. I crept to the top of it and lay there on the slant of the muck to watch. But it was too dark to see anything. As for sounds, there were none. The stillness was deathlike. True, there were the usual night-sounds of the country—the whir of night birds, the buzzing of insects, the barking of distant dogs, the mellow lowing of far-off kine—but these didn't seem to break the stillness, they only intensified it, and added a gruesome melancholy to it into the bargain.

I presently gave up looking, the night shut down so black, but I kept my ears strained to catch the least suspicious sound, for I judged I had only to wait and I shouldn't be disappointed. However, I had to wait a long time. At last I caught what you may call indistinct glimpses of sound—dulled metallic sound. I pricked up my ears, then, and held my breath, for this was the sort of thing I had been waiting for. This sound thickened, and approached—from toward the north. Presently I heard it at my own level—the ridgetop of the opposite embankment, a hundred feet or more away. Then I seemed to see a row of black dots appear along that ridge—human heads? I couldn't tell; it mightn't be anything at all; you can't depend on your eyes when your imagination is out of focus. However, the question was soon settled. I heard that metallic noise descending into the great ditch. It augmented fast, it spread all along, and it unmistakably furnished me this fact: an armed host was taking up its quarters in the ditch. Yes, these people were arranging a little surprise party for us. We could expect entertainment about dawn, possibly earlier.

I groped my way back to the corral, now; I had seen enough. I went to the platform and signaled to turn the current onto the two inner fences. Then I went into the cave, and found everything satisfactory there—nobody awake but the working watch. I woke Clarence and told him the great ditch was filling up with men, and that I believed all the knights were coming for us in a body. It was my notion that as soon as dawn approached we could expect the ditch's ambuscaded thousands to swarm up over the embankment and make an assault, and be followed immediately by the rest of their army.

Clarence said:

"They will be wanting to send a scout or two in the dark to make preliminary observations. Why not take the lightning off the outer fences, and give them a chance?"

"I've already done it, Clarence. Did you ever know me to be inhospitable?"

"No, you are a good heart. I want to go and—"

"Be a reception committee? I will go, too."

We crossed the corral and lay down together between the two inside fences. Even the dim light of the cave had disordered our eyesight somewhat, but the focus straightway began to regulate itself and soon it was adjusted for present circumstances. We had had to feel our way before, but we could make out to see the fence posts now. We started a whispered conversation, but suddenly Clarence broke off and said:

"What is that?"

"What is what?"

"That thing yonder?"

"What thing—where?"

"There beyond you a little piece—a dark something—a dull shape of some kind—against the second fence."

I gazed and he gazed. I said:

"Could it be a man, Clarence?"

"No, I think not. If you notice, it looks a lit—why, it *is* a man—leaning on the fence!"

"I certainly believe it is; let's us go and see."

We crept along on our hands and knees until we were pretty close, and then looked up. Yes, it was a man—a dim great figure in armor, standing erect, with both hands on the upper wire—and of course there was a smell of burning flesh. Poor fellow, dead as a doornail, and never knew what hurt him. He stood there like a statue—no motion about him, except that his plumes swished about a little in the night wind. We rose up and looked in through the bars of his visor, but couldn't make out whether we knew him or not—features too dim and shadowed.

We heard muffled sounds approaching, and we sank down to the ground where we were. We made out another knight vaguely; he was coming very stealthily, and feeling his way. He was near enough, now, for us to see him put out a hand, find an upper wire, then bend and step under it and over the lower one. Now he arrived at the first knight—and started slightly when he discovered him. He stood a moment—no doubt wondering why the other one didn't move on; then he said, in a low voice, "Why dreamest thou here, good Sir Mar—" then he laid his hand on the corpse's shoulder—and just uttered a little soft moan and sunk down dead. Killed by a dead man, you see—killed by a dead friend, in fact. There was something awful about it.

These early birds came scattering along after each other, about one every five minutes in our vicinity, during half an hour. They brought no armor of offense but their swords; as a rule they carried the sword ready in the hand, and put it forward and found the wires with it. We would now and then see a blue spark when the knight that caused it was so far away as to be invisible to us; but we knew what had happened, all the same, poor fellow; he had touched a charged wire with his sword and been elected. We had brief intervals of grim stillness, interrupted with piteous regularity by the clash made by the falling of an ironclad; and this sort of thing was going on, right along, and was very creepy, there in the dark and lonesomeness.

We concluded to make a tour between the inner fences. We elected to walk upright, for convenience sake; we argued that if discerned, we should be taken for friends rather than enemies, and in any case we should be out of reach of swords, and these gentry did not seem to have any spears along. Well, it was a curious trip. Everywhere dead men were lying outside the second fence—not plainly visible, but still visible; and we counted fifteen of those pathetic statues—dead knights standing with their hands on the upper wire.

One thing seemed to be sufficiently demonstrated: our current was so tremendous that it killed before the victim could cry out. Pretty soon we detected a muffled and heavy sound, and next moment we guessed what it was. It was a surprise in force coming! I whispered Clarence to go and wake the army, and notify it to wait in silence in the cave for further orders. He was soon back, and we stood by the inner fence and watched the silent lightning do its awful work upon that swarming host. One could make out but little of detail; but he could note that a black mass was piling itself up beyond the second fence. That swelling bulk was dead men! Our camp was enclosed with a solid wall of the dead—a bulwark, a breastwork, of corpses, you may say. One terrible thing about this thing was the absence of human voices; there were no cheers, no war cries: being intent upon a surprise, these men moved as noiselessly as they could; and always when the front rank was near enough to their goal to make it proper for them to begin to get a shout ready, of course they struck the fatal line and went down without testifying.

I sent a current through the third fence, now; and almost immediately through the fourth and fifth, so quickly were the gaps filled up. I believed the time was come, now, for my climax; I believed that that whole army was in our trap. Anyway, it was high time to find out. So I touched a button and set fifty electric suns aflame on the top of our precipice.

Land, what a sight! We were enclosed in three walls of dead men! All the other fences were pretty nearly filled with the living, who were stealthily working their way forward through the wires. The sudden glare paralyzed this host, petrified them, you may say, with astonishment; there was just one instant for me to utilize their immobility in, and I didn't lose the chance. You see, in another instant they would have recovered their faculties, then they'd have burst into a cheer and made a rush, and my wires would have gone down before it; but that lost instant lost them their opportunity forever; while even that slight fragment of time was still unspent, I shot the current through all the fences and struck the whole host dead in their tracks! *There* was a groan you could *hear!* It voiced the death pang of eleven thousand men. It swelled out on the night with awful pathos.

A glance showed that the rest of the enemy—perhaps ten thousand strong—were between us and the encircling ditch, and pressing forward to the assault. Consequently we had them *all!* and had them past help. Time for the last act of the tragedy. I fired the three appointed revolver shots—which meant:

"Turn on the water!"

There was a sudden rush and roar, and in a minute the mountain brook was raging through the big ditch and creating a river a hundred feet wide and twenty-five deep.

"Stand to your guns, men! Open fire!"

The thirteen gatlings began to vomit death into the fated ten thousand. They halted, they stood their ground a moment against that withering deluge of fire, then they broke, faced about and swept toward the ditch like chaff before a gale. A full fourth part of their force never reached the top of the lofty embankment; the three-fourths reached it and plunged over—to death by drowning.

Within ten short minutes after we had opened fire, armed resistance was totally annihilated, the campaign was ended, we fifty-four were masters of England! Twenty-five thousand men lay dead around us.

But how treacherous is fortune! In a little while—say an hour—happened a thing, by my own fault, which—but I have no heart to write that. Let the record end here.

CHAPTER XLIV
A Postscript by Clarence

I, CLARENCE, must write it for him. He proposed that we two go out and see if any help could be afforded the wounded. I was strenuous against the project. I said that if there were many, we could do but little for them; and it would not be wise for us to trust ourselves among them, anyway. But he could seldom be turned from a purpose once formed; so we shut off the electric current from the fences, took an escort along, climbed over the enclosing ramparts of dead knights, and moved out upon the field. The first wounded man who appealed for help, was sitting with his back against a dead comrade. When the Boss bent over him and spoke to him, the man recognized him and stabbed him. That knight was Sir Meliagraunce, as I found out by tearing off his helmet. He will not ask for help any more.

We carried the Boss to the cave and gave his wound, which was not very serious, the best care we could. In this service we had the help of Merlin, though we did not know it. He was disguised as a woman, and appeared to be a simple old peasant goodwife. In this disguise, with brown-stained face and smooth-shaven, he had appeared a few days after the Boss was hurt, and offered to cook for us, saying her people had gone off to join certain new camps which the enemy were forming, and that she was starving. The Boss had been getting along very well, and had amused himself with finishing up his record.

We were glad to have this woman, for we were short-handed. We were in a trap, you see—a trap of our own making. If we stayed where we were, our dead would kill us; if we moved out of our defenses, we should no longer be invincible. We had conquered; in turn we were conquered. The Boss recognized this; we all recognized it. If we could go to one of those new camps and patch up some kind of terms with the enemy—yes, but the Boss could not go, and neither could I, for I was among the first that were made sick by the poisonous air bred by those dead thousands. Others were taken down, and still others. Tomorrow—

Tomorrow. It is here. And with it the end. About midnight I awoke, and saw that hag making curious passes in the air about the Boss's head and face, and wondered what it meant. Everybody but the dynamo-watch lay steeped in sleep; there was no sound. The woman ceased from her mysterious foolery, and started tiptoeing toward the door. I called out—

"Stop! What have you been doing?"

She halted, and said with an accent of malicious satisfaction:

"Ye were conquerors; ye are conquered! These others are perishing—you also. Ye shall all die in this place—every one—except *him.* He sleepeth, now —and shall sleep thirteen centuries. I am Merlin!"

Then such a delirium of silly laughter overtook him that he reeled about like a drunken man, and presently fetched up against one of our wires. His mouth is spread open yet; apparently he is still laughing. I suppose the face will retain that petrified laugh until the corpse turns to dust.

The Boss has never stirred—sleeps like a stone. If he does not wake today we shall understand what kind of a sleep it is, and his body will then be borne to a place in one of the remote recesses of the cave where none will ever find it to desecrate it. As for the rest of us—well, it is agreed that if any one of us ever escapes alive from this place, he will write the fact here, and loyally hide this Manuscript with the Boss, our dear good chief, whose property it is, be he alive or dead.

SARAH ORNE JEWETT

Sarah Orne Jewett, although far less known than either Mark Twain or Stephen Crane, was nevertheless an important author of her era. Her devotion to themes drawn from the "down east" section of Maine, where she was born and raised, reflects her feelings about the value of regional writing. In fact, Jewett took it upon herself to educate the larger American public about the values of rural life. As she put it: "I determined to teach the world that country people were not the awkward ignorant set those persons [literary critics, specifically and readers, generally] seemed to think. I wanted to know their grand and simple lives and so far as I had a mission when I first began to write, I think that was it."

Condemning what she called "the destroying left hand of progress," Jewett wrote a number of works, elegiac in tone, praising the people and culture of her native Maine. In *A Country of Pointed Firs* (1896), Jewett transcended mere regional writing and produced what Willa Cather called "one of the unquestioned classics of American prose writing." In the sections reproduced below, Captain Littlepage talks about how Maine has changed and then tells the narrator a tale about "The Waiting Place," which some critics see as Jewett's metaphor for the modern world.

5 Captain Littlepage

It was a long time after this; an hour was very long in that coast town where nothing stole away the shortest minute. I had lost myself completely in work, when I heard footsteps outside. There was a steep footpath between the upper and the lower road, which I climbed to shorten the way, as the children had taught me, but I believed that Mrs. Todd would find it inaccessible, unless she had occasion to seek me in great haste. I wrote on, feeling like a besieged miser of time, while the footsteps came nearer, and the sheep-bell tinkled away in haste as if some one had shaken a stick in its wearer's face. Then I looked, and saw Captain Littlepage passing the nearest window; the next moment he tapped politely at the door.

"Come in, sir," I said, rising to meet him; and he entered, bowing with much courtesy. I stepped down from the desk and offered him a chair by the window, where he seated himself at once, being sadly spent by his climb. I returned to my fixed seat behind the teacher's desk, which gave him the lower place of a scholar.

"You ought to have the place of honor, Captain Littlepage," I said.

"A happy, rural seat of various views," he quoted, as he gazed out into the sunshine and up the long wooded shore. Then he glanced at me, and looked all about him as pleased as a child.

"My quotation was from Paradise Lost; the greatest of poems, I suppose you know?" and I nodded. "There's nothing that ranks, to my mind, with Paradise Lost; it's all lofty, all lofty," he continued. "Shakespeare was a great poet; he copied life, but you have to put up with a great deal of low talk."

I now remembered that Mrs. Todd had told me one day that Captain Littlepage had overset his mind with too much reading; she had also made dark reference to his having "spells" of some unexplainable nature. I could not help wondering what errand had brought him out in search of me. There was something quite charming in his appearance: it was a face thin and delicate with refinement, but worn into appealing lines, as if he had suffered from loneliness and misapprehension. He looked, with his careful precision of dress, as if he were the object of cherishing care on the part of elderly unmarried sisters, but I knew Mari' Harris to be a very commonplace, inelegant person, who would have no such standards; it was plain that the captain was his own attentive valet. He sat looking at me expectantly. I could not help thinking that, with his queer head and length of thinness, he was made to hop along the road of life rather than to walk. The captain was very grave indeed, and I bade my inward spirit keep close to discretion.

"Poor Mrs. Begg has gone," I ventured to say. I still wore my Sunday gown by way of showing respect.

"She has gone," said the captain,—"very easy at the last, I was informed; she slipped away as if she were glad of the opportunity."

I thought of the Countess of Carberry and felt that history repeated itself.

"She was one of the old stock," continued Captain Littlepage, with touching sincerity. "She was very much looked up to in this town, and will be missed."

I wondered, as I looked at him, if he had sprung from a line of ministers; he had the refinement of look and air of command which are the heritage of the old ecclesiastical families of New England. But as Darwin says in his autobiography, "there is no such king as a sea-captain; he is greater even than a king or a schoolmaster!"

Captain Littlepage moved his chair out of the wake of the sunshine, and still sat looking at me. I began to be very eager to know upon what errand he had come.

"It may be found out some o' these days," he said earnestly. "We may know it all, the next step; where Mrs. Begg is now, for instance. Certainty, not conjecture, is what we all desire."

"I suppose we shall know it all some day," said I.

"We shall know it while yet below," insisted the captain, with a flush of impatience on his thin cheeks. "We have not looked for truth in the right direction. I know what I speak of; those who have laughed at me little know how much reason my ideas are based upon." He waved his hand toward the village below. "In that handful of houses they fancy that they comprehend the universe."

I smiled, and waited for him to go on.

"I am an old man, as you can see," he continued, "and I have been a shipmaster the greater part of my life,—forty-three years in all. You may not think it, but I am above eighty years of age."

He did not look so old, and I hastened to say so.

"You must have left the sea a good many years ago, then, Captain Littlepage?" I said.

"I should have been serviceable at least five or six years more," he answered. "My acquaintance with certain—my experience upon a certain occasion, I might say, gave rise to prejudice. I do not mind telling you that I chanced to learn of one of the greatest discoveries that man has ever made."

Now we were approaching dangerous ground, but a sudden sense of his sufferings at the hands of the ignorant came to my help, and I asked to hear more with all the deference I really felt. A swallow flew into the schoolhouse at this moment as if a kingbird were after it, and beat itself against the walls for a minute, and escaped again to the open air; but Captain Littlepage took no notice whatever of the flurry.

"I had a valuable cargo of general merchandise from the London docks to Fort Churchill, a station of the old company on Hudson's Bay," said the captain earnestly. "We were delayed in lading, and baffled by head winds and a heavy tumbling sea all the way north-about and across. Then the fog kept us off the coast; and when I made port at last, it was too late to delay in those northern waters with such a vessel and such a crew as I had. They cared for nothing, and idled me into a fit of sickness; but my first mate was a good, excellent man, with no more idea of being frozen in there until spring than I had, so we made what speed we could to get clear of Hudson's Bay and off the coast. I owned an eighth of the vessel, and he owned a sixteenth of her. She was a full-rigged ship, called the Minerva, but she was getting old and leaky. I meant it should be my last v'y'ge in her, and so it proved. She had been an excellent vessel in her day. Of the cowards aboard her I can't say so much."

"Then you were wrecked?" I asked, as he made a long pause.

"I wa'n't caught astern o' the lighter by any fault of mine," said the captain gloomily. "We left Fort Churchill and run out into the Bay with a light pair o' heels; but I had been vexed to death with their red-tape rigging at the company's office, and chilled with stayin' on deck an' tryin' to hurry up things, and when we were well out o' sight o' land, headin' for Hudson's Straits, I had a bad turn o' some sort o' fever, and had to stay below. The days were getting short, and we made good runs, all well on board but me, and the crew done their work by dint of hard driving."

I began to find this unexpected narrative a little dull. Captain Littlepage spoke with a kind of slow correctness that lacked the longshore high flavor to which I had grown used; but I listened respectfully while he explained the winds having become contrary, and talked on in a dreary sort of way about his voyage, the bad weather, and the disadvantages he was under in the lightness of his ship, which bounced about like a chip in a bucket, and would not answer the rudder or properly respond to the most careful setting of sails.

"So there we were blowin' along anyways," he complained; but looking at me at this moment, and seeing that my thoughts were unkindly wandering, he ceased to speak.

"It was a hard life at sea in those days, I am sure," said I, with redoubled interest.

"It was a dog's life," said the poor old gentleman, quite reassured, "but it made men of those who followed it. I see a change for the worse even in our own town here; full of loafers now, small and poor as 't is, who once would have followed the sea, every lazy soul of 'em. There is no occupation so fit for just that class o' men who never get beyond the fo'cas'le. I view it, in addition, that a community narrows down and grows dreadful ignorant when it is shut up to its own affairs, and gets no knowledge of the outside world except from a cheap, unprincipled newspaper. In the old days, a good part o' the best men here knew a hundred ports and something of the way folks lived in them. They saw the world for themselves, and like's not their wives and children saw it with them. They may not have had the best of knowledge to carry with 'em sight-seein', but they were some acquainted with foreign lands an' their laws, an' could see outside the battle for town clerk here in Dunnet; they got some sense o' proportion. Yes, they lived more dignified, and their houses were better within an' without. Shipping's a terrible loss to this part o' New England from a social point o' view, ma'am."

"I have thought of that myself," I returned, with my interest quite awakened. "It accounts for the change in a great many things,—the sad disappearance of sea-captains,—doesn't it?"

"A shipmaster was apt to get the habit of reading," said my companion, brightening still more, and taking on a most touching air of unreserve. "A captain is not expected to be familiar with his crew, and for company's sake in dull days and nights he turns to his book. Most of us old shipmasters came to know 'most everything about something; one would take to readin' on farming topics, and some were great on medicine,—but Lord help their poor crews!—or some were all for history, and now and then there'd be one like me that gave his time to the poets. I was well acquainted with a shipmaster that was all for bees an' bee-keepin'; and if you met him in port and went aboard, he'd sit and talk a terrible while about their havin' so much information, and the money that could be made out of keepin' 'em. He was one of the smartest captains that ever sailed the seas, but they used to call the Newcastle, a great bark he commanded for many years, Tuttle's beehive. There was old Cap'n Jameson: he had notions of Solomon's Temple, and made a very handsome little model of the same, right from the Scripture measurements, same's other sailors make little ships and design new tricks of rigging and all that. No, there's nothing to take the place of shipping in a place like ours. These bicycles offend me dreadfully; they don't afford no real opportunities of experience such as a man gained on a voyage. No: when folks left home in the old days they left it to some purpose, and when they got home they stayed there and had some pride in it. There's no large-minded way of thinking now: the worst have got to be best and rule everything; we're all turned upside down and going back year by year."

"Oh no, Captain Littlepage, I hope not," said I, trying to soothe his feelings.

There was a silence in the schoolhouse, but we could hear the noise of the water on a beach below. It sounded like the strange warning wave that gives notice of the turn of the tide. A late golden robin, with the most joyful and eager of voices, was singing close by in a thicket of wild roses.

6 The Waiting Place

"How did you manage with the rest of that rough voyage on the Minerva?" I asked.

"I shall be glad to explain to you," said Captain Littlepage, forgetting his grievances for the moment. "If I had a map at hand I could explain better. We were driven to and fro 'way up toward what we used to call Parry's Discoveries, and lost our bearings. It was thick and foggy, and at last I lost my ship; she drove on a rock, and we managed to get ashore on what I took to be a barren island, the few of us that were left alive. When she first struck, the sea was somewhat calmer than it had been, and most of the crew, against orders, manned the long-boat and put off in a hurry, and were never heard of more. Our own boat upset, but the carpenter kept himself and me above water, and we drifted in. I had no strength to call upon after my recent fever, and laid down to die; but he found the tracks of a man and dog the second day, and got along the shore to one of those far missionary stations that the Moravians support. They were very poor themselves, and in distress; 't was a useless place. There were but few Esquimaux left in that region. There we remained for some time, and I became acquainted with strange events."

The captain lifted his head and gave me a questioning glance. I could not help noticing that the dulled look in his eyes had gone, and there was instead a clear intentness that made them seem dark and piercing.

"There was a supply ship expected, and the pastor, an excellent Christian man, made no doubt that we should get passage in her. He was hoping that orders would come to break up the station; but everything was uncertain, and we got on the best we could for a while. We fished, and helped the people in other ways; there was no other way of paying our debts. I was taken to the pastor's house until I got better; but they were crowded, and I felt myself in the way, and made excuse to join with an old seaman, a Scotchman, who had built him a warm cabin, and had room in it for another. He was looked upon with regard, and had stood by the pastor in some troubles with the people. He had been on one of those English exploring parties that found one end of the road to the north pole, but never could find the other. We lived like dogs in a kennel, or so you'd thought if you had seen the hut from the outside; but the main thing was to keep warm; there were piles of birdskins to lie on, and he'd made him a good bunk, and there was another for me. 'T was dreadful dreary waitin' there; we begun to think the supply steamer was lost, and my poor ship broke up and strewed herself all along the shore. We got to watching on the headlands; my men and me knew the people were short of supplies and had to pinch themselves. It ought to read in the Bible, 'Man cannot live by fish alone,' if they'd told the truth of things; 'tain't bread that wears the worst on you! First part of the time, old Gaffett, that I lived with, seemed speechless, and I didn't know what to make of him, nor he of me, I dare say; but as we got acquainted, I found he'd been through more disasters than I had, and had troubles that wa'n't going to let him live a great while. It used to ease his mind to talk to an understanding person, so we used to sit and talk together all day, if it rained or blew so that we couldn't get out. I'd got a bad blow on the back of my head at the time we came ashore, and it pained me at times, and my strength was broken, anyway; I've never been so able since."

Captain Littlepage fell into a reverie.

"Then I had the good of my reading," he explained presently. "I had no books; the pastor spoke but little English, and all his books were foreign; but I used to say over all I could remember. The old poets little knew what comfort they could be to a man. I was well acquainted with the works of Milton, but up there it did seem to me as if Shakespeare was the king; he has his sea terms very accurate, and some beautiful passages were calming to the mind. I could say them over until I shed tears; there was nothing beautiful to me in that place but the stars above and those passages of verse.

"Gaffett was always brooding and brooding, and talking to himself; he was afraid he should never get away, and it preyed upon his mind. He thought when I got home I could interest the scientific men in his discovery: but they're all taken up with their own notions; some didn't even take pains to answer the letters I wrote. You observe that I said this crippled man Gaffett had been shipped on a voyage of discovery. I now tell you that the ship was lost on its return, and only Gaffett and two officers were saved off the Greenland coast, and he had knowledge later that those men never got back to England; the brig they shipped on was run down in the night. So no other living soul had the facts, and he gave them to me. There is a strange sort of a country 'way up north beyond the ice, and strange folks living in it. Gaffett believed it was the next world to this."

"What do you mean, Captain Littlepage?" I exclaimed. The old man was bending forward and whispering; he looked over his shoulder before he spoke the last sentence.

"To hear old Gaffett tell about it was something awful," he said, going on with his story quite steadily after the moment of excitement had passed. " 'T was first a tale of dogs and sledges, and cold and wind and snow. Then they begun to find the ice grow rotten; they had been frozen in, and got into a current flowing north, far up beyond Fox Channel, and they took to their boats when the ship got crushed, and this warm current took them out of sight of the ice, and into a great open sea; and they still followed it due north, just the very way they had planned to go. Then they struck a coast that wasn't laid down or charted, but the cliffs were such that no boat could land until they found a bay and struck across under sail to the other side where the shore looked lower; they were scant of provisions and out of water, but they got sight of something that looked like a great town. 'For God's sake, Gaffett!' said I, the first time he told me. 'You don't mean a town two degrees farther north than ships had ever been?' for he'd got their course marked on an old chart that he'd pieced out at the top; but he insisted upon it, and told it over and over again, to be sure I had it straight to carry to those who would be interested. There was no snow and ice, he said, after they had sailed some days with that warm current, which seemed to come right from under the ice that they'd been pinched up in and had been crossing on foot for weeks."

"But what about the town?" I asked. "Did they get to the town?"

"They did," said the captain, "and found inhabitants; 't was an awful condition of things. It appeared, as near as Gaffett could express it, like a place where there was neither living nor dead. They could see the place when they were approaching it by sea pretty near like any town, and thick with habitations; but all at once they lost sight of it altogether, and when they got close inshore they could see the shapes of folks, but they never could get near them,—all blowing gray figures that would pass along alone, or sometimes gathered in companies as if they were watching. The men were frightened at first, but the shapes never came near them,—it was as if they blew back; and at last they all got bold and went ashore, and found birds' eggs and sea fowl, like any wild northern spot where creatures were tame and folks had never been, and there was good water. Gaffett said that he and another man came near one o' the fog-shaped men that was going along slow with the look of a pack on his back, among the rocks, an' they chased him; but, Lord! he flittered away out o' sight like a leaf the wind takes with it, or a piece of cobweb. They would make as if they talked together, but there was no sound of voices, and 'they acted as if they didn't see us, but only felt us coming towards them,' says Gaffett one day, trying to tell the particulars. They couldn't see the town when they were ashore. One day the captain and the doctor were gone till night up across the high land where the town had seemed to be, and they came back at night beat out and white as ashes, and wrote and wrote all next day in their notebooks, and whispered together full of excitement, and they were sharp-spoken with the men when they offered to ask any questions.

"Then there came a day," said Captain Littlepage, leaning toward me with a strange look in his eyes, and whispering quickly. "The men all swore they wouldn't stay any longer; the man on watch early in the morning gave the alarm, and they all put off in the boat and got a little way out to sea. Those folks, or whatever they were, come about 'em like bats; all at once they raised incessant armies, and come as if to drive 'em back to sea. They stood thick at the edge o' the water like the ridges o' grim war; no thought o' flight, none of retreat. Sometimes a standing fight, then soaring on main wing tormented all the air. And when they'd got the boat out o 'reach o' danger, Gaffet said they looked back, and there was the town again, standing up just as they'd seen it first, comin' on the coast. Say what you might, they all believed 't was a kind of waiting-place between this world an' the next."

The captain had sprung to his feet in his excitement, and made excited gestures, but he still whispered huskily.

"Sit down, sir," I said as quietly as I could, and he sank into his chair quite spent.

"Gaffett thought the officers were hurrying home to report and to fit out a new expedition when they were all lost. At the time, the men got orders not to talk over what they had seen," the old man explained presently in a more natural tone.

"Weren't they all starving, and wasn't it a mirage or something of that sort?" I ventured to ask. But he looked at me blankly.

"Gaffett had got so that his mind ran on nothing else," he went on. "The ship's surgeon let fall an opinion to the captain, one day, that 't was some condition o' the light and the magnetic currents that let them see those folks. 'T wa'n't a right-feeling part of the world, anyway; they had to battle with the compass to make it serve, an' everything seemed to go wrong. Gaffett had worked it out in his own mind that they was all common ghosts, but the conditions were unusual favorable for seeing them. He was always talking about the Ge'graphical Society, but he never took proper steps, as I view it now, and stayed right there at the mission. He was a good deal crippled, and thought they'd confine him in some jail of a hospital. He said he was waiting to find the right men to tell, somebody bound north. Once in a while they stopped there to leave a mail or something. He was set in his notions, and let two or three proper explorin' expeditions go by him because he didn't like their looks; but when I was there he had got restless, fearin' he might be taken away or something. He had all his directions written out straight as a string to give the right ones. I wanted him to trust 'em to me, so I might have something to show, but he wouldn't. I suppose he's dead now. I wrote to him, an' I done all I could. 'T will be a great exploit some o' these days."

I assented absent-mindedly, thinking more just then of my companion's alert, determined look and the seafaring, ready aspect that had come to his face; but at this moment there fell a sudden change, and the old, pathetic, scholarly look returned. Behind me hung a map of North America, and I saw, as I turned a little, that his eyes were fixed upon the northernmost regions and their careful recent outlines with a look of bewilderment.

4

OVERSEAS EXPANSION
CHRONOLOGY, CAUSATION,
AND ESSAY WRITING

In 1898, U.S. troops fought what John Hay called "a splendid little war" to free Cuba from Spanish rule. In 1917, following a congressional declaration of war, Woodrow Wilson dispatched American soldiers to Europe in an effort to "make the world safe for democracy." By 1945, the United States had more than 15 million men in arms, had pioneered in the development of the most awesome weapon of destruction in the history of humankind, and stood ready to combat aggression against human freedom wherever it might occur in the world. Clearly, by the end of World War II, the United States was the most powerful nation in the world. Thus, in less than fifty years, the role of the United States in the world had undergone a startling and rapid transformation.

This chapter focuses on the period between 1890 and 1920 when, put simply, the United States became a world power. In this period, and for the first time, the United States maintained a formal overseas colonial empire, defined its interests in terms of the entire globe, played a major role in the outcome of a war in Europe, and—in the peace conference that followed—helped to revise the map of the world.

The expanding role of the United States in the affairs of the world produced heated political controversies then and is prompting heated historical debate now. At the time, many Americans pointed to the United States's traditional isolation from Europe's political affairs and its historical affinity with those who struggled against imperialism; these Americans argued that the United States was violating ethical principles of republicanism and liberty central to its existence as a nation. Moreover, they warned, such violations would certainly threaten and perhaps destroy democracy and self-government at home. Using these arguments, some historians have labeled this period the "great aberration" or the "great departure" in the history of U.S. foreign policy.

Other historians have used the expansionist arguments of those who favored American imperialism and concluded that the supposed departures of the 1890–1920 era were more apparent than real. In conquering and dispossessing the Indians, fighting a war with Mexico, and extending its domain westward to the Pacific Ocean, the United States had, prior to 1900, shaped a long tradition of aggressive expansion. It had an equally long history of involvement in European affairs whenever its interests were at stake. Moreover, many Americans at the time maintained, imperialism was the responsibility of "civilized" nations, and the events of 1914–1917 left the United States with no choice but to take up arms to defend its way of life.

Although historians debate over whether the emergence of the United States as a world power changed the essence of the nation's foreign policy, there is more general agreement that the scope of U.S. foreign relations expanded dramatically. The material that follows attempts to acquaint you with some of the events and processes by which the United States became a great power; whatever side of the historical debate you take, you need to understand the process.

CHRONOLOGY AND CAUSATION

America's rise to great-power status did not take place overnight and cannot be simply explained by a single fact or set of circumstances. Any effort to analyze this progression requires an understanding of a host of complex issues and their interaction, especially the ability to place events in their correct *chronology*—that is, their proper sequence in time. This chapter is partially designed to help you use chronology as an analytical tool to solve problems of historical causation.

Causation is history's most perplexing and fascinating problem. Historical events seldom have a single "cause." Usually, they result from a multiplicity of factors that are related to each other in the realms of time and space. Moreover, an event that is the result of a series of past events can simultaneously be one of the causes of a future event. If you are to understand fully such causes and consequences of a particular event, you must know the relationship between it and all the relevant events that both preceded and followed it in time. The failure to put these events in proper chronological order hinders your understanding of causation and often leads to inaccuracy and distortion.

These problems are clearly illustrated by an examination of the two wars in which the United States participated during this era—the Spanish-American War and World War I. The Spanish-American War, which had been preceded by and also resulted in the acquisition of overseas territory and influence, was both a cause and a result of American imperialism during this era. Similarly, American entry into World War I was both a result of preceding overseas interests and a cause of additional overseas interests. Moreover, major dissent arose against American participation in and the results of both conflicts. And while that dissent had a few successes, most notably the Senate refusal to ratify the Versailles treaty, it failed to prevent American participation in either conflict or the general extension of American influence in the aftermath of those conflicts. This is very puzzling, especially in light of the fact that the antiwar and anti-imperialist forces had numerous American traditions and beliefs on their side, as well as sound logic to buttress their arguments. Equally puzzling, although both wars resulted in an extension of American influence, in neither conflict was such extension a stated goal or a justification.

To begin to understand such apparent paradoxes, one must first categorize different causes and consequences of an event and then see how those causes and consequences relate to each other over time. In general, these causes and consequences can be divided into *long-range* and *immediate* factors. The most famous immediate causes of the Spanish-American War, for example, were the sinking of the U.S. battleship *Maine* in Havana harbor and the publication of the deLome letter. The long-range causes of that conflict are quite different, however. They include the traditional American interest in Cuba and desire to remove Spain from that island, the equally long-standing history of American expansion in North America, the growth of American overseas economic interests in general and in Cuba in particular, and the crisis atmosphere within the United States during the 1890s. The results of the war beyond Spain's forced agreement to Cuban independence (i.e., the acquisition of the Philippines, Guam, Hawaii, and Puerto Rico) seem to have no relationship whatsoever to the immediate causes of the war. They are clearly related, however, to some of the long-range causes of the war as well as to some of the events of the war itself. However alien to imperialism the immediate causes of the war may have been, the very act of fighting that war led to the conquest and occupation of some of these territories, recognition of the importance of others, and an emotional reaction by many Americans against giving back what had already been taken by blood. Anti-imperialist arguments proved insufficient to overcome these *faits accomplis* and such emotionalism; the subsequent decision to acquire these territories became, in turn, a cause of continued American imperialism and overseas involvement. The process reached an apogee of sorts after the building of the Panama Canal, a project with such enormous economic and strategic implications that it led all future presidents, no matter what their previous stand on imperialism, to insist on American domination of all Caribbean and Central American countries astride the canal's access routes. This bias led even the Reagan administration to wield a decidedly big stick in Central America, despite the fact that the strategic rationale for such an approach may no longer really exist.

An understanding of these relationships requires not only a complete listing of the factors involved but also the ability to place them in their proper chronological order so that the true cause-and-effect relationships between them become clear. For example, the publication of the deLome letter preceded the sinking of the *Maine* by a week and thereby influenced the public's perception of the latter event; a full understanding of the American reaction to the sinking of the *Maine* is thus impossible if one does not know that publication of the deLome letter, as well as numerous other events, preceded it. Similarly, the Senate voted in favor of the peace treaty that ended the war and gave the United States the Philippines after they had been conquered and one day after word arrived that fighting had broken out between American troops and Filipino guerrillas intent on independence; obviously, the events had an impact on the vote—and the failure of the anti-imperialists—that cannot be understood unless one knows that they preceded the vote. In analyzing why America entered World War I, one cannot understand the full impact of the publication of the Zimmerman telegram unless one realizes that it had been preceded by the German declaration of unrestricted submarine warfare and by an American punitive expedition into Mexico that had almost resulted in war with that country. Moreover, none of these events makes explanatory sense if one does not first understand the overall *context* that had been created by long-range factors previously discussed.

The assignments that follow are designed to help you understand that context, as well as chronology, and the role that both play in clarifying the causes and consequences of specific events. But while historical context and proper chronology for specific events can be determined fairly straightforwardly, the actual analysis of causes and consequences is much more complex and is subject to differing interpretations, as described in Chapter 1. Of the many long-range and immediate causes of the Spanish-American War you can cite and relate to each other, for example, which would you choose to emphasize as most important, and why? If different relationships between events are possible, which relationships would you choose, and why? Once you make such decisions, you are interpreting the past rather than simply studying it, and such interpretation requires the writing of a historical essay to explain your logic. So far, your written assignments in this volume have been limited to questions, summaries, and brief explanations. You now have an opportunity to write a real historical essay by answering one of the questions listed in assignment 2 and, in the process, to grapple with the problems of causation and interpretation.

OUTLINING AND REVISION

As with most historical problems, the evidence you uncover to answer your question will not lead to a simple, single conclusion, and you will need some method of organizing and synthesizing the different points you wish to make. The primary method of organizing and synthesizing historical material in preparation for writing a paper is to create an *outline.* An outline is also a useful tool to help clarify your thoughts and is thus of value for *all* writing exercises—including essay examination questions.

Your first step in creating an outline is to write a *thesis* statement. This statement will provide you, in sentence form, with the basic points you wish to make and will serve as a guide for your outline and subsequent paper. For the essay you will be writing, your summary answer to the question you have chosen from assignment 2 would be your thesis statement.

Your second step is to organize your information in outline form. Some students find less formal outlines or lists more useful than what we suggest below; others prefer to write a very rough draft before outlining and then proceed to more polished versions. If one of these methods works for you, by all means use it in the future. Only experience will make clear which form is most appropriate for you, however, and in this essay you should use a formal outline if only to experiment with it.

In formal outlines, Roman numerals (I) and capital letters (A) are used for major points and concepts; arabic numerals (1) and lowercase letters (a) are used for subordinate, minor points. You can use an indefinite number of subheadings, depending upon the complexity of the subject, but you should seldom, if ever, carry subheadings beyond five or six levels. However many you use, headings and subheadings should be consistent. Do not, for example, make capital letter "A" a major issue and then make letter "B" a minor, related event; the less important event should be a numerical subheading under "A." You should also try not to phrase "A" as a complete sentence, "B" as a clause or phrase, and "C" as a single noun; any of these forms is acceptable, but whichever one is chosen should be used consistently. Furthermore, every heading should have at least two citations; in other words, if you have an "A" there should also be a "B," and if you have a 1 there should also be a 2.

The first Roman numeral for any essay should indicate the outline of your introduction; the last Roman numeral should contain the outline of your conclusion. Roman numerals and subheadings in between should organize your major points and evidence in a logical, consistent, and coherent manner. For examples and more detailed information, consult one of the writer's guides listed in Chapter 1.

After you complete an outline, you are ready to begin writing. But do not assume that your first draft is what you should hand in. Most writers, no matter how skilled, find that they go through numerous drafts before their written work accurately reflects their thoughts. Indeed, many writers can clarify their thoughts *only* by examining and editing early drafts of their work; revising enables them to recognize weaknesses in logic and presentation, to alter their interpretations accordingly, and to strengthen their prose. In reading your first draft, for example, you may very well discover not merely grammatical and spelling errors but also illogical conclusions; such problems may call for additional thought or research that would lead to changes in your thesis. These problems with logic did not emerge earlier because you had not yet spelled out in detail what you thought. Once you did, previously unnoticed flaws in your generalizations became apparent. Correction of such problems may very well require a new outline and draft. It may even require a new thesis statement, for in many ways your first thesis statement was merely a hypothesis whose weaknesses emerged in the process of outlining and writing. (In this regard, it is advisable to let some time pass before you read and revise your first draft, so that you can clear your mind and rethink your conclusions.)

Redrafting should continue until you are convinced that your most recent version is logical, readable, and an accurate reflection of your final thoughts. You should then make sure to *proofread* your paper prior to submission. Constantly remember that your readers can understand only what you present to them on paper, not what is going on inside your head. Moreover, as previously implied, an illogical or sloppy paper often reflects illogical, incomplete, or sloppy thinking. If you are uncertain after the first or after numerous drafts as to how a reader would react to your paper, ask a friend or classmate to read, summarize, and comment on it. The summary should reflect accurately what you were trying to say, and the comments should note whether or not the paper is clearly argued, written, and presented.

ASSIGNMENTS

1. At the end of this chapter you will find four separate lists of events relating to American imperialism and the Spanish-American War: one for important events in the history of American imperialism prior to the war, one for the specific events that led to the war, one for the specific events that influenced the peace treaty and the Senate vote on it, and one for important events in the later history of American imperialism. Using the information provided in your textbook, class lectures, and, when necessary, appropriate reference works cited in Chapter 1, provide the date for each event and rearrange each list so that the events are in proper chronological order. Hand in a copy of these rearranged lists if so instructed by your professor, making sure to keep a copy for yourself.

2. Examine the relationship between these events, now that they are in proper chronological order, and use this information to write a thesis statement and outline for an essay that would answer one of the following questions:

    a. Why did the United States go to war with Spain in April of 1898?

    b. Why did the United States acquire an overseas empire as a result of the war with Spain?

    c. How and why were the anti-imperialists unable to stop the acquisition of an overseas empire?

    d. How and why did the Spanish-American War and resulting peace treaty lead to additional overseas imperialism between 1899 and 1917?

3. Compose the first draft of a two- to three-page (500- to 750-word) essay from this outline. Revise it as you see fit.

4. On the direction of your professor, either meet with him or her or a teaching assistant or with another member of the class to receive commentary and criticism on your outline and draft.

5. Revise your essay again and produce a final copy. Submit this along with your original outline and first draft as instructed.

ADDITIONAL QUESTIONS TO CONSIDER

1. In writing your essay, which particular event or events did you consider to be the most important factors? Why? Could someone else have chosen other events as the most important? If so, why do you consider your choice the better one?

2. As previously stated, the anti-imperialists argued that the acquisition of an overseas empire was immoral, a violation of American traditions, and a danger to American democracy at home. Were their criticisms justified? Why?

3. One of the most common and popular historical questions people ask involves predicting how the past and present would change if one past event had occurred differently. If, for example, President McKinley had not ordered Admiral Dewey to Manila Bay, would the United States have acquired the Philippines? And if the answer is no, would the United States still have wound up going to war with Japan in 1941? While such questions are fascinating and fun, most historians argue that the complexities of chronology and causation, often referred to as the "seamless web" of history, make these questions unanswerable. Do you agree? If so, can you explain why they are unanswerable? If you disagree, how can you answer such an argument?

4. In all of its wars, the United States has justified its intervention on moral grounds while in actuality extending its power and influence. Are such justifications merely hypocritical lies to cover up the truth or real beliefs that can be considered important causes of the wars and their aftermaths?

5. Was American foreign policy from 1890 to 1920 a "great departure" from past U.S. history?

AMERICAN IMPERIALISM AND THE SPANISH-AMERICAN WAR

A. American Imperialism Prior to the Spanish-American War

Publication of Alfred Thayer Mahan's *The Influence of Seapower*
The Hawaiian Revolution

The Venezuelan Crisis and the Olney Corollary to the Monroe Doctrine
The Depression of 1893
First U.S. treaty with Samoa
Bureau of the Census declares frontier has ended
Social Darwinism and "white man's burden" publications of Josiah Strong, John Fiske, et al.
Beginnings of U.S. naval construction program
Samoan crisis with Germany and England
Chilean crisis
The McKinley Tariff
The Hawaiian Reciprocity Trade Treaty
The Hawaiian Pearl Harbor Treaty
Beginnings of American fears that Europeans are about to partition China
Formation of National Association of Manufacturers to foster increased foreign trade

B. *Specific Events Leading to the Spanish-American War*

Destruction of the *U.S.S. Maine*
Wilson-Gorman Tariff
President Cleveland's Neutrality Proclamation regarding Cuba
Development of contingency plan for War with Spain
The "yellow press" begins to report and distort events in Cuba
Congress declares Cuba free and authorizes the president to employ force
General Weyler initiates the "concentration" policy in Cuba
Outbreak of the second Cuban revolution
Publication of the deLome letter
McKinley's inauguration and mediation offer
U.S.S. Maine sent to Havana
McKinley's demand for an armistice in Cuba, negotiations, and an end to the "concentration" policy
Antiautonomy riots in Havana
Senator Proctor's Senate speech on Cuba
President McKinley's request for congressional authority to use force to end hostilities in Cuba
Spain's reply to President McKinley's demands
Spain's recall of General Weyler, modification of the concentration policy, and moves toward Cuban autonomy

C. *Specific Events Influencing Terms of Treaty of Paris and Senate Vote*

Annexation of Hawaii
British request for U.S. support in preventing partition of China
Arrival of German fleet in Manila Bay
Congress passes the Teller Amendment
Admiral Dewey's victory at Manila Bay
Armistice signed ending Spanish-American hostilities
Aguinaldo declares Philippine independence
U.S. ground forces and Philippine guerrillas capture Manila

Treaty of Paris signed
Battle of Santiago Bay
Battles of El Caney and San Juan Hill
Formation of the Anti-Imperialist League
Word arrives of U.S.-Philippine clashes
William Jennings Bryan announces support for Treaty of Paris
McKinley squelches the Turpie-Foraker Amendment recognizing the Cuban
   rebels as a government
U.S. conquest of Puerto Rico
Senate passes Treaty of Paris 57–27
McKinley directs U.S. negotiators at Paris conference to obtain entire Philip-
   pine archipelago
Senate debate on Treaty of Paris begins
Formation of American Asiatic Association

D. *American Imperialism After Spanish-American War and Treaty of
Paris*

Roosevelt Corollary to the Monroe Doctrine
Passage of Platt Amendment for Cuba
U.S. acquisition of Virgin Islands
The first Open Door Note
Panamanian Revolution and Canal Treaty
U.S. military intervention in Mexican revolution
U.S. joins European forces in suppressing Boxer Rebellion in China
U.S. protectorate over Nicaragua
U.S.-German Division of Samoa
The second Open Door Note
U.S. military intervention in and protectorates over Dominican Republic and
   Haiti
U.S. Army suppression of Philippine Insurrection
Completion of Panama Canal

5
PROGRESSIVISM
BIOGRAPHY IN HISTORY

On September 6, 1901, President William McKinley was shot in Buffalo, New York, by a young self-styled anarchist named Leon Czolgosz. Eight days later McKinley died and Vice-President Theodore Roosevelt, whom Mark Hanna had once called "that damned cowboy," became the twenty-sixth president of the United States. Symbolically at least, this ascension to power of the young, dynamic, and reform-minded Roosevelt altered American politics. While progressive reformers had already achieved many successes on the state and local levels, Roosevelt brought progressivism to the presidency. For the next two decades the movement would dominate and transform national politics. To this day, however, historians have problems explaining just what this movement was.

"Progressivism," as your lectures and textbook readings suggest, is one of those terms that is historically useful but fraught with problems of definition. It is useful because it brings together in a single word all the substantial, conscious efforts on the local, state, and national levels to grapple with the social, economic, and political problems of an emerging industrial economy. In the years from the turn of the century to American entry into World War I, reformers sought to use the power of government to remedy an enormous range of specific problems, from trees to tenement houses. They also sought, in the words of Herbert Croly, one of the intellectual mentors of the movement, a "civilized democracy," a new type of politics in which "the common citizen must be something of a saint and something of a hero."

All human beings, however, even progressives, make individual decisions about how and why they will seek sainthood or heroism. The incredibly diverse backgrounds and motives that these reformers brought to their task—and the equally diverse ways in which they sought to ameliorate the social, economic, and political conditions of the early twentieth century—make "progressivism" extremely difficult to define. Historian Walter T. K. Nugent recently concluded that "many different people—one is tempted to say practically anybody alive then—could claim to be progressive at least at some point and on some issue." However useful the term may be in describing the general thrust of this era, "progressive" must thus be applied very cautiously in describing individual lives and in trying to reach some meaningful conclusions about what took place during this time period.

The study of individual lives belongs to a special and highly popular form of history known as *biography*. In the process of carefully examining specific individuals, biography can also provide useful guidelines for broader historical definitions. Society is, after all, composed of individuals who share common beliefs and experiences, and the study of specific individuals thus involves examination of the broader environment within which the subjects lived. No one living in the progressive era, for example, could completely escape the impact of industrialization or imperialism. A study of the lives of individual progressives can thus offer you a number of insights into the social environment in which they lived and the patterns of their responses to that environment; such insights are of critical importance in any effort to define a movement or era.

According to some historians in the field of psychohistory, biographies can also reveal the subconscious motivations that ruled both individuals and their societies. Studies of certain types of progressives, for example, emphasize the fact that the dramatic changes in social status and values caused by industrialization led many members of the old middle class into progressive reform as a means of recovering their lost status in society and reasserting some of their most deeply held values. Such psychological motivations by no means affected all progressive reformers, however; in a movement so widespread and diverse, the historian must be extremely careful before reaching any generalizations.

One way to avoid faulty generalizations is to examine a series of prominent individuals in a single movement who came from different backgrounds and espoused different causes. Following the "Assignments" section of this chapter are biographical sketches of three such individuals from the progressive movement. Florence Kelley was a genuine radical, a socialist who attempted to use the legislative authority of the state to eliminate child labor and protect working women from industrial exploitation. Gifford Pinchot was a political moderate who, as one of the nation's preeminent foresters, was a pioneer in using the power of the federal government to protect the nation's woodland resources. Leonard Wood was a high-ranking army officer and politician who, while conservative on many issues, sought to reform the army to make it both effective in light of America's overseas interests and influential in the development of the civilized democracy sought by Herbert Croly and so many other progressives.

Despite their enormous differences in terms of background, issues, and political outlook, Kelley, Pinchot, and Wood had some things in common that lead us to label them "progressive." At the very least they were all political activists who shared an acceptance of and desire for change in American society as well as a deep commitment to making the system work. They also shared a series of more specific beliefs but were divided by an equally large number of differences. Careful examination of the similarities and differences in their beliefs and activities should provide you with sufficient information to form some tentative hypotheses about the progressive movement—hypotheses you can then test through biographical examination of a fourth individual of your own choosing.

ASSIGNMENTS

1. Read the biographical sketches and documents at the end of this chapter.
2. Select a fourth individual who was in some way active during the progressive era (1900–1917) and who produced some documentary evidence (i.e., book, pamphlet, memoir, song, painting, diary, speech) of that activity. The individual can be chosen from your textbook, class notes, or your own reading.
3. Using the library as described in Chapter 1 of this volume, collect biographical data on this individual and find and reproduce a portion of the documentary evidence the individual produced. The biographical works available in reference represent a logical starting point for this research.
4. Write a two- to three-page (500- to 750-word) biographical sketch of the individual and append the reproduced document or excerpt. Organize your biographical material and emphasize relevant factors in such a way that the sketch serves as an *introduction to the document.* You can use the three sketches provided as guides in this regard, but make sure you include footnotes and bibliography as well as the duplication.

ADDITIONAL QUESTIONS TO CONSIDER

1. Putting together the information you gathered for your biographical sketch with the other sketches in this chapter and material from your textbook and lectures, how would you define progressivism? Does your definition depart significantly from the textbook definition or from that offered by your professor?
2. What previously unknown aspects of progressivism did you discover in preparing your biographical sketch? What generalizations could you and could you not make from this new information? In general terms, what have you found to be the strengths and weaknesses of the biographical approach to history and the relationship between the two? Why is biography such a popular form of historical writing?

3. If the structure and format of your class permit, you may be able to approach this assignment collaboratively. This can be done by getting together with some of your classmates and identifying either a *group* of progressives to focus on or a series of individuals representing very different groups within the progressive movement. Either method will enable you to draw important comparisons and contrasts and thereby help you to define "progressivism." The sketches provided in this chapter would suggest that settlement workers, conservationists, and soldier-diplomats would be three possibilities. Other groups that could be studied include mayors, governors, social scientists, labor leaders, poets and novelists, journalists, and national politicians. Your imagination, combined with some thought and discussion, will suggest innumerable other possibilities.

GIFFORD PINCHOT

In 1909, President William Howard Taft's newly appointed Secretary of the Interior Richard A. Ballinger reopened certain public lands in Wyoming and Montana for public sale. Gifford Pinchot, head of the U.S. Forest Service, immediately accused Ballinger of abandoning sound conservation practices in favor of corporate interests. Shortly thereafter, a former employee of the Interior Department charged in *Collier's* magazine that Ballinger was trying to abet certain fraudulent corporate claims to Alaskan coal lands. Charges and countercharges swirled through the Interior Department. Finally, President Taft upheld Secretary Ballinger and fired Gifford Pinchot. Subsequently, a congressional investigation exonerated Ballinger of charges of wrongdoing but condemned the secretary as hostile to conservation.

This Ballinger-Pinchot controversy split the Taft administration and certainly contributed to Theodore Roosevelt's decision to divide the Republican party and run a separate Progressive party campaign for the presidency in 1912. The controversy also converted Pinchot to political activism on behalf of a national Progressive party coalition. Yet he had long been destined to activism of one sort or another.

Pinchot was born to a wealthy New York family on August 11, 1865. His father, James Wallace Pinchot, was a wealthy merchant, a Republican, and a Presbyterian who named his firstborn son after his close friend, Sanford Gifford, the American landscape painter. James Pinchot was also a Francophile: his children were tutored in French as well as English; the family frequently traveled in France; and they often lived in a country villa outside Milford, Pennsylvania, modeled after a French chateau. Gifford Pinchot attended a series of private schools in New York and Paris. After preparatory school at Phillips Exeter Academy, he entered Yale in 1885.

At Yale, following the urgings of his father, Gifford studied botany, meteorology, and other sciences to prepare himself for a career in forestry. After graduating from Yale in 1889, he went to study at the French National Forestry School at Nancy. There, he absorbed European ideas about managing public resources for the use of future generations. In 1890, Pinchot returned to the United States determined to introduce public forestry programs.

Pinchot wanted American forests to "produce the largest amount of whatever crop or service will be most useful and keep on producing it for generation after generation of men and trees." Clearly, he favored commercial use of public as well as private forests; his leading role in conservation circles was based on his insistence that forests be used scientifically. He emphasized selective harvesting, planning for future growth, and fire prevention. In 1896, Pinchot served on the National Forest Commission of the National Academy of Sciences, which was charged with making recommendations for how the forest reserves of the American West should be used. The commission's conclusions were embodied in the Forest Management Act of 1897, which established the legal guidelines for use of these western lands. Pinchot's pragmatic views on using natural resources occasionally led to confrontations with more ardent conservationists, like the naturalist John Muir, who sought to preserve wilderness areas.

In 1898, Pinchot was appointed head of the insignificant Division of Forestry within the Department of Agriculture. His convictions and ambitions argued for a larger role for that division and, in 1905, with the active support of President Roosevelt, Pinchot embarked on a clever bureaucratic campaign to persuade Congress to transfer the nation's vast forest reserves from the General Land Office of the Department of the Interior to his section of the Department of Agriculture. Pinchot succeeded, and his revamped division, now called the Forestry Service, became a powerful force within the government. The Forest Service, in line with Pinchot's progressive convictions, argued for federal regulation of natural resources and pioneered new techniques for resolving economic conflicts over the use of public lands. The dynamic and personable Pinchot, working with a sympathetic president, firmly established conservation as an important item on the nation's agenda. The 1908 White House Conference on the Conservation of Natural Resources marked a pinnacle for the conservation movement in the progressive era.

To defend the conservation movement he had done so much to create, Pinchot became embroiled in his feud with Ballinger. And when Taft fired him, Pinchot determined to defeat Taft. He was one of the founders, in January 1911, of the National Progressive Republican League, designed to challenge Taft's renomination in 1912. Pinchot first supported the presidential ambitions of Wisconsin progressive Robert M. LaFollette, but he turned to his friend and mentor Theodore Roosevelt after the latter became a candidate in 1912. When the Republicans renominated Taft, Pinchot left the party and participated in founding the Progressive party, which nominated Roosevelt. With Roosevelt's defeat in 1912 and the demise of the Progressive party in 1916, Pinchot was forced to play a lesser role in national politics. Although he had presidential ambitions and on several occasions ran for the United States Senate, his impact on national politics ended with Roosevelt's defeat.

Pinchot remained active in politics and conservation for the rest of his long life. He was twice elected to the governorship of Pennsylvania and served as professor of forestry at Yale and as founder and president of the Society of American Foresters. He wrote an autobiography, *Breaking New Ground,* which was published posthumously in 1947. Gifford Pinchot died of leukemia at the age of 81 in 1946.

The passages that follow are from two sources. The first selection is from Pinchot's book *The White Pine* (1896). It provides evidence of the conservationist principles that Pinchot held throughout his life. The second passage is a brief section of his autobiography in which he none too modestly assesses his work on the white pine.

FIRE AND WIND[1]

The worst enemy of the Pennsylvania woodlands, and especially of the coniferous forests, is fire. Very few of the Pine woods visited in the course of this investigation were without traces of it. Although many of the fires run only upon the surface and do no direct harm to the timber itself, the indirect injury which results from burning the humus layer and drying out the soil is very serious, and should not be overlooked. Such fires are often followed by a decrease in the rate of annual growth from which it may take the trees several years to recover. In very many other cases the injury to the tree is both direct and important. Often the bark of the butt is scorched or burned, and the cambium layer below it killed by heat. Then the bark loosens or drops away, and decay sets in soon afterward.

When exposed to fire the young growth, with its delicate bark and foliage, is killed at once. Later on, when the trees have reached an age of forty to sixty years, and have formed thick corky bark, many of them are comparatively safe from direct injury from moderate surface fires. But if a fire reaches the crown and burns the leaves, the tree does not survive. Large bodies of second-growth Pine were examined which had been killed in this way.

After lumbering the danger from fire is very great, and especially where Hemlock has been cut, because of its heavy crown and great quantity of fine spray. As the tops lie on the ground, a large surface is thus exposed to the action of the wind and sun, and the whole mass becomes exceedingly inflammable. The crown of the Pine, on the other hand, is not only shorter, but it is generally very much broken by the fall of the tree. It furnishes, in consequence, far less material to feed a fire. It may be said in passing that a very considerable source of danger would be removed if it were possible for lumbermen to break down the tops of lumbered trees. Standing, as they often do

[1]Gifford Pinchot and Henry S. Graves, *The White Pine* (New York: Century, 1896), pp. 33–36.

at present, propped clear of the ground on their leg-like branches, they become as dry as tinder and burn with an intense heat. The danger lasts long, for the tops rot very slowly. If they could be brought in contact with the ground their menace to the forest would speedily disappear.

In the spring, under the influence of the warm dry southwest wind, fires are easily started. They burn most readily, and are most frequent, on south and southwest slopes, and upon mountain-tops and ridges. Fires running down hill are often stopped by the damp moss and other vegetation under the dense cover of Hemlock and Pine. When started at the bottom of a slope, a fire may either run up over the hillside or it may follow some narrow ravine, which acts almost like a chimney to increase its power.

The chief causes of fires are the desire for better pasture or a richer crop of huckleberries, the carelessness of campers, recklessness in clearing land or burning a fallow, railroads, and malice. The country is so sparsely populated that, even when the incendiary is known, it is practically impossible to secure evidence sufficient to convict.

The usual method of fighting fires is backfiring, but the scanty population makes it both costly and difficult, in most lumber regions, to assemble men enough to offer successful resistance to extensive fires. Effective measures must look toward localizing the danger by cutting fire-lines, and the organization of systems of fire wardens or fire patrols. But these precautions are expensive, and without a strong public sentiment behind them they can never fully succeed. When the inhabitants of any region where fires occur become thoroughly alive and earnest in the desire to prevent and extinguish them, then the danger from that source will be in a fair way to disappear.

White Pine is fairly wind-firm; much more so than Hemlock. Still it is often thrown by tornadoes and extraordinarily strong winds. In such cases lumbermen peel a strip of bark from the top of the stem throughout the lumber length. The rest of the bark becomes loosened and falls off, and the wood is saved from the attacks of borers.

FROM THE AUTOBIOGRAPHY[2]

One of the first studies which [Henry] Graves and I undertook was concerned with the management of White Pine, the most important commercial timber tree of those days. It resulted in the first professional forester's account of the growth of a North American tree. Its purpose was to enable forest students (who were beginning to appear), lumbermen, and others, to ascertain the volume of individual White Pine trees and of whole stands, in cubic feet and in board feet, more easily and accurately, and to predict the yield at any desired number of years.

[2]Gifford Pinchot, *Breaking New Ground* (New York: Harcourt Brace, 1947), p. 73.

The White Pine [the book of that name] appeared in 1896. It kept in mind both the forest and its owner—did not forget interest, taxes, and other expenses in relation to forest production. It also proved two points which the lumbermen of that day uniformly denied . . . , that the *White Pine* was coming back; and that the new growth would in time produce good lumber like the old. The annual rings in the young trees were going through the same cycles of growth as their elders before them.

I still think it was a workmanlike job, but very technical for its time, as was not unnatural in view of the youth and inexperience of its authors. Incidentally, it made nobody rich. Before long, the annual royalties on the sale of it came in postage stamps because they were too small for checks.

FLORENCE KELLEY

Florence Kelley, according to Frances Perkins, Franklin Roosevelt's secretary of labor, "was no gentle saint." She brought an incisive mind, a clear intelligence, and a forceful personality to her lifelong concern with the issues confronting working women in industrial America. When, for example, while working as a factory inspector for the State of Illinois, she experienced difficulty getting cases prosecuted in state courts, she enrolled in law school at Northwestern University, completed her course of study, and was admitted to the Illinois bar within two years. Such energy and ability made Kelley a formidable advocate of those progressive causes she espoused.

Kelley was born in Philadelphia on September 12, 1859. She was the daughter of William D. Kelley, an Irish Protestant, self-educated lawyer and abolitionist. He served in the House of Representatives from 1861 to 1890, where his ardent defense of the protective tariff earned him the nickname "Pig Iron." Her mother was from an established Quaker family with a long-standing commitment to the abolition of slavery and other social reforms. Later in life, Kelley fondly recalled that her Great Aunt Sarah had refused to permit cotton or sugar products into her house because they were produced by slave labor. Kelley was educated largely at home, reading widely in her father's library.

In 1876 she entered Cornell University. Illness forced her to drop out for a time, but in 1882 she completed her degree program, and her thesis on the changing legal status of children was published in the *International Review* in August of that year. Kelley then applied to the University of Pennsylvania Graduate School, where she was denied admission because she was a woman. She then started teaching evening classes for working women in Philadelphia. In 1883, while traveling in Europe, Kelley met with M. Carey Thomas, later a feminist reformer and longtime president of Bryn Mawr, and learned that the University of Zurich was offering advanced degrees to qualified women. She proceeded to Zurich, where she became a convert to the socialist ideas popular among university students there.

Socialism, Kelley testified, enabled her to understand much that previously had baffled her about the exploitation of women and child labor in industrial society.

In Zurich Kelley also met and married Lazare Wischnewetzky, a Russian medical student and socialist. In 1886 the young couple with their firstborn son returned to New York, where Wischnewetzky struggled to establish a medical practice. Despite the birth of two more children, it soon became clear that the marriage was in trouble. In 1889, Florence Kelley moved to Illinois, divorced her husband, took custody of their three children, and resumed her maiden name.

In 1891 Kelley took up residence at Hull House, which had been established by Jane Addams two years earlier in Chicago's Nineteenth District to combat the problems of urban poverty. A year later Kelley was hired by the Illinois Bureau of Labor to undertake a study of working conditions in the garment industry sweatshops that infested Chicago's tenements. At the same time, the federal commissioner of labor employed Kelley to investigate living conditions in Chicago's slums. Much of the data that Kelley collected were used to persuade Illinois state legislators of the need for a new law; this proved to be the Factory Act, which was enacted in 1893. Illinois Governor John Peter Altgeld hired her as factory inspector to enforce the provisions of this act, which limited the number of hours women could work, forbade child labor, and attempted to regulate the sweatshops of the tenements. Despite difficulties—which included getting shot at and being exposed to smallpox in the 1893 epidemic—Kelley worked determinedly to enforce the law. Her annual reports forcefully and clearly described the grim conditions under which women and children were often compelled to work. When Altgeld was defeated for reelection in 1896, Kelley was forced to resign. She returned to Hull House and supported her children by working evenings in a Chicago public library.

In 1899, Kelley accepted a position as secretary for the newly formed National Consumer's League, a position she held to her death in 1932. To accept this job meant moving back to New York City, where Kelley joined the Henry Street Settlement House; this had been established by Lillian Wald. As secretary to the Consumer's League, Kelley traveled thousands of miles and delivered countless speeches. In time, she organized over sixty consumer leagues in more than twenty states. In 1905, Kelley published *Some Ethical Gains Through Legislation,* a book that succinctly argued her views on how the enactment of wage-and-hour laws could benefit working women and why consumers needed the protection of state and federal legislation.

Kelley, while active for the Consumer's League, continued her work on other causes. When the U.S. Supreme Court proposed to hear a case on an Oregon law that limited the workday for women to ten hours, Kelley and her collaborators compiled a mass of sociological and medical statistics to show the negative impact of long hours on working women. These data became the basis for the brief that attorney Louis D. Brandeis used to defend Oregon's law. The court upheld the right of the state to regulate working hours for women—a major victory for Kelley and her supporters. Kelley also continued to oppose child labor; she served on both the New York State and national child labor committees and applauded President Taft's decision in 1912 to set up a child labor bureau. Kelley was also a leading supporter of the Keating-Owen Child Labor Act of 1916, in which Congress used its authority under the commerce clause to regulate the sale and production of goods produced by child labor.

Kelley embraced other progressive causes as well. She was one of the founding members of the National Association for the Advancement of Colored People in 1909. A pacifist, she was also an outspoken opponent of U.S. overseas expansion and a founding member of the Woman's International League for Peace and Freedom. She continued to be an active socialist, advocating not the violent overthrow of the government but an increased role for the state in directing and regulating the economy. Kelley also spent the last years of her life combating a proposed equal rights amendment to the U.S. Constitution, fearing that it would endanger the hard-won protective laws for working women.

The excerpt from *Some Ethical Gains Through Legislation* reproduced below, which argues the need for the Pure Food and Drug Act, illustrates not only Kelley's commitment to progressive reforms but also something of her research methods and her enormous knowledge of consumer issues.

CHAPTER VI
The Rights of Purchasers[3]

In any given community every person is directly or indirectly a purchaser. From birth to death choice is made for us or we ourselves choose objects of purchase daily, even hourly. As we do so, we help to decide, however unconsciously, how our fellow men shall spend their time in making what we buy. Few persons can give much in charity; giving a tithe is, perhaps, beyond the usual custom. But whatever our gifts may be, they are less decisive for the weal or woe of our fellow beings than are our habitual expenditures. For a man is largely what his work makes him—an artist, an artisan, a handicraftsman, a drudge, a sweater's victim or, scarcely less to be pitied, a sweater. All these and many more classes of workers exist to supply the demand that is incarnate in their friends and fellow citizens, acting as the purchasing public. All of us, all the time, are deciding what industries shall survive, and under what conditions.

Obviously the purchaser ultimately decides all production, since any

[3]Florence Kelley, *Some Ethical Gains Through Legislation* (New York: Macmillan, 1905), pp. 209–228.

article must cease to be produced if consumers cease to purchase it. The horsehair furniture of the early part of the nineteenth century has now virtually ceased to be manufactured. On the other hand, any article, however injurious to human life and health the conditions of its production may be, or with whatsoever risk they may be attended, continues to be placed on the market so long as there is an effective demand for it; *e.g.*, nitro-glycerine, phosphorous matches, and mine products of all kinds.

This great purchasing public, embracing the whole people, which ultimately decides everything, does so, on the whole, blindly, and in a manner injurious to itself, and particularly to that portion of itself which is engaged in production and distribution.

It would seem an obvious right of the purchaser that the food which he buys at the price asked should be pure and clean; that the garment purchased of an entirely reputable dealer should be free from poisonous dyes, vermin, and the germs of disease; and that both food and garments should leave his conscience free from participation in the employment of young children or of sweaters' victims.

Yet these seemingly obvious rights were, perhaps, never farther from attainment than to-day, in the opening years of the twentieth century. Adulteration of foods has never, in the history of the human race, been carried on upon a scale so vast as at present. The sweating system with its inevitable accompaniment of filth and disease conveyed in the product, persists and increases in spite of sixty years of effort of the philanthropists and the needleworkers to check it.

The oldest recognized legal right of the purchaser is to have his goods as they are represented. To sell goods under false pretenses has long been an offense punishable with more or less severity. But of late this right, if it was ever widely enforceable, has become largely illusory. In the vast complications of modern production and distribution, conditions have arisen such that the individual purchaser at the moment of buying, cannot possibly ascertain for himself whether the representation of the seller is accurate or not. The rule *caveat emptor* fails when the purchaser is prevented by the nature of the case from exercising *enlightened* care. Thus in the case of adulterated foods, or of foods exposed to filth or disease in the course of preparation, and in the case of garments sewed in tenements, the purchaser is at the mercy of the producer and the distributer, and is debarred from exercising care in these respects at the moment of purchasing.

Not only may a department store advertise with impunity in a dozen daily newspapers that "all our goods are made in our own factory," when it neither owns nor controls a factory, but the sales-clerks may safely reiterate the assurance over the counter in regard to an individual garment which, in truth, was finished in a tenement house by a bedridden consumptive. The machinery for identification is so imperfect, the difficulties in the way of tracing a garment are so many and so subtle, that the law has no more terrors for a mendacious sales-clerk than for the reckless advertising agent, or for the business office of those daily papers which thrive upon the wholesale mendacity of retail commerce.

Yet the demand for opportunity to obtain garments and food which may be purchased with a clear conscience grows imperative, has become, indeed, an ardent and abiding desire of enlightened purchasers who long for some trustworthy assurance that they are free from participation in the employment of children, in starvation wages and in the continuance of the sweating system. Granted that this new aspiration may be far from general, far from achieving its own gratification on any large scale, the mere fact that it is present in the minds of thousands of purchasers involves a new ethical standard on their part and must, in the course of time, bring fundamental changes throughout wide reaches of production and distribution.

The relation of this aspiration to certain legislation forms the subject of this and the ensuing chapter.

Ignorance of Conditions of Production

The most serious obstacle to the realizing of this aspiration is the willing ignorance of the masses, particularly of the masses of women who constitute the direct purchasers of the largest portion of the articles used for personal consumption. Even the producers, themselves, suffer so keenly from the lack of intelligence of their customers, that they are fitting out museums for the purpose of educating them, the Commercial Museum of Philadelphia being a promising type of such undertakings.

Recognizing no duty in this matter, asserting no right, the unintelligent purchasers tempt the greed of producers and distributors. Devoid of enlightened imagination, these purchasers exert no stimulus favorable to the honest manufacturer.

Because the germs of the deadliest diseases are not discernible by the eye, because they have no conspicuous and offensive smell, a shopping public devoid of imagination remains easily unaware of their presence on the counters of reputable merchants. In the same way, ices and syrups colored in tints and shades unknown to the fruits and flowers of nature, arouse no imaginative wonder. Peas of brilliant green in January, corn taken as yellow from the can in March as from the ear in July, these impossible objects are credulously accepted by the buying multitude. Why? Because it prefers not to know the truth.

Because the purchasing public, on the whole, prefers at present not to know the facts, we are all in danger of eating aniline dyes in tomatoes, jams, jellies, candies, ices, fruit syrups, flavoring and coloring extracts; and salicylic acid in our canned peas and other vegetables which we insist upon having preserved of midsummer hue at midwinter. We wear more or less arsenic in our print goods and the germs of tuberculosis and of countless other diseases in our outer garments.

A physician who visits among the poorest of the poor in New York City recently found a woman in the last stages of consumption, making, as she lay propped among her pillows, little boxes for wedding cake, licking the edges to moisten the gum to make it hold together. The teacher of a class of defective children in the same city, while visiting the home of a lad whose left arm and right hand had been amputated by reason of cancerous growths, found the father suffering from tuberculosis, but making a trivial addition to the family income by cracking walnuts (for which he was paid seven cents a pound if no kernels were broken and three cents a pound if his work was imperfect). The father complained that he lost much time in fetching and carrying the nuts and kernels between the store and his home, and could crack but fifteen pounds in three days.

The individual purchaser would doubtless prefer to eat nuts cracked in a workroom not frequented by a father afflicted with tuberculosis and little son mutilated by the ravages of cancer. The individual has, however, at present no method of enforcing this reasonable preference.

We are all much in the position of the Italian immigrants in any of our great cities. They support at least one store for the sale of imported maccaroni, vermicelli, sausage (bologna and other sorts), olive oil, Chianti wine, and Italian cheese and chestnuts. These articles are all excessively costly, by reason of transportation charges and the import duties involved; but the Italians are accustomed to using them and prefer a less quantity of these kinds of food to a greater abundance of those cheaper and more accessible supplies by which they are surrounded. The pitiful result is that the importer buys the least quantity of the Italian produce requisite for the purpose of admixture with American adulterants. The most flagrant example of this is, perhaps, the use of Italian olive oil, of which virtually none really pure is placed upon the market for sale at retail. What the Italian immigrant gets is the familar Italian label, the well-known package with its contents tasting more or less as it tasted at home in Italy. What the actual ingredients are he knows no more than an American knows what he is eating when he places his so-called butter or honey upon his so-called wheat-cakes. The demand of the Italians in America for Italian food-products, although large, persistent, and maintained at a heavy sacrifice on the part of the purchasers, is not an effective demand, because the immigrants have neither the knowledge nor the organization wherewith to enforce it, while the legislation of the various states affords them virtually no redress.

The privilege of remaining thus unintelligent costs the shopping public uncounted thousands of lives and other uncounted thousands of invalids. But it is a privilege dear to modern crowds. Indeed, the preference for things which come from afar, whose industrial history cannot be known to the purchasers, appears to be almost universal. Thus the writer has seen in a filthy hovel, in the grimiest street in Chicago, Sicilian peasant women sewing into the waistbands of the cheapest little knee pants, tags bearing the words *New York,* because the purchasers like the illusion that all garments sold in the United States are made in New York. The same illusion is cherished as to numerous food products—the purchaser will have it that they came from some other place than their real source. Figs from California must be labeled Smyrna; cotton seed oil from South Carolina must bear French or Italian labels calling it olive oil.

Why all these queer mendacities? Because the purchasing public will have it so! Because the number is still sadly small of those who perceive the duty to know their sources of supply and assert their right to know them; who are willing to sacrifice that deadly privilege of remaining ignorant, which the careless majority exercise at frightful cost of disease spread among innocent families, and of poverty, illness and death among the workers. The willingly ignorant purchaser carries a heavy share of the guilt of the exploiting manufacturer and the adulterating distributer. . . .

Among all the cherished forms of ignorance, none is more tenacious than that of the prosperous purchaser able and willing to pay for the best that the market affords and convinced that, whatever the sorrows of purchasers of ready-to-wear goods, he is safe, because he gets his garments only of the merchant tailor and pays a high price for the assurance that they are made up under conditions which guard him against disease, and enable the merchant tailor to pay the working tailor a fair price for his labor. But this customer is really no better off than the well-instructed club woman making her ineffectual search for righteously made ready-to-wear goods for her boys. For example, as factory inspector of Illinois, the writer was one day in search of a cigarmaker who was said to have smallpox in his family, during the terrible epidemic of 1894. Quite by accident a tailor was discovered newly moved into the suspected house, and not yet registered with the department or with the local board of health. In this tailor's shop, which was his dwelling, there was a case of smallpox. In the same shop there was, also, a very good overcoat, such as gentlemen were paying from sixty to seventy dollars for in that year. In the collar was a hang-up strap bearing the name of a merchant tailor in Helena, Montana. Now, that merchant tailor had had, in his store window in Helena, excellent samples of cloth from which the customer had ordered his coat. The Helena tailor had taken the necessary measurements and had telegraphed them, together with the sample-number of the cloth, to the wholesale house in Chicago, of which he was an agent. The wholesaler had had the coat cut and had sent it to the kitchen-tailor in whose sickroom in an infected house in Chicago it was fortunately discovered. But for the happy accident of the finding of the tailor during a search for an entirely different person, the purchaser in Helena, Montana, would surely have bought smallpox germs in his expensive coat.

Beside this fatuous belief that his custom-work, because it is costly, is made under clean and wholesome conditions, the purchaser of expensive garments usually comforts his conscience with the assumption that the working tailor who makes them receives some substantial share of the high price in the form of wages. While it is true that the tailors who do custom work have a more stable trade union than workingmen in the ready-to-wear branches, and command, therefore, somewhat better pay, it is also true that the tailor in this case, as in scores of others during the same epidemic, was driven by extreme poverty to conceal the dreadful fact that he had smallpox in his family, through fear of losing a few days' or a few weeks' work. So the high price of the coat did not even entitle the customer in Helena, Montana, to an easy conscience on the score of the wages paid to the people who worked upon it.

In the matter of wages, however, there is no longer an available excuse for ignorance on the part of the purchaser as to the wages paid for the manufacture of his garments; and to-day, he who remains ignorant upon this important point does so by his own choice. For the tailors were already, at that time, offering a label attached to goods made under conditions of pay and of hours of work satisfactory to both the employer and the worker.

Efforts to Enlighten Purchasers

Clearly the first step towards the assertion of the rights of the purchaser is the acquisition of knowledge; and it is an idiosyncrasy of the present industrial situation that a large part of the effort exerted for the enlightenment of purchasers has come, not from themselves, but from manufacturers, physicians and philanthropists (in the form of restrictions upon the sale of drugs, or recommendations in favor of municipally prepared vaccine, anti-toxine, etc.), from public authorities in the shape of official reports, from the Consumers' League in its endeavor to form a large and stable body of organized purchasers, and finally and chiefly from the trade unions, disseminating information in the interest of better working conditions for themselves.

Among all these agencies, the press and the advertising merchants might be expected to appear. These have, however, little claim to any educational quality in their endeavor. Their exertions have been directed distinctly not toward education. Rather they have been meant to stimulate, to persuade, incite, entice, and induce the indifferent to purchase. Much of the current advertising, of which the patent medicine advertisement may be taken as the type, is aimed directly at the ignorance of the purchaser. Nearly all of it is aimed at the cupidity of the public and it, therefore, offers cheapness as the one great characteristic. It is immoral rather than ethical.

Such measures as exist for the inspection and testing of food products have usually been obtained either by hygienists and physicians for philanthropic purposes, or by producers who were furthering their own interests while nominally promoting those of the purchaser. Such is the requirement that oleomargarine shall be colored pink when offered for sale in certain states, nominally for the protection of consumers, who may not care whether the substance which they use for frying or for spreading on bread is made of the milk of the cow or the fat of the steer. The people who obtained the enactment of this law were not the outraged consumers of oleomargarine, demanding to be protected against it, but the farmers whose butter market was threatened by the invasion of the oleomargarine.

Similar protection to American purchasers of foreign food products is afforded by the federal bureau with its laboratories for the investigation of imported articles, nominally in the interest of the public health, but really in the interest of the American producer, whose adulterations are left by the federal government to the varying efficiency and honesty of local boards of health, and state chemists, and food and dairy commissions.

In consequence of these diverse and multifarious exertions on behalf of the purchasers, there have grown up regulations of strangely unequal effectiveness. Thus in many cities the sale of a small number of well-known deadly drugs is hedged about with precautions intended to prevent murder and suicide by the ancient method of poisoning. In some cases, the purchaser of such drugs must be identified, and must state the purpose for which the purchase is made. Arsenic and strychnine, having an old established reputation as possible enemies of human life, and but slight profit for the retailer in the quantities in which they are sold to individual purchasers, are surrounded by precautions; and the package may even have to be conspicuously labeled with skull and crossbones, so that no careless third party can unintentionally come to harm.

Meanwhile the milk sold by the grocer next door to the druggist may be conveying typhoid germs in every bottle, and his cream may be so thickened with corn-starch and other substances as to starve any baby depending upon it; or serve as a gradual poison to a diabetic patient conscientiously endeavoring to follow his prescribed diet of fats and to avoid starch in all its forms. The products of the dairy have an excellent reputation as bases of wholesome feeding for infants and invalids; the purchaser is not habitually on guard against them, as he is forewarned against the corner druggist's arsenic and strychnia, nor has he any available means of personal self-defense. The typhoid germ and the thickening substance added to his cream and milk he cannot discover for himself at will. He must take his chances of protection through the intelligence and faithfulness of the municipal officials who deal with the milk supply. The constant appalling death rate of infants who depend upon milk, in all great cities, demonstrates the insufficiency of this agency, under present conditions.

Only the intelligent farmer, managing his own dairy, or the coöperative society owning its dairies and buying its own product, can be certain of avoiding poisons, quite as dangerous to life and health as strychnia and arsenic, with which American society has not yet learned to deal by any effective summary procedure. The experience of some of the English cities, and of Rochester, New York, seems to indicate that the difficulties of the milk supply can be met only by the institution of municipal milk, analogous to the municipal water supply; and municipal provision of all useful drugs, analogous to the present municipal supplies of vaccine and antitoxin serum.

On the other side from the dairyman, the druggist's next door neighbor, perhaps, is a tailor, who may be actively engaged in poisoning society in yet a different manner, by the sale of garments made in places in which there is infectious disease transmissible in articles exposed to it. In this case, also, as in the case of the dairyman's milk, the customer is at the mercy of the community and its officials. For when he orders a suit, it is out of his power to sit in the tailor's shop while the garment is cut, and then follow it whithersoever the merchant tailor may send it, first to a workshop to be stitched, afterward to a second place in which the buttonholes may be made, and then to a third place, commonly a tenement-dwelling, in which the vest and trousers are felled and otherwise completed before the garment is sent back to the tailor for the removal of whatever grease and vermin it may have acquired in its travels. For the tailor, as for the dairyman, there has never yet been brought to bear any precautionary measure adequately protective for the customer.

Scarcely more availing than the restrictions upon strychnia and arsenic in the wilderness of modern retail trade, are the efforts of the public officials to protect the purchasing public by the dissemination of information. The Department of Labor at Washington, the state bureaus of labor, the state inspectors of factories, the municipal and state boards of health, the state chemists and dairy commissions, all publish annually or biennially (some of them quarterly, monthly, and weekly) information for the enlightenment of the citizens. But very little of this information has, hitherto, served the purpose of the individual purchaser. If I have read the reports of all these officers, I am not only in as great danger as before of buying glucose for sugar, acetic acid for vinegar, and paper in the soles of my shoes; but I am in as great danger as before of buying smallpox, measles, scarlet fever, infectious sore eyes and a dozen forms of disease of the skin in my new garments. For not one of these officials publishes the list of the kitchen-tailors to whom the merchant tailor gives his goods to be made up; just as not one of them can possibly give information whereby adulterations of foods can be successfully detected in the private kitchen.

On the other hand, the available official information already existing has hitherto remained largely ineffectual. In vain has the fact been printed that a certain bouillon (so extensively advertised as particularly delicate and suitable for the use of aged persons and little children) is boiled in such close proximity to the fertilizer storage of the packing establishment that the factory inspectors fall ill on the days of inspection of these premises. The bouillon continues to be served at the luncheons of the socially aspiring. Official statements on all these matters, safely buried in official reports, do not reach and influence the great mass of the buyers. . . .

For certain great modern industries men have devised tests for the product, and warships, locomotives, railway bridges, and electrical installations can all be tried and tested before the bills are paid. But for the bulk of the products intended for personal use, nothing effective has been designed corresponding to these tests. Especially is this true of all those branches of manufacture which were once carried on by women in the home, and have now gone out into shops and factories. Concerning these products, purchasers must still rely upon their individual skill as buyers. The old rule *caveat emptor* is here carried out to its utmost application.

The most promising step forward in the effort to educate the purchasing public has been taken whenever a state has required the manufacturer of an article of food or medicine to state clearly and truthfully the ingredients composing each package offered for sale. This is a direct appeal to the intelligence of the purchasing public. Such measures become effective just in proportion as the purchasers coöperate with the officials who are charged with the duty of testing and analyzing samples bought in the ordinary course of trade. A community in which this coöperation is well sustained protects the life and health of its citizens, stimulates their intelligence in a direction of ever-increasing industrial importance, and enforces honesty upon producers who are under the heaviest moral strain when left unsustained under the pressure of competition.

The same principle underlies a bill entitled "An Act for Preventing the Adulteration or Misbranding of Foods or Drugs, and for Regulating Traffic Therein," which has twice passed the House of Representatives only to fail each time of passage by the Senate. This is the attempted application of the principle that the purchaser is of right entitled to trustworthy information furnished by the producer and guaranteed by the ceaseless activity of officials created for the purpose of examining the products and testing the veracity of the labels attached to them.

By providing for a continuous appeal to the intelligence of the individual purchaser, and an ever present warning to the producer to tell the truth as to his product, this bill promises an important ethical gain through legislation.

LEONARD WOOD

A soldier, doctor, administrator, reformer, imperialist, propagandist, and politician, Leonard Wood clearly ranks as one of the most accomplished officers of his era. He is best remembered for his governance of Cuba after the Spanish-American War and his efforts as army chief of staff to reform U.S. military policy and make the U.S. Army a vital component of a revived, progressive America.

Born in Winchester, New Hampshire, on October 9, 1860, Leonard was the first of three children born to Dr. Charles Jewett Wood and Caroline Hagar Wood. He spent his youth in the Massachusetts seaside village of Pocasset and was educated both by a private tutor and at Pierce Academy in Middleboro. When his father died in 1880, Leonard decided to adopt his father's profession and entered Harvard Medical School. He successfully completed his course work and an internship at Boston City Hospital, and in 1884 received his M.D. degree. He found private practice to be boring and unprofitable, however, and instead took an appointment as a contract surgeon in the army. Here he would find his true calling.

Ordered to Arizona, Wood quickly became involved in the brutal campaign against the Apaches that eventually resulted in the capture of Geronimo. During this campaign, in addition to fulfilling his medical duties, he commanded troops admirably and was, for a time, taken hostage. For his exploits, he was commissioned, promoted to the captaincy, and awarded the Congressional Medal of Honor.

In 1890 Wood married Louise A. Condit Smith. Five years later, he was transferred to Washington, where he raised his family of three children and established important political connections. President and Mrs. McKinley became his patients. Equally if not more important, Theodore Roosevelt became his close friend, and he was thereby drawn into that extraordinary circle of young men who would play a major role in the transformation of American domestic, foreign, and military policy.

Including individuals like Henry Cabot Lodge, Brooks Adams, and Alfred Thayer Mahan as well as Roosevelt, this group avidly embraced overseas imperialism. Some of them felt that such imperialism had to be an integral component of any effort to reform America domestically. Industrial capitalism's overemphasis on moneymaking, they believed, was destroying the strength and foundations of American society, and reform would be possible only if individual greed could be replaced by a new spirit of nationalism and sacrifice for the common good. Philosopher William James later echoed similar thoughts when he called for a "moral equivalent of war" that could bring out the military virtues of sacrifice and sharing without the bloodshed of the battlefield. So did Herbert Croly in his call for a citizenry of saints and heroes. For Wood and Roosevelt, however, the realities of domestic and international life necessitated not merely a "moral equivalent" for war but war itself—as well as overseas imperialism—to provide Americans with a new national crusade and mission. By this American version of the "white man's burden," sometimes known as the "warrior critique of business civilization," the reform of American society at home became inseparable from a "righteous" war and reform of "backward" peoples abroad.

When Congress in 1898 fulfilled the wishes of these men by declaring war on Spain, Roosevelt and Wood organized the volunteer cavalry regiment that became known as the "Rough Riders." Although Roosevelt is popularly associated with this colorful group and its exploits, it was Wood who was given command by virtue of his position and experience and who led the Rough Riders in their first battle. By the time Roosevelt achieved notoriety for his charge up San Juan Hill, Wood had been given command of a full brigade.

Wood's military exploits were soon overshadowed by his administrative abilities. Appointed military governor of the recently besieged city of Santiago, he was so successful in relieving starvation and in beginning major sanitation and public works programs to rid the city of its notorious filth and disease that he was soon placed in charge of the entire province and eventually the entire island. As military governor of Cuba from 1899 to 1902, he expanded on the programs he had initiated in Santiago, establishing educational, police, and fiscal systems; starting an electoral process and a government; modernizing the judicial system; chartering and regulating railroads; and setting up a major sanitation and disease control program. It was as part of that program that Major Walter Reed and his associates instituted their successful effort to eradicate yellow fever.

After brief stays in the United States and Europe, Wood in 1903 was appointed governor of the Moro province of the Philippines. Here he repeated his Cuban exploits but simultaneously conducted a vicious war against Moro guerrillas and virtually destroyed Moro institutions. Although criticized for his actions, Wood felt them justified by both military necessity and the "backwardness" of what he considered a "barbaric" people in need of American institutions.

For his numerous achievements between 1898 and 1903, the ambitious and able Wood received very rapid promotion. A captain in 1898, he was a major general by 1903. Some saw his rise—that of a non-West Pointer trained as a doctor—as the product of Wood's friendship with now-President Theodore Roosevelt. This engendered deep resentment among many high-ranking officers and their supporters in Congress—a resentment that would explode when Wood was appointed army chief of staff in 1910 and tried to use his position to reorganize and reform the army and American military policy.

Progressive reform of the antiquated and undersized American army had begun a decade earlier when Secretary of War Elihu Root had pressed for change as necessary to defend America's increased overseas interests. Beyond expanding the regular army and increasing officer education, Root pressed for a managerial revolution similar to the one that had taken place in business and in European armies, so that the government could have a large, federally trained reserve to call upon in times of emergency as well as a general staff to supervise an expanded American military establishment. Opposition to such plans came both from reformers sincerely concerned about the dangers of militarism and from individuals with vested interests in the existing system—most notably the state-controlled National Guard, the old army bureau chiefs, and their numerous allies in Congress. By 1903 Root had succeeded in getting congressional approval for a modest general staff and increased federal regulation of the National Guard, but these were halfway measures and much still remained to be done.

Wood was determined upon his appointment as chief of staff to complete Root's work. This combined with the controversy surrounding his rapid promotion to bring about a series of explosive confrontations. The best-known of these was his struggle with Adjutant General Frederick Ainsworth. Backed by Secretary of War Henry L. Stimson, Wood won this battle and forced Ainsworth into retirement, but Ainsworth's friends in Congress combined with state supporters of the National Guard to stymie many of Wood's efforts to complete Root's reforms. Politically checked, nearing the end of his tenure as chief of staff, and out of sympathy with the new Wilson administration, Wood in 1913–14 decided to go public. He set up civilian training camps and began to speak publicly for military preparedness, replacing the National Guard with some form of universal military training, and the positive aspects of military service to American society. By 1916 he had become, according to historian Walter Millis, a "military evangelist." He had also become a candidate for the Republican presidential nomination and a thorn in the side of President Wilson.

The Wilson administration censured Wood and, when the United States entered World War I, refused to appoint him to a European command. To many Americans, Wood was one of Wilson's victims. In 1920, as heir to Theodore Roosevelt's political legacy, he held the largest number of delegates at the Republican convention. But to many other Americans, Wood appeared to be a dangerous militarist. Moreover, the Republican leadership generally thought him too controversial and independent. Warren G. Harding was nominated instead.

In the 1920s, Wood's health began to fail, and on August 7, 1927, he died in Washington while undergoing surgery for a paralyzing brain tumor. Opposed throughout his career by an odd assortment of progressives and conservatives, Leonard Wood clearly represented one variety of progressive thought, a variety concerned with overseas expansion as well as domestic reform and with turning the army into a modern instrument capable not only of defending America but also of fulfilling its overseas "mission" and of transforming American citizens themselves.

Reprinted below is a speech Wood gave in 1915 at St. Paul's School in New Hampshire. It illustrates his concern with preparedness and his belief that the army could play a very positive, progressive role both at home and abroad.

THE CIVIL OBLIGATION OF THE ARMY[4]

It is always an inspiration to meet a body of enthusiastic youngsters who have the world ahead of them, and if one can do anything to make more clear the responsibilities and obligations which confront them and suggest a way to meet and overcome them, it is a duty which should be performed. What I wish to say to you may sound a bit harsh and inject an element of seriousness into this occasion which will tend a little to take from it the spirit of joyousness. I am going to say something to you about your obligations to the country as soldiers, for you come of the stock and represent a class whose responsibility to the country in time of war has always been generous.

I noticed today your fine soldiers' monument, erected in honor of the graduates of the school who gave their lives in the nation's service in the Spanish War. Among them are the names of men of my regiment. The response of these men is indicative of the response which is going to be made by men of their kind in the future. You are going to respond whether you are trained or not. What I want to bring home to you is that to be a really good citizen of a republic which is dependent upon its citizen army you must be not only willing but prepared, and I want to say to the parents and friends assembled here tonight that they must remember that these youngsters are going to respond to the call of the country whether they wish it or not; that it is a duty which the great majority of right minded boys will not attempt to shirk, and the question I want to ask them is—Are they going to send these boys to us prepared to be efficient soldiers or are they going to send them to us untrained and unprepared to make such sacrifice as they may have to make effective?

This subject was brought home to me very forcibly the other day by a letter received from a friend in the West, who had just lost his boy in the battle at Ypres. He said:

"You remember the last time we met that I told you of my 17-year-old boy at school in England. Well, he left school and went into the Home Defense force, but this was not enough, and he transferred and joined a regiment at the front—one of the new regiments—and was killed at Ypres. It was sad enough and hard enough to lose the boy, but I shall never be able to get rid of the feeling that neither he nor his mates had a sporting chance; they were unprepared and untrained."

Before going into the details of this subject I want to impress one fact

[4]Leonard Wood, *The Military Obligation of Citizenship* (Princeton, N.J.: Princeton University Press, 1915), pp. 50–76.

upon you, and that is that our country has never yet in its entire history met single handed a first-class country prepared for war. The shrinkage in enlistments and steady diminution in the strength of our military establishment during our struggle for independence points out clearly and conclusively to any fair-minded person the invaluable assistance of France in the Revolution. In the War of 1812–1814 we were, from a military standpoint, a minor issue, for Great Britain was engaged in that tremendous struggle with Napoleon— a struggle which required the great bulk of her forces on sea and land and prohibited her from concentrating her efforts upon the war in America.

The question is—Shall we drift on, regardless of the teachings of history, making no adequate preparation for the possibilities of the hour, or shall we take heed from the experiences of the past, not only of our own country, but of all lands since history was written, which is, that preparedness is the best insurance against war, or shall we accept as our guide for the future the theory of those deluded people who tell us that wars are over and that this is the last great war, forgetful of the fact that these same people, or people of the same type of intelligence, announced that the Russo-Japanese War was the last war, then that the Balkan War was the last war? The answer is no. We must judge the future by the past and make wise preparation to protect and safeguard those rights which our forefathers handed down to us. It seems to me that no right-minded person can hesitate in deciding which is the path of wisdom and which is the path of folly.

We do not want war, but we must not forget that there is many a peace which is infinitely worse than war, such as a peace which results from failure to do our clear duty to fight for what we believe is right or to support our honest convictions. We in this country do not want a large standing army, nor do we desire anything which savors of militarism. We do need and those who are intelligent enough to appreciate the situation want, an adequate army. By this I mean an army sufficient for the peace needs of the nation, which means the garrisoning of the Philippines, Panama, Hawaii, Alaska and Porto Rico, together with such force in the United States as will be sufficient for an expeditionary force, such as we sent to Cuba, or to deal with internal disorders which neither the police nor militia may be adequate to control. We must have an adequate navy, sufficient to perform a navy's function—on one ocean in any case, and, if we are wise, on both oceans. Both the army and navy must be supported by adequate reserves—the navy with a reserve strong enough to completely man the second line ships ordinarily out of commission and the many supply ships and auxiliary ships which must be put into commission in time of war, and in addition men enough to make good the losses of the first six months of war. We must also have a good Militia with reserves, under a large measure of federal control—a Militia whose response to the calls of the nation will be prompt and certain—one which will come well trained and well equipped. This can only be accomplished through the Federal Government fixing the standards and exercising the necessary power of inspection. Unless this can be done the Militia cannot be considered a dependable force. Back of it is that great force of citizen soldiers, ordinarily known as volunteers— a force which must be trained in time of peace, in order to be promptly available in time of war. In any case the officers of this force must be provided in time of peace and their provision must include thorough, systematic training.

We cannot depend upon volunteers in future wars, as we have in past wars, for the simple reason that the onrush of a modern war is so sudden and all our possible antagonists, concerning whom we need have any serious apprehension, are so thoroughly prepared that there will be no time to train volunteers, and certainly no time to train officers. Washington and the officers of his time were convinced of the folly of depending upon volunteers. They come with a rush from the best of the population during the early stages of war, but their enthusiasm soon passes away and the bounty and the draft follow. In the Revolution our greatest force was, in 1776, about 89,000 men. It dwindled year by year so that in 1781 we had in the field only a little over 29,000 men, and this notwithstanding large bounties of money and land and the strongest efforts on the part of individuals and Colonial assemblies. The same thing took place in the War of 1812–1814. Men came for a short time, but new men had to take their places; 527,000 different men were in the field during this war. Of this number something over 33,000 were officers.

The frequent change of personnel resulted in demoralization and inefficiency. It was again attempted through the bounty to produce effects which should have been produced by patriotism. In the Revolution, which was really the birth struggle of the nation, the falling off in volunteering is worthy of the most serious consideration, as is the chaotic condition which resulted from the working of the same system in the War of 1812–1814. This war on land was highly discreditable to us. With the exception of a drawn battle at Lundy's Lane and an unimportant victory on the Thames, our land operations were not only disastrous, but generally highly discreditable. We abandoned Washington to a force of only about sixty per cent of that of the defenders, with a loss on our side of eight killed and eleven wounded. The greatest force of regulars which England had in this country at any time during the war was a little over 16,800. There was, of course, a considerable number of Indians and Militia, but this combined force was only a small fraction of our numerically great force. At the battle of New Orleans (fought after the war) we won a highly creditable victory. Our troops were well handled and the enemy attempted the impossible. Moreover, the bulk of the men who composed Jackson's army were expert with the rifle.

On the water we had many highly creditable individual ship actions and some creditable fleet actions, but generally speaking, on the high seas our commerce was destroyed and our gallant but small navy bottled up.

In the Civil War we of necessity continued the volunteer system, no general policy looking to military efficiency having been inaugurated, and the two armies, each undisciplined and untrained, learned the game of war together, and after several years were moulded into excellent fighting machines. In this war, as in preceding wars, the volunteer system failed absolutely, and both the North and the South had to go to the draft and every attendant evil of the bounty system, with its accompanying desertions, bounty jumping, etc., which tended to demoralize the public conscience in all which pertained to the sacredness of the military obligation. The number of desertions was enormous. Charles Francis Adams places it as high as 523,000 out of a total enlistment in the northern armies of something over 2,700,000, or nearly one in five.

In the Mexican War we met an unprepared and rather ineffective enemy and the theater of war was so remote that our men were in hand long enough to get them into reasonably good shape, at least to meet an enemy of the type which confronted us. We had, moreover, an unusually able body of officers, many of whom distinguished themselves greatly in the Civil War; but again, as in all our wars, had we met a prepared and efficient enemy the system would have been our undoing.

You must never for a moment accept the very common idea, brought into being largely by the politicians and the Fourth of July orator, that we as a nation have peculiar military ability and that without thorough training we can meet equally good men who have been well trained.

The cowardly abandonment of our capital almost without loss on our part shows how unsafe it is to trust untrained troops in combat with well-organized, well-disciplined troops. You must remember also that this particular action occurred almost within a generation of the Revolutionary War, and that the men who made up the force defending Washington were drawn from sections which produced many of the best troops of the Revolution. Old Light-Horse Harry Lee summed the situation as follows:

"That government is a murderer of its citizens which sends them to the field uninformed and untaught, where they are to meet men of the same age and strength, mechanized by education and discipline for battle."

Those words are just as true and just as applicable today as they were when they were uttered. We are no longer an Anglo-Saxon race, but a very mixed one. Blood strains from all parts of Europe run through our people, and their influence is felt in the descendants of the new-comers. Everything indicates the necessity today, more than ever before, of thorough preparation. Now, while we do not desire a large standing army, we must have the kind of army and an army of the strength referred to above. We must have also a great body of 35,000 or 40,000 reserve officers trained and ready to serve as officers of volunteers. We must have a sound military system—one which tends to produce in the heart of every boy the consciousness of the fact that he is one of the defenders of the country and impels him to make the necessary preparation.

The military systems of Switzerland or Australia appeal to me very strongly as models which we could follow to our advantage in all which pertains to military training. Switzerland has had her system in operation long enough to make its application general, and as a result, while a peaceful, orderly country, she stands always ready to defend her rights and to guard her territory. She is absolutely free from all indication of militarism, as ordinarily understood, and yet every man in Switzerland who is physically fit has received a sufficient amount of training to make him an effective and efficient soldier; that this has served to benefit and uplift the people is conclusively shown by her low criminal rate, which is only a fraction of ours, and by the admitted conservatism of her people, their law-abiding habits, their patriotism and their respect for the rights of others. Contrast her position of today with that of another small European country, which, unlike her, had not made due preparation. In both Switzerland and Australia a large amount of instruction is given through public schools or during the school period of the youth—so much, indeed, that only two or three months of intensive training in camp are necessary to complete the training of the soldier. The officers take a longer and more intensive course, but the system in both countries is worked out so that there is practically no interference with the industrial or educational careers of those under training.

As I have said before, there has been little or no interest in this country in this great question of military training. There has been a general haphazard policy and a blind dependence upon volunteers; in other words, a dependence upon someone else doing one's work. It is an illogical system. There is no reason why one group of the population should assume that another group is going to voluntarily perform their military duties. The obligation to military service is universal. It is a tax upon which all others depend, and a nation which fails to recognize this prepares its own downfall. This general training can all be effected as has been done in Switzerland and Australia, without a trace of militarism, without any departure from ideals, and with a great resulting improvement in the morals, physique and character of our youth. In Switzerland and Australia the training of young boys is principally of a calisthenic character. Later they pass to rifle shooting and military formations. The final finish is put upon them in training at the camps which immediately precede their entry into the first line of the country's defense.

You must not think that war is one of the great destroyers of human life. It does take many lives, but it is among the lesser causes of loss of life. Our industrial casualties, not deaths necessarily, but casualties of all kinds, amount to something over 450,000 a year. Of these, about 78,000 or 79,000 result fatally—a loss rather exceeding the average loss of life of two years of the Civil War. Most of these accidents are preventable. The public interest in life saving is not sufficiently keen to insist on adequate legislation to this end. The losses in the war are more dramatic, more startling, but the lives lost in every day work in the struggle for existence exceed them vastly in number and run on without ceasing, both during peace and war.

The following is a little illustration of the case of our own country, namely, in ten peaceful Fourths of July (the last July 4, 1910), approximately 1,800 persons were killed and something over 35,000 wounded in celebrating the success of a war which ended nearly 130 years before. The number killed equals the number killed in battle or who died of wounds in the Spanish-American War, the Philippine rebellion and the Indian wars of a number of years preceding. The wounded of these ten peaceful days aggregate seven and a half times the wounded of all these wars. I tell you these things not to prove that war is any less dreadful, or that you should strive less to avoid it, but simply to present to you the truth with reference to the causes which bring about loss of life. Do not give up your ideals. Strive for universal peace, but while striving do not forget the conditions under which you are living, and, however much you may hope to obtain a condition of world peace, remember that there is no evidence of it today and that if we want to preserve the institutions which have been handed down to us we must be ready to defend them or, as Lord Roberts said:

"Strive to stir up, to foster and develop the manly and more patriotic spirit in the nation—a spirit which will induce our youth to realize that they must be not only ready but prepared to guard the heritage handed down to them."

Abandon the theory of chance and adopt that of probability in making wise provisions for peace through preparedness for war.

You hear a great deal about the destructive work of the soldier. I am going to say just a word with reference to his constructive and life saving work, which has really been his principal function since the close of the Spanish-American War, and indeed it was one of his principal activities during that war. Starting with Porto Rico, we find that, principally due to the efforts of a medical officer of the army, Dr. Bailey K. Ashford, tropical anemia, or hook-worm disease, as it is ordinarily called, has been about eliminated. Not only was this discovery of value in Porto Rico, but it was made use of throughout our own southern states, with a result of revitalizing and reënergizing hundreds of thousands of people afflicted with this disease. The annual death rate in Porto Rico alone was reduced by a number exceeding the total number of men killed during the Spanish-American War, and a recent inquiry made of all planters in the island with reference to their workers indicates that, in their opinion, the average increase in efficiency is 60 per cent—a truly startling figure, and one which illustrates very well the far-reaching and wonderful effects of sanitary measures and preventative medicine.

Passing on to Cuba, here we have the wonderful discovery of Major Walter Reed and his associates, Carroll and Lezear, which resulted in discovering the method of transmission of yellow fever and the means of controlling it, and the eventual elimination of that dread disease not only from Cuba, but from all the American troops, with the resulting saving in life, which runs into many thousands each year, and a saving in money so vast that it is difficult to estimate it; for the days of yellow fever, with the consequent quarantine, which tied up the movement of men and materials throughout the entire South, limited the movements of ships coming from yellow fever countries, and the costly disinfection, resulted in an expenditure running into hundreds of millions. Indeed, it is safe to say that the saving from yellow fever alone every year in life and money has exceeded the cost in each of the Spanish-American War and the Philippine rebellion.

In the Philippines splendid sanitary work has been done by the army and later by the civil government. Berri berri, one of the most dreaded of the eastern diseases, has been done away with. Malaria has been brought under control. Infant mortality has been halved. Most of this latter work has been done under the civil government, but the foundations were laid by the medical officers of the army who at first had charge of the work. In Panama we see the direct effect of this work in the completion of the Panama Canal. This great and splendid piece of engineering, remarkable as it is from an engineering standpoint, and conducted with wonderful efficiency by General Goethals and his assistants, could not have been built had it not been for the application by General Gorgas of the results of the sanitary discoveries made in Cuba which made it possible to carry on this great work under conditions of health which equalled those anywhere in the United States. It may be truly said without taking one atom of credit from the engineers that this great work was built on a sanitary foundation. Had we not got rid of yellow fever and learned to control malaria, the death rate would have been so heavy that the work could only have resulted in our hands as it did in the hands of the French, for nothing demoralizes working forces more effectively than great epidemics. They are worse than battles in some ways.

The mobilization on the Mexican frontier has not been without its great and lasting benefits. It enabled us, because of the prevalence of typhoid in the Mexican villages and along the Rio Grande, to insist upon general typhoid inoculation of officers and men, and the result has been the removal of typhoid from the army. Last year there were 100,000 men scattered from Tientsin to Panama, through the Hawaiian Islands and the Philippines, from Alaska to

Porto Rico, as well as all over the United States, and there was not a single death among them from typhoid. When one remembers thousands of cases in the camps of the Spanish-American War, the importance of this discovery is appreciated. The general application was made possible only by the mobilization of troops and in the struggle to protect them. So it was with the discovery concerning yellow fever and the elaboration of the methods employed in controlling malaria. The results of these discoveries are now all of general application, not only to the population in our own country, but to the population of all countries in and bordering on the American tropics, as well as in the insular possessions. Not only were great sanitary results secured through the military arms of the government, but it should be remembered also that it, the military arm, established and maintained a civil government in Porto Rico, Cuba and the Philippines, and conducted these governments with great success—in Cuba up to the point of the transfer to the Cuban people of a completely organized republic, and in Porto Rico until the transfer to the American civil government; likewise in the Philippines the military authorities were in full charge during the most trying period and turned over to the civil commission which followed them a well-organized government and a well-filled treasury.

I tell you all this in order that you may understand more fully what the real work of the army has been—that its life saving has counterbalanced scores of times its work as a destructive force, if one may apply the term "destructive forces" to a force used to terminate intolerable conditions and to establish humane, just and equitable governments among dependent people.

6

WORLD WAR I
AND ITS IMPACT
PRIMARY SOURCES AND
DOCUMENT ANALYSIS

World War I changed the face of the world. The once mighty German, Russian, Austro-Hungarian, and Ottoman empires could not withstand the strains of four years of war and collapsed. At the end of the war, even the supposedly victorious powers faced disillusion, debt, and the rebellion of their colonial peoples against continued imperial rule. Revolution threatened much of Europe, and in imperial Russia, once the most autocratic of the European powers, a victorious Communist government claimed to be the headquarters of the inevitable revolution that would overthrow Western capitalism and eventually govern the world. Europe's hegemony over much of that world, once an accepted fact of Western civilization, had been seriously impaired. Consequently, the easy optimism and faith in progress that had characterized much of European civilization was lost at war's end. Many now looked with a new pessimism and despair at a world they had not anticipated and did not understand. In the words of one participant, "No road. No thoroughfare. Neither race had won, nor could win, the War. The War had won, and would go on winning."

The impact of World War I on the United States was less dramatic but no less profound. And it is likely that some of the ways in which the "Great Crusade" of 1917–1918 affected American society are still not fully understood. Americans, initially at least, had hoped that their intervention could make the Great War "a war to end all wars" and that their participation could "make the world safe for democracy" (although the words were Wilson's, the sentiments were American). Yet twenty years after Versailles, they faced a distinctly undemocratic world which, after suffering a severe economic depression, found itself once more engulfed in a global war with consequences that have dominated modern history.

One of the ways in which World War I affected all nations, including the United States, was the linkage between industrialization and military effort to produce what scholars call "total war." War, of course, by placing nations under enormous stress, has often accelerated change within those societies. Many military historians are convinced that total war intensifies the process of change. Rather than rely on small professional armies to achieve limited territorial objectives, as eighteenth- and nineteenth-century nations had done, total war has demanded that nations use the tools of an industrial society to mobilize all their people and resources for an unlimited effort aimed at defeating and transforming their enemies. In this process, twentieth-century nations, the United States chief among them, have transformed themselves. The conscription of millions of men for the armed forces, the consequent need for an increased number of women in the work force, the mobilization of scientists to create new weapons of war, all require that extraordinary powers be given to the government to control the nation's economy.

During World War I, the U.S. government assumed previously unimagined authority over the nation's resources. For example, the government ran the railroads to assure that troops could be transported and supplied. It built defense plants, allocated food resources, intervened in disputes between labor and management—in short, the government controlled the economic life of the nation. Moreover, most of this control was given to the executive branch. In fact, the Overman Act of 1917 gave President Wilson such broad authority that one senator suggested jokingly that the act be amended so that "if any power, constitutional or not, has been inadvertently omitted from this bill, it is hereby granted in full."

This concentration of power raised serious constitutional issues that were ignored in the effort to win the war. Traditional American guarantees of freedom of speech and freedom of the press virtually disappeared once the nation went to war. The Committee on Public Information helped to create and continued to agitage an anti-German hysteria, which led to numerous incidents of mob violence. German books were burned outside libraries, Beethoven was banned in Boston, and in Los Angeles three pacifist ministers were beaten by an angry mob. The government also passed a series of Espionage Acts in 1917 and 1918 which led to the arrests of more than 1,500 Americans who criticized the war. These efforts at waging total war obviously had profound consequences which did not evaporate at the end of the war.

The war also had a profound impact on the nation's cultural imagination. The closing passages of F. Scott Fitzgerald's novel *This Side of Paradise,* published in 1920, suggest something of this impact by referring to "a new generation . . . grown up to find all Gods dead, all wars fought, all faiths in man shaken." Clearly, the nation's faith in human progress was challenged in significant ways by the blood, barbed wire, and mud of European battlefields. The war disillusioned many American intellectuals (although surprisingly few of them opposed it) and provoked a skeptical questioning of traditional American assumptions about the nature of the world and the nature of humanity that reverberate into our own time.

Culturally, economically, politically, and socially the United States's involvement in World War I affected American society profoundly and often in unforeseen ways. Historians try to understand the impact of the war on society by studying the documents and artifacts of the period. These artifacts and documents are *primary sources*—the basic building blocks of all historical research and writing.

Clearly, an enormous variety of primary material is available to students of history. Poetry, literature, songs (a 1917 popular song, "Over There," displaced the 1916 hit "I Didn't Raise My Son to be a Soldier"), photographs, maps, blueprints, even tools, to suggest some examples, can all be used as primary sources. Even secondary writing done by historians can be a primary source provided the right questions are asked of it. Charles Beard's *The Rise of American Civilization* (1927), which was basically a synthesis of American history emphasizing economic motives, might also be read for clues to the attitudes and convictions that had led Beard to oppose U.S. participation in World War I.

Preceding chapters in this volume have already exposed you to some types of primary sources, such as literature. This chapter is designed to introduce you to a wider range of primary material and to the methods of analysis historians apply to such material in their efforts to understand the past.

Working with primary sources demands thought, imagination, and analysis. Primary sources vary not only in form but also in reliability. Moreover, different types of primary sources provide different kinds of information. And, unfortunately, all primary sources are biased and incomplete. It is not possible for the historical witness to see everything, and even the best witness can tell the historian only what he or she has perceived. Questions about limited knowledge and biased perception are profoundly important to the student of history.

Historians assess the reliability of documents in a variety of ways. A good way to begin is to consider some basic questions that apply to any primary source. How much evidence does it supply? How believable is this information? Is there any evidence of bias in this source? Why does this source exist at all? In examining the primary sources at the end of this chapter, you may find it helpful to keep these questions in mind.

The questions that one asks of a source do more than help to assess its reliability. They also help to determine what that source can tell you about the era under study. In the Supreme Court's 1919 *Schenck* decision upholding the 1918 Espionage Act, for example, Justice Oliver Wendell Holmes stated the Court's famous caveat on the First Amendment: freedom of speech does not give one the right to falsely shout "fire" in a crowded theater. One question a historian can ask is: "Just what constitutes such a false shout in such a theater?" Since the case concerned dissent in wartime, the Court's decision reveals a belief that such dissent is intolerable when the nation is at war (a "clear and present danger," in Holmes's words), and that the existence of war severely limits the basic rights American citizens are supposed to possess. But just what are those limits? Do they apply to all wars or just those that threaten the existence of the nation? If the latter, who determines the category of the war, and on what basis? Does the Court's decision deal with any of these issues? If not, have they been dealt with since?

Such questioning can reveal that the *Schenck* case, while setting a key precedent in Americal legal history and providing future scholars with two marvelous clichés, is also very illustrative of the wartime hysteria that swept the United States. Although Justice Holmes made clear that the Espionage Act did not supersede the First Amendment, his distinction offered little comfort to socialist leader Eugene V. Debs, who was sentenced to ten years in jail for merely urging Americans to "resist militarism wherever found."

The primary sources reproduced below have been chosen to encourage such questioning and analysis as well as to illustrate the varieties of primary material available to the historian. This questioning and analysis should also enable you to understand the tremendous impact of World War I on American society.

ASSIGNMENTS

1. Read or examine carefully each primary source reproduced below.
2. After reading each source, summarize its contents for your own later use. You should note the essential points this source makes, jot down any details you find interesting, and list any questions the source suggests to you. You should also ask yourself whether the evidence the source provides supports or contradicts information you have received from the text or in class.
3. Choose *one* of these sources as instructed or at your own discretion and prepare a list of *four* historical questions you could generate from it. You may apply the questioning formula used in Chapter 1 of this volume or simply list the questions that occurred to you as you read and thought about the source.
4. Using the questions listed, write a one- to two-page (250- to 500-word) essay on the reliability of your source and what it tells you about the impact of World War I on American society. Remember that the accuracy of a source and what it tells you are partly determined by the questions asked of it.

ADDITIONAL QUESTIONS TO CONSIDER

1. Be prepared to discuss the reliability of all the primary sources listed below as well as what they can tell you about the impact of World War I on American society.
2. What changes in American society caused by World War I are still with us today?
3. Can you deduce any general rules for determining the reliability of a primary source? Is there such a thing as a completely reliable primary source? Why, or why not?
4. In light of the problems you have encountered with reliability, how should an individual go about using primary sources to write a good history?

PRIMARY SOURCE   1

On April 2, 1917, President Wilson went before Congress to request a declaration of war against Germany. Congress complied five days later, thereby making the United States an official belligerent in World War I. Reproduced below is the address Wilson delivered to Congress on April 2, in which he states his version of the events leading to his request, what the United States hoped to achieve by fighting, and what would be necessary to win.

GENTLEMEN OF THE CONGRESS: I have called the Congress into extraordinary session because there are serious, very serious, choices of policy to be made, and made immediately, which it was neither right nor constitutionally permissible that I should assume the responsibility of making.

On the third of February last I officially laid before you the extraordinary announcement of the Imperial German Government that on and after the first day of February it was its purpose to put aside all restraints of law or of humanity and use its submarines to sink every vessel that sought to approach either the ports of Great Britain and Ireland or the western coasts of Europe or any of the ports controlled by the enemies of Germany within the Mediterranean. That had seemed to be the object of the German submarine warfare earlier in the war, but since April of last year the Imperial Government had somewhat restrained the commanders of its undersea craft in conformity with its promise then given to us that passenger boats should not be sunk and that due warning would be given to all other vessels which its submarines might seek to destroy, when no resistance was offered or escape attempted, and care taken that their crews were given at least a fair chance to save their lives in their open boats. The precautions taken were meagre and haphazard enough, as was proved in distressing instance after instance in the progress of the cruel and unmanly business, but a certain degree of restraint was observed.

The new policy has swept every restriction aside. Vessels of every kind, whatever their flag, their character, their cargo, their destination, their errand, have been ruthlessly sent to the bottom without warning and without thought of help or mercy for those on board, the vessels of friendly neutrals along with those of belligerents. Even hospital ships and ships carrying relief to the sorely bereaved and stricken people of Belgium, though the latter were provided with safe conduct through the proscribed areas by the German Government itself and were distinguished by unmistakable marks of identity, have been sunk with the same reckless lack of compassion or of principle.

I was for a little while unable to believe that such things would in fact be done by any government that had hitherto subscribed to the humane practices of civilized nations. International law had its origin in the attempt to set up some law which would be respected and observed upon the seas, where no nation had right of dominion and where lay the free highways of the world. By painful stage after stage has that law been built up, with meagre enough results, indeed, after all was accomplished that could be accomplished, but always with a clear view, at least, of what the heart and conscience of mankind demanded. This minimum of right the German Government has swept aside under the plea of retaliation and necessity and because it had no weapons which it could use at sea except these which it is impossible to employ as it is employing them without throwing to the winds all scruples of humanity or of respect for the understandings that were supposed to underlie the intercourse of the world. I am not now thinking of the loss of property involved, immense and serious as that is, but only of the wanton and wholesale destruction of the lives of noncombatants, men, women, and children, engaged in pursuits which have always, even in the darkest periods of modern history, been deemed innocent and legitimate. Property can be paid for; the lives of peaceful and innocent people cannot be. The present German submarine warfare against commerce is a warfare against mankind.

It is a war against all nations. American ships have been sunk, American lives taken, in ways which it has stirred us very deeply to learn of, but the ships and people of other neutral and friendly nations have been sunk and overwhelmed in the waters in the same way. There has been no discrimination. The challenge is to all mankind. Each nation must decide for itself how it will meet it. The choice we make for ourselves must be made with a moderation of counsel and a temperateness of judgment befitting our character and our motives as a nation. We must put excited feeling away. Our motive will not be revenge or the victorious assertion of the physical might of the nation, but only the vindication of right, of human right, of which we are only a single champion.

When I addressed the Congress on the twenty-sixth of February last I thought that it would suffice to assert our neutral rights with arms, our right to use the seas against unlawful interference, our right to keep our people safe against unlawful violence. But armed neutrality, it now appears, is impracticable. Because submarines are in effect outlaws when used as the German submarines have been used against merchant shipping, it is impossible to defend ships against their attacks as the law of nations has assumed that merchantmen would defend themselves against privateers or cruisers, visible craft giving chase upon the open sea. It is common prudence in such circumstances, grim necessity indeed, to endeavour to destroy them before they have shown their own intention. They must be dealt with upon sight, if dealt with at all. The German Government denies the right of neutrals to use arms at all within the areas of the sea which it has proscribed, even in the defense of rights which no modern publicist has ever before questioned their right to defend. The intimation is conveyed that the armed guards which we have placed on our merchant ships will be treated as beyond the pale of law and subject to be dealt with as pirates would be. Armed neutrality is ineffectual enough at best; in such circumstances and in the face of such pretensions it is worse than ineffectual: it is likely only to produce what it was meant to prevent; it is practically certain to draw us into the war without either the rights or the effectiveness of belligerents. There is one choice we cannot make, we are incapable of making: we will not choose the path of submission and suffer the most sacred rights of our nation and our people to be ignored or violated. The wrongs against which we are now array ourselves are no common wrongs; they cut to the very roots of human life.

With a profound sense of the solemn and even tragical character of the step I am taking and of the grave responsibilities which it involves, but in unhesitating obedience to what I deem my constitutional duty, I advise that the Congress declare the recent course of the Imperial German Government to be in fact nothing less than war against the government and people of the United States; that it formally accept the status of belligerent which has thus been thrust upon it; and that it take immediate steps not only to put the country in a more thorough state of defense but also to exert all its power and employ all its resources to bring the Government of the German Empire to terms and end the war.

What this will involve is clear. It will involve the utmost practicable cooperation in counsel and action with the governments now at war with Germany, and, as incident to that, the credits, in order that our resources may so far as possible be added to theirs. It will involve the organization and mobilization of all the material resources of the country to supply the materials of war and serve the incidental needs of the nation in the most abundant and yet the most economical and efficient way possible. It will involve the immediate full equipment of the navy in all respects but particularly in supplying it with the best means of dealing with the enemy's submarines. It will involve the immediate addition to the armed forces of the United States already provided for by law in case of war at least five hundred thousand men, who should, in my opinion, be chosen upon the principle of universal liability to service, and also the authorization of subsequent additional increments of equal force so soon as they may be needed and can be handled in training. It will involve also, of course, the granting of adequate credits to the Government, sustained, I hope, so far as they can equitably be sustained by the present generation, by well conceived taxation.

I say sustained so far as may be equitable by taxation because it seems to me that it would be most unwise to base the credits which will now be necessary entirely on money borrowed. It is our duty, I most respectfully urge, to protect our people so far as we may against the very serious hardships and evils which would be likely to arise out of the inflation which would be produced by vast loans.

In carrying out the measures by which these things are to be accomplished we should keep constantly in mind the wisdom of interfering as little as possible in our own preparation and in the equipment of our own military forces with the duty,—for it will be a very practical duty,—of supplying the nations already at war with Germany with the materials which they can obtain only from us or by our assistance. They are in the field and we should help them in every way to be effective there.

I shall take the liberty of suggesting through the several executive departments of the Government, for the consideration of your committees, measures for the accomplishment of the several objects I have mentioned. I hope that it will be your pleasure to deal with them as having been framed after very careful thought by the branch of the Government upon which the responsibility of conducting the war and safeguarding the nation will most directly fall.

While we do these things, these deeply momentous things, let us be very clear, and make very clear to all the world what our motives and our objects are. My own thought has not been driven from its habitual and normal course by the unhappy events of the last two months, and I do not believe that the thought of the nation has been altered or clouded by them. I have exactly the same things in mind now that I had in mind when I addressed the Senate on the twenty-second of January last; the same that I had in mind when I addressed the Congress on the third of February and on the twenty-sixth of February. Our object now, as then, is to vindicate the principles of peace and justice in the life of the world as against selfish and autocratic power and to set up amongst the really free and self-governed peoples of the world such a concert of purpose and of action as will henceforth ensure the observance of those principles. Neutrality is no longer feasible or desirable where the peace of the world is involved and the freedom of its peoples, and the menace to that peace and freedom lies in the existence of autocratic governments backed by organized force which is controlled wholly by their will, not by the will of their people. We have seen the last of neutrality in such circumstances. We are at the beginning of an age in which it will be insisted that the same standards of conduct and of responsibility for wrong done shall be observed among nations and their governments that are observed among the individual citizens of civilized states.

We have no quarrel with the German people. We have no feeling towards them but one of sympathy and friendship. It was not upon their impulse that their government acted in entering this war. It was not with their previous knowledge or approval. It was a war determined upon as wars used to be determined upon in the old, unhappy days when peoples were nowhere consulted by their rulers and wars were provoked and waged in the interest of dynasties or of little groups of ambitious men who were accustomed to use their fellow men as pawns and tools. Self-governed nations do not fill their neighbour states with spies or set the course of intrigue to bring about some critical posture of affairs which will give them an opportunity to strike and make conquest. Such designs can be successfully worked out only under cover and where no one has the right to ask questions. Cunningly contrived plans of deception or aggression, carried, it may be, from generation to generation, can be worked out and kept from the light only within the privacy of courts or behind the carefully guarded confidences of a narrow and privileged class. They are happily impossible where public opinion commands and insists upon full information concerning all the nation's affairs.

A steadfast concert for peace can never be maintained except by a partnership of democratic nations. No autocratic government could be trusted to keep faith within it or observe its covenants. It must be a league of honour, a partnership of opinion. Intrigue would eat its vitals away; the plottings of inner circles who could plan what they would and render account to no one would be a corruption seated at its very heart. Only free peoples can hold their purpose and their honour steady to a common end and prefer the interests of mankind to any narrow interest of their own.

Does not every American feel that assurance has been added to our hope for the future peace of the world by the wonderful and heartening things that have been happening within the last few weeks in Russia? Russia was known by those who knew it best to have been always in fact democratic at heart, in all the vital habits of her thought, in all the intimate relationships of her people that spoke their natural instinct, their habitual attitude towards life. The autocracy that crowned the summit of her political structure, long as it had stood and terrible as was the reality of its power, was not in fact Russian in origin, character, or purpose; and now it has been shaken off and the great, generous Russian people have been added in all their naive majesty and might to the forces that are fighting for freedom in the world, for justice, and for peace. Here is a fit partner for a League of Honour.

One of the things that has served to convince us that the Prussian autocracy was not and could never be our friend is that from the very outset of the present war it has filled our unsuspecting communities and even our offices of government with spies and set criminal intrigues everywhere afoot against our national unity of counsel, our peace within and without, our industries and our commerce. Indeed it is now evident that its spies were here even before the war began; and it is unhappily not a matter of conjecture but a fact proved in our courts of justice that the intrigues which have more than once come perilously near to disturbing the peace and dislocating the industries of the country have been carried on at the instigation, with the support, and even under the personal direction of official agents of the Imperial Government accredited to the Government of the United States. Even in checking these things and trying to extirpate them we have sought to put the most generous interpretation possible upon them because we knew that their source lay, not in any hostile feeling or purpose of the German people towards us (who were, no doubt as ignorant of them as we ourselves were), but only in the selfish designs of a Government that did what it pleased and told its people nothing. But they have played their part in serving to convince us at last that Government entertains no real friendship for us and means to act against our peace and security at its convenience. That it means to stir up enemies against us at our very doors the intercepted note to the German Minister at Mexico City is eloquent evidence.

We are accepting this challenge of hostile purpose because we know that in such a government, following such methods, we can never have a friend; and that in the presence of its organized power, always lying in wait to accomplish we know not what purpose, there can be no assured security for the democratic governments of the world. We are now about to accept gauge of battle with this natural foe to liberty and shall, if necessary, spend the whole force of the nation to check and nullify its pretensions and its power. We are glad, now that we see the facts with no veil of false pretence about them, to fight thus for the ultimate peace of the world and for the liberation of its peoples, the German peoples included: for the rights of nations great and small and the privilege of men everywhere to choose their way of life and of obedience. The world must be made safe for democracy. Its peace must be planted upon the tested foundations of political liberty. We have no selfish ends to serve. We desire no conquest, no dominion. We seek no indemnities for ourselves, no material compensation for the sacrifices we shall freely make. We are but one of the champions of the rights of mankind. We shall be satisfied when those rights have been made as secure as the faith and the freedom of nations can make them.

Just because we fight without rancour and without selfish object, seeking nothing for ourselves but what we shall wish to share with all free peoples, we shall, I feel confident, conduct our operations as belligerents without passion and ourselves observe with proud punctilio the principles of right and of fair play we profess to be fighting for.

I have said nothing of the governments allied with the Imperial Government of Germany because they have not made war upon us or challenged us to defend our right and our honour. The Austro-Hungarian Government has, indeed, avowed its unqualified endorsement and acceptance of the reckless and lawless submarine warfare adopted now without disguise by the Imperial German Government, and it has therefore not been possible for this Government to receive Count Tarnowski, the Ambassador recently accredited to this Government by the Imperial and Royal Government of Austria-Hungary; but that Government has not actually engaged in warfare against citizens of the United States on the seas, and I take the liberty, for the present at least, of postponing a discussion of our relations with the authorities at Vienna: We enter this war only where we are clearly forced into it because there are no other means of defending our rights.

It will be all the easier for us to conduct ourselves as belligerents in a high spirit of right and fairness because we act without animus, not in enmity towards a people or with the desire to bring any injury or disadvantage upon them, but only in armed opposition to an irresponsible government which has thrown aside all considerations of humanity and of right and is running amuck. We are, let me say again, the sincere friends of the German people, and shall desire nothing so much as the early re-establishment of intimate relations of mutual advantage between us,—however hard it may be for them, for the time being, to believe, that this is spoken from our hearts. We have borne with their present government through all these bitter months because of that friendship,—exercising a patience and forbearance which would otherwise have been impossible. We shall, happily, still have an opportunity to prove that friendship in our daily attitude and actions towards the millions of men and women of German birth and native sympathy who live amongst us and share our life, and we shall be proud to prove it towards all who are in fact loyal to their neighbours and to the Government in the hour of test. They are, most of them, as true and loyal Americans as if they had never known any other fealty or allegiance. They will be prompt to stand with us in rebuking and restraining the few who may be of a different mind and purpose. If there should be disloyalty, it will be dealt with with a firm hand of stern repression; but, if it lifts its head at all, it will lift it only here and there and without countenance except from a lawless and malignant few.

It is a distressing and oppressive duty, Gentlemen of the Congress, which I have performed in thus addressing you. There are, it may be, many months of fiery trial and sacrifice ahead of us. It is a fearful thing to lead this great peaceful people into war, into the most terrible and disastrous of all wars, civilization itself seeming to be in the balance. But the right is more precious than peace, and we shall fight for the things which we have always carried nearest our hearts,—for democracy, for the right of those who submit to authority to have a voice in their own governments, for the rights and liberties of small nations, for a universal dominion of right by such a concert of free peoples as shall bring peace and safety to all nations and make the world itself at last free. To such a task we can dedicate our lives and our fortunes, everything that we are and everything that we have, with the pride of those who know that the day has come when America is privileged to spend her blood and her might for the principles that gave her birth and happiness and the peace which she has treasured. God helping her, she can do no other.

PRIMARY SOURCE 2

According to the editors of his papers, President Wilson personally supervised the drafting of the Overman Act of 1917, which gave him absolute authority over the bureaus, agencies, and departments of the federal government.

May 20, 1918.
[S. 3771.]

[Public, No. 152.]

CHAP. 78.—An Act Authorizing the President to coordinate or consolidate executive bureaus, agencies, and offices, and for other purposes, in the interest of economy and the more efficient concentration of the Government.

) Consolidation of executive bureaus, etc.

Authority vested in the President during present war to utilize more effectively functions, etc., of the Government.

Be it enacted by the Senate and House of Representatives of the United States of America in Congress assembled, That for the national security and defense, for the successful prosecution of the war, for the support and maintenance of the Army and Navy, for the better utilization of resources and industries, and for the more effective exercise and more efficient administration by the President of his powers as Commander in Chief of the land and naval forces the President is hereby authorized to make such redistribution of functions among executive agencies as he may deem necessary, including any functions, duties, and powers hitherto by law conferred upon any executive department, commission, bureau, agency, office, or officer, in such manner as in his judgment shall seem best fitted to carry out the purposes of this Act, and to this end is authorized to make such regulations and to issue such orders as he may deem necessary, which regulations and orders shall be in writing and shall be filed with the head of the department affected and constitute a public record: *Provided,* That this Act shall remain in force during the continuance of the present war and for six months after the termination of the war by the proclamation of the treaty of peace, or at such earlier time as the President may designate: *Provided further,* That the termination of this Act shall not affect any act done or any right or obligation accruing

Written regulations, etc., to be issued.

Provisos.
Duration of authority.

Termination not to affect acts done, etc.

or accrued pursuant to this Act and during the time that this Act is in force: *Provided further,* That the authority by this Act granted shall be exercised only in matters relating to the conduct of the present war.

> **Limited to acts affecting conduct of the war.**

Sec. 2. That in carrying out the purposes of this Act the President is authorized to utilize, coordinate, or consolidate any executive or administrative commissions, bureaus, agencies, offices, or officers now existing by law, to transfer any duties or powers from one existing department, commission, bureau, agency, office, or officer to another, to transfer the personnel thereof or any part of it either by detail or assignment, together with the whole or any part of the records and public property belonging thereto.

> **Transfer of powers, duties, and personnel of departments, etc., authorized.**

Sec. 3. That the President is further authorized to establish an executive agency which may exercise such jurisdiction and control over the production of aeroplanes, aeroplane engines, and aircraft equipment as in his judgment may be advantageous; and, further, to transfer to such agency, for its use, all or any moneys heretofore appropriated for the production of aeroplanes, aeroplane engines, and aircraft equipment.

> **Aircraft.**
> **Agency for entire control of production, etc., established.**
> **Appropriations to be used.**

Sec. 4. That for the purpose of carrying out the provisions of this Act, any moneys heretofore and hereafter appropriated for the use of any executive department, commission, bureau, agency, office, or officer shall be expended only for the purposes for which it was appropriated under the direction of such other agency as may be directed by the President hereunder to perform and execute said function.

> **All moneys restricted to uses for which appropriated.**

Sec. 5. That should the President, in redistributing the functions among the executive agencies as provided in this Act, conclude that any bureau should be abolished and it or their duties and functions conferred upon some other department or bureau or eliminated entirely, he shall report his conclusions to Congress with such recommendations as he may deem proper.

> **Report to Congress on bureaus recommended to be abolished, etc.**

Sec. 6. That all laws or parts of laws conflicting with the provisions of this Act are to the extent of such conflict suspended while this Act is in force.

> **Conflicting laws suspended.**

Upon the termination of this Act all executive or administrative agencies, departments, commissions, bureaus, offices, or officers shall exercise the same functions, duties, and powers as heretofore or as hereafter by law may be provided, any authorization of the President under this Act to the contrary notwithstanding.

> **Status to be restored on termination of Act.**

Approved, May 20, 1918.

PRIMARY SOURCE 3

The Great War also had an impact on American life, from the playing fields to the nursery, as the two cartoons from *Harper's Magazine* of 1920 attest.

Auto Polo in 1950

SHE: " *Do be careful, dear, remember you sprained your shoulder in the game last week* "

Reprinted by permission from the April 1920 issue of *Harper's Magazine*.

PRIMARY SOURCE 4

Not all Americans responded to the nation's call to arms in 1917 with patriotic vigor. Over a quarter of a million draftees failed to respond at all to their conscription notices and thousands went AWOL (absent without leave) within days of their induction. This account of war resistance in one rural Arkansas town was printed in *The Literary Digest* in 1919.

"UNCLE SAM'S LITTLE WAR IN THE ARKANSAS OZARKS"

When the United States entered the war with Germany, Cecil Cove did not. This little valley in the remote fastnesses of the North Arkansas Ozarks practically seceded from the Union for the duration of the war. The older men cooperated with the eligibles to resist the draft. They defied Uncle Sam, being well stocked with arms and prepared to hold out indefinitely in their hiding-places. When they finally gave up it was by no means an unconditional surrender, for the authorities accepted all the terms of the slacker gang, after a number of attempts to round them up had proved unsuccessful. A writer in the Kansas City *Star* attributes the incident to "a combination of plain igno-

MOTHER: "*What do you want the alarm clock for?*"
"*We're pretendin' Sammy Jones is a German spy
an' we got to get up an' shoot him at sunrise*"

Reprinted by permission from the February 1920 issue of *Harper's Magazine.*

rance, Jeff Davis politics, *The Appeal to Reason,* and mountain religion." He adds that another fact may throw some light on the happenings in Cecil Cove, namely, that "it was a notorious hiding-place for men who were neither Federals nor Confederates in the Civil War," and who "found a refuge in the caves and fastnesses of the Cove exactly as did the slacker gang of 1917–1918."

Cecil Cove—some twelve miles long and eight miles wide—lies high up in Newton County, which has not been penetrated by the railroad. The people there form an isolated mountain community, suspicious yet hospitable, reticent, "trained and accustomed to arms," and also trained and accustomed, boys and girls, men and women alike, to using tobacco, as snuffers, smokers, and chewers. If we are to believe *The Star,* they are "unerring spitters," and "the youngest of the family is considered deserving of a reprimand if he can not hit the fireplace at ten paces."

When the news of the draft came the Cove prepared for war, but not with Germany. To quote *The Star:*

The country roundabout was scoured for high-power rifles. Stocks of the Harrison and Jasper stores were pretty well depleted. Repeating rifles of 30–30 caliber and great range and precision began to reach the Cove from mail-order houses. Quantities of ammunition were bought—report has it that "Uncle Lige" Harp bought nearly $60 worth at one time in Harrison.

A number of young men were drafted, but refused to report for duty. The sheriff sent word he was coming after them, but seems to have thought better of it when he received the answer: "Come on, but look out for yourself!" Four United States marshals or deputies, several special investigators, and an army colonel all visited Newton County in turn, did some questioning and searching, and alike returned empty handed. We read in *The Star* that the people in the Cove were all related through intermarriage, and practically all of them were in sympathy with the slackers. They agreed to stick together, and it has been reported that some sort of covenant was signed. The Cove, we are told, "is a region of multifarious hiding-places, studded with boulders and pocketed with caves; a searcher might pass within six feet of a dozen hidden men and see none of them." It is reached and penetrated only by steep mountain-trails, which are easily threaded by the "sure-footed mountain horses and mules and their equally sure-footed owners," but which are almost impassable to strangers. Moreover, continues the writer in *The Star:*

> So perfect were means of observation and communication a stranger could not enter the Cove at any point without that fact being known to all its inhabitants before the intruder had got along half a mile.
>
> Nearly all the families in the Cove have telephones. It is a remarkable fact that these mountaineers will do without the meanest comforts of life, but they insist upon having telephones. This and the other varied methods of intercourse, peculiar to the mountains, gave the Cecil Cove slackers an almost unbeatable combination. They always knew where the searchers were and what they were doing, but the searchers never were able to find anything except a blind trail.
>
> The telephone-lines might have been cut, but that would have served little purpose. News travels by strange and devious processes in the mountains. The smoke of a brush-fire high up on a peak may have little significance to the uninitiated, but it may mean considerable to an Ozark mountaineer. The weird, long-drawn-out Ozark yell, "Hia-a-ahoo-o-o" may sound the same always to a man from the city, but there are variations of it that contain hidden significances. And the mountaineer afoot travels with amazing speed, even along those broken trails. Bent forward, walking with a characteristic shuffle, he can scurry over boulder and fallen log like an Indian.

A deputy marshal "with a reputation as a killer" spent a month in Newton County, but made no arrests, telling some one that it would be "nothing short of suicide" for an officer to try to capture the slacker gang. The officer second in command at Camp Pike, Little Rock, took a hand in the affair and told the county officials that some of his men who were "sore at being unable to go across to France" would be very glad to "come up and clear out these slackers." But about this time the War Department offered something like amnesty to the Cove gang and apparently promised that a charge of desertion would not be prest if the men were to give themselves up. Word was passed around, whether or not from official sources, that the boys would be "gone only from sixty to ninety days, that they would all get a suit of clothes and a dollar a day." At the same time a new sheriff, Frank Carlton, came into office. He knew the neighborhood and its people. He got in touch with some of the leaders of the hiding men and finally had an interview with two of them. They agreed to give themselves up if certain concessions were made and finally told the sheriff to meet them alone and unarmed and thus accompany them to Little Rock. As we read:

> The next day the gang met the sheriff at the lonely spot agreed upon. They caught a mail-coach and rode to Harrison and then were taken to Camp Pike.
> The morning after their arrival Joel Arnold asked the sheriff:
> "Do they feed like this all the time?"
> The sheriff replied that they had received the ordinary soldier fare.
> "We've been a passel of fools," Arnold replied.

The slackers are still held in custody at Camp Pike, and, according to the writer in *The Star,* authorities there will make no statement as to the procedure contemplated in the case. In showing how such different influences as religion, socialism, and sheer ignorance operated, the writer lets certain of the Cove leaders speak for themselves. Uncle Lige Harp backed up the slackers strongly with all of his great influence in the community. "Uncle Lige" is now an old man, but in his younger days had the reputation of being a "bad man." He tells with glee of a man who once said he would "just as soon meet a grizzly bear on the trail as meet Lige Harp." In his heyday Uncle Lige "was accounted a dead shot—one who could put out a turkey's left eye at one hundred yards every shot." Here are Uncle Lige's views:

> "We-all don't take no truck with strangers and we didn't want our boys takin' no truck with furriners. We didn't have no right to send folks over to Europe to fight; 'tain't a free country when that's done. Wait till them Germans come over here and then fight 'em is what I said when I heard 'bout the war. If anybody was to try to invade this country ever' man in these hills would git his rifle and pick 'em off."
> "Aunt Sary" Harp, between puffs at her clay pipe, nodded her approval of "Uncle Lige's" position.

France Sturdgil and Jim Blackwell say they are Socialists. They have read scattering copies of *The Appeal to Reason.* To be fair, it should be added that this Socialist paper, now *The New Appeal,* has taken an attitude in support of the Government's war-policy. Said Sturdgil:

> "It's war for the benefit of them silk-hatted fellers up in New York. We don't want our boys fightin' them rich fellers' battles and gittin' killed just to make a lot of money for a bunch of millionaires. Why, they own most of the country now."

To the writer of the *Star* article this sounds very much like the sort of argument which Jeff Davis used for many years in persuading the "hill billies" of Arkansas to elect him regularly to the United States Senate. George Slape, the Cove's religious leader, is "a prayin' man."

> "The good book says, 'Thou shalt not kill.' We didn't want our boys takin' nobody's life. It ain't right 'cause it's contrary to the Bible and the good Lord's teachin's," declared Slape.
> Asked to explain the difference between fighting Germans and preparing to resist the draft authorities, both likely to result in death, Slape said:
> "The boys wasn't goin' to kill nobody unless they had to. It's different killing a man who tries to make you do wrong and killin' somebody in war."

None of these leaders ever admitted they knew anything about where the boys were hiding. It was a common report that the slackers "lived at home except on those occasions when an officer was discovered to be prowling about." It is the Ozark way: "nobody ever has seen a hunted man, tho a rustling of the leaves, the crackling of a dead twig, might betray the fact that the fugitive was there only a moment before."

Cecil Cove had its loyal men. At least one young man defied home opinion and threats of violence by reporting for duty when he was drafted. He was sent to France and became an excellent soldier. Loyal citizens living on the fringe of the Cove were shot at and threatened on a number of occasions, and several were ordered to keep away from the community. "Uncle Jimmy" Richardson, a Confederate veteran, loyal and fearless, was not afraid to go straight to some of the parents of the slackers and tell them what he thought of them.

> "You're a gang of yellow bellies," he said. "If you've got any manhood in you, them boys will be made to go and serve their country."
> "Uncle Jimmy" got his answer one day when he ventured a little way into the Cove. A shot rang out and a bullet whistled past his ear.
> "The cowardly hounds wouldn't fight fair," he said. "In the old days of the Civil War them kind was swung up to the nearest tree. I'm past seventy-three now, but I'd have got down my rifle and gone in with anybody that would have went after them. I don't like to live near folks who ain't Americans."
> "Uncle Jimmy" does not speak to the slacker folks in the Cove now. He says he never will again. If he did, he says, he would feel ashamed of the more than a dozen wounds that he received in the Civil War.

Loyalists in the Cove were forced by fear into what amounted to a state of neutrality. "We couldn't risk having our homes burned down or our stock killed, let alone anything worse," said one of them, who added "I'm not afraid of any man face to face, but it is a different proposition when you're one against thirty-six, and them with all the advantage and willin' to go anything." . . .

PRIMARY SOURCE 5

Scott Nearing was one of a small number of university professors who opposed U.S. entry into World War I. As a result, Nearing lost his post at the Wharton School of Business Administration and, after two years of teaching at the municipally owned University of Toledo, was unable to find academic employment. During the 1930s, Nearing and his wife, Helen, pioneered in what the 1960s would call a "back to the land" movement by homesteading in Vermont. The excerpts that follow are from Nearing's *The Making of a Radical: A Political Autobiography*, begun in 1963 when Nearing was eighty.

War is an attempt of one group to impose its will upon another group by armed violence. This is the immediate object of a war. But war has wider implications. War offers those in power a chance to rid themselves of opposition while covering up their designs with patriotic slogans.

Our Wharton School Eight tried to learn the truth, teach it, and build it into community life. War not only stopped us, it scattered us so completely that we never got together again.

I did not take a direct part in the war of 1914–18. Although I was of draft age, I was not drafted because I had been under Federal indictment for a felony. Had I been drafted I would certainly have gone to jail as a conscientious objector. Yet the guns shattered my career as completely as though I had been under an artillery barrage.

There is an old saying that truth is the first casualty in any war. From personal experience I can bear witness that war not only negates truth, decency, and human kindness, but brings disaster also to truth-seekers and those who are devoting their energies to social improvement.

War is hell. More than that, war drags human beings from their tasks of building and improving, and pushes them en masse into the category of destroyers and killers. . . .

Meanwhile the war makers, whose profession is wholesale destruction and mass murder, had taken over control of the United States and its policies, were writing the words, calling the tune, and helping to wreck the structure of western civilization.

The United States of my youth was slipping from under my feet and vanishing from my sight. The Mayflower Covenant, William Penn's charter of love and good human relations, Thomas Jefferson's Bill of Rights, the Constitution of 1789 which as a schoolboy I had learned word for word, Lincoln's Gettysburg Address and Second Inaugural had become obsolete scraps of paper. They were appropriate and valid to a degree three score and seven years ago. As the pages of history were turned, one by one, the doctrine of "life, liberty and the pursuit of happiness" propounded by the founders of the Republic became irrelevant, annoying, obstructive verbiage. We had become part and parcel of another kind of social procedure. We had begun beating our plowshares into swords and our pruning hooks into spears, transforming tools into weapons and techniques of destruction and murder.

What so proudly we hailed in my school and college days was gone. In its place was a new nation, not as Lincoln had envisaged it "under God" but under Mammon, under arms, one of a group of warfare states, struggling for wealth and power. It had become a nation that was making sport of the Bill of Rights, trampling on the Constitution, squandering its rich economic and political heritage in frantic efforts to mark out and destroy all who stood in the way or even questioned its mad race to affluence, conquest, power, and destruction.

Could this be the country I had loved, honored, worked for, believed in? The general welfare was forgotten. The land had become a happy hunting ground for adventurers, profiteers, and pirates who called history "bunk" and used their privileged positions to promote their careers and fill their pockets at public expense. Peace, progress, and prosperity had become scraps of raw meat, thrown to a pack of venal, military minded ravenous wolves. Inquiry, education, legislation, reconstruction, improvement, betterment, progress were words strung together by prewar liberals. Now, in the era of the Great War, all such ideas were obsolete. In their places appeared America's unmatched wealth, American interests, national security, the American Way, to be forced down the throats of mankind in the American Century.

My own career lay in ruins; my experience and competence as a professional teacher were brushed aside, but these personal frustrations, disappointments and disasters were only straws in a whirlwind that was starting to blow through the whole country. The significant wreckage resulted from the abandonment of the American dream and the replacement of American idealism by the hard-headed, hard-fisted policy of the American Century imposed on mankind by hucksters and their strong-arm squads operating on land and sea and in the air.

The higher education for which I was now prepared could be obtained in only one existing institution—the College of Hard Knocks. The University of Pennsylvania had conferred on me the degree of Doctor of Philosophy in Economics. Since then I have been working for two additional degrees: Doctorate of Imperialism and of Civilization. Needless to say, these degrees will not be conferred by any existing university.

More than half a century has passed since I was fired from my last academic post. For me the years 1917 to 1971 have provided a satisfying and richly rewarding higher education. At first from state to state in the United States, then from nation to nation and from continent to continent I have had an opportunity to observe, record, report, and draw my own conclusions.

Since I was born, in 1883, mankind has been supplied with a series of inventions and discoveries so revolutionary in character that one now duplicates in a few hours the planet-girdling tour on which Marco Polo, Magellan, and their contemporaries spent years or even lifetimes. With telescope, microscope, spectroscope, and spacecraft one can now enter realms of nature, modify and refurbish levels of society that have been opened to detailed inspection only during my adult lifetime.

In this period, mankind has learned not only to unmake many aspects of nature but to unmake and remake human society and human beings. I could not adopt a doctrinaire attitude toward this problem. The science and art of association (sociology) and the science and art of man's understanding, redirection, and reconstruction of himself (psychology in the West and yoga in the East) were opening new vistas and blazing new trails in what had been a wilderness. . . .

PRIMARY SOURCE 6

About 400,000 black Americans served in the U.S. Army during World War I despite a persistent pattern of racial discrimination against them. Occasionally black-white tensions erupted into violence. The events described in the NAACP's petition to President Wilson took place in Houston, Texas, in August 1917. Apparently the arrest and beating of Cpl. Charles W. Baltimore led a number of black soldiers to seek reprisal against the Houston police. In the shooting that followed, two blacks and seventeen whites, including five Houston policemen, were killed. Sixty-three black soldiers were court-martialed and, on December 11, 1917, thirteen of them were hanged. Incidentally, it should be noted that lynching, despite the best efforts of the NAACP to oppose it, continued to be endemic in the South well into the 1930s.

A PETITION

[Feb. 19, 1918]

We come as a delegation from the New York Branch of the National Association for the Advancement of Colored People, representing the twelve thousand signers to this petition which we have the honor to lay before you. And we come not only as the representatives of those who signed this petition, but we come representing the sentiments and aspirations and sorrows, too, of the great mass of the Negro population of the United States.

We respectfully and earnestly request and urge that you extend executive clemency to the five Negro soldiers of the Twenty-Fourth Infantry now

Permission granted by the NAACP. Authority by Ronald A. Gregg, Assistant General Counsel.

under sentence of death by court martial. And understanding that the cases of the men of the same regiment who were sentenced to life imprisonment by the first court martial are to be reviewed, we also request and urge that you cause this review to be laid before you and that executive clemency be shown also to them.

We feel that the history of this particular regiment and the splendid record for bravery and loyalty of our Negro soldiery in every crisis of the nation give us the right to make this request. And we make it not only in the name of their loyalty, but also in the name of the unquestioned loyalty to the nation of twelve million Negroes—a loyalty which today places them side by side with the original American stocks that landed at Plymouth and James-town.

The hanging of thirteen men without the opportunity of appeal to the Secretary of War or to their Commander-in-Chief, the President of the United States, was a punishment so drastic and so unusual in the history of the nation that the execution of additional members of the Twenty-Fourth Infantry would to the colored people of the country savor of vengeance rather than justice.

It is neither our purpose nor is this the occasion to argue whether this attitude of mind on the part of colored people is justified or not. As representatives of the race we desire only to testify that it does exist. This state of mind has been intensified by the significant fact that, although white persons were involved in the Houston affair, and the regiment to which the colored men belonged was officered entirely by white men, none but colored men, so far as we have been able to learn, have been prosecuted or condemned.

We desire also respectfully to call to your attention the fact that there were mitigating circumstances for the action of these men of the Twenty-Fourth Infantry. Not by any premeditated design and without cause did these men do what they did at Houston; but by a long series of humiliating and harassing incidents, culminating in the brutal assault on Corporal Baltimore, they were goaded to sudden and frenzied action. This is borne out by the long record for orderly and soldierly conduct on the part of the regiment throughout its whole history up to that time.

And to the end that you extend the clemency which we ask, we lay before you this petition signed by white as well as colored citizens of New York; one of the signers being a white man, president of a New York bank, seventy-two years of age, and a native of Lexington, Kentucky.

And now, Mr. President, we would not let this opportunity pass without mentioning the terrible outrages against our people that have taken place in the last three-quarters of a year; outrages that are not only unspeakable wrongs against them, but blots upon the fair name of our common country. We mention the riots at East St. Louis, in which the colored people bore the brunt of both the cruelty of the mob and the processes of law. And we especially mention the savage burnings that have taken place in the single state of Tennessee within nine months; the burnings at Memphis, Tennessee; at Dyersburg, Tennessee; and only last week at Estill Springs, Tennessee, where a Negro charged with the killing of two men was tortured with red-hot irons, then saturated with oil and burned to death before a crowd of American men, women, and children. And we ask that you, who have spoken so nobly to the whole world for the cause of humanity, speak against these specific wrongs. We realize that your high position and the tremendous moral influence which you wield in the world will give a word from you greater force than could come from any other source. Our people are intently listening and praying that you may find it in your heart to speak that word.

PRIMARY SOURCE 7

World War I also marked the beginning of a black exodus to northern cities, and sometimes patriotism produced not the violence described in Source #6 but racial cooperation, as in the integrated Liberty Bond concert described in James Weldon Johnson's autobiography, *Along This Way,* first published in 1933. Johnson was an author, educator, and one of the early twentieth century's most prominent advocates of civil rights for blacks.

My work on the road carried me into the far South, and I had opportunity to observe closely the operation of two powerful forces that were at work on the Negro's status—the exodus and the war. Negroes were migrating to the North in great numbers, and I observed the anomaly of a premium being put on this element of the population that had generally been regarded as a burden and a handicap to the South. Here, it seemed, was a splendid chance to get rid of a lot of "lazy, worthless people," but some communities were so loath to lose them that they obliged railroad ticket agents to adopt a policy of not selling tickets to Negroes to go North. In many instances Negroes were forcibly restrained from leaving.

The demands of the war were also working great changes. A train that I was on stopped at Waycross, Georgia. I saw a great crowd around the station and on the tracks, and got out of my coach to see what it was all about. I found a long train loaded with Negro troops who were on their way "over there," and witnessed the incredible sight of white women, together with colored women, all dressed alike in a Red Cross looking uniform, busy distributing to the men neatly wrapped packages of whatever things such committee gave to soldiers leaving for the front.

I reached Jacksonville a day or two before the date of a mass meeting that was being held in the National Guard armory. Let me here go back to a time when I was in Jacksonville three or four years prior to this meeting. The armory, built, of course, out of the tax funds of Duval County, was then brand-new. The drill room was the finest and largest auditorium in Jacksonville; its use as a municipal auditorium was among the advantages set forth in the project for building the armory. Its first use under this head was for a musical affair that had been promoted by a committee of white women. These ladies had arranged to have Coleridge-Taylor's *Hiawatha* sung, and for the principal rôle had engaged a tenor from Atlanta. A small group of colored people wanted very much to hear the cantata, and they asked me if I would not see if it could be arranged for them to do so. I telephoned Mrs. Lund, who was on the committee, and stated the case. She seemed very much pleased that there were colored people who wanted to hear the class of music that was to be sung. She asked how many there would be. I told her, probably twenty-five. She assured me that seats would be arranged for them and they would be welcome. The group was delighted. They asked me if I was going with them. I answered that I had been lucky enough to hear *Hiawatha* under better circumstances, and would not go. The next day, Mrs. Lund rang me up. She was very much perturbed. She gave me to know that the militia officer in charge of the armory had countermanded the arrangements that had been made; he had declared that Negroes could not be allowed in the armory. I asked Mrs. Lund if she thought the militia officer knew that the music to be sung was the work of a Negro composer. She did not answer that. Indeed, it is doubtful whether Mrs. Lund, as competent a musician as she was, or any other lady of the committee, knew that Coleridge-Taylor was a Negro.

The mass meeting that was to be held at the armory was for the purpose of stimulating the sale of Liberty Bonds. Fully a half of the auditorium was filled with colored people, and they subscribed liberally. On the platform was a large committee composed of white and colored citizens. Both white and colored speakers addressed the audience. By the white speakers, especially, great emphasis was laid on *"our* country" and "what *we* must do" to win the war for democracy. I don't know whether the same militia officer was still in charge of the armory or not.

PRIMARY SOURCE 8

Radicals were the principal victims of proceedings by the U.S. Justice Department during and after the war. William Z. Foster, labor organizer and long-time Communist party leader, recounts here his trial experience in Michigan in 1922. This anecdote is taken from Foster's *Pages from a Worker's Life,* published in 1939.

THE WOMAN JUROR

The Communist Party, being illegal at the time, held its national convention of August, 1922, secretly at Bridgman, Michigan. Tipped off by undercover men, the Department of Justice agents and local police raided the convention, arresting thirty-two delegates, for violation of the state's criminal syndicalism law. Later forty more were indicted. I was among the number. The country was then being torn with the greatest series of strikes in its whole history, the war-time anti-red hysteria still lingered, and so the occasion was deemed opportune to railroad most of the top leadership of the Communist Party to the penitentiary for long terms.

The Communist Party, which had united front movements with the Farmer-Labor Party and many trade unions, launched a national mass defense movement, hired Frank P. Walsh as chief attorney, while the Department of Justice and the Michigan police gathered together a choice collection of frameup witnesses to convict us. The State, believing that I, because of my long activity in the trade union and revolutionary movements, would be the easiest to convict, chose me as the first to be tried. The charge was unlawful assembly and the penalty was five to ten years imprisonment in Jackson penitentiary. The trial took place in St. Joseph.

The Michigan authorities confronted us with a list of prospective jurors made up almost entirely of small businessmen, professionals and farmers. Consequently, we soon exhausted our peremptory challenges.

Then came a woman to be examined for the jury. Her name was Mrs. Minerva Olson and she was a militant leader in all the local patriotic work in St. Joseph. She had had two sons killed in France and was a member of the D.A.R. During her examination she defined a "red" as "an ignorant foreigner." She appeared very eager to get on the jury, manifestly to help carry out the prosecutor's aim of organizing the jury to convict me. To us she was so much poison, and Walsh exhausted all his skill to disqualify her. But in spite of our charges of bias, she was accepted as a juror. Our hopes sank, and the prosecution was obviously pleased.

The hard-fought trial lasted a week and attracted national attention. As it progressed, I naturally spent no little time studying the jurors, trying to figure out their reactions to the testimony. But there was small reassurance in this. The twelve faces in the jury box, especially Mrs. Olson's, looked cold and hostile. I could not perceive a friendly glance anywhere among them.

When the case duly went to the jury we expected a quick decision of guilty. But the hours dragged along, and no verdict came. What could be up? Our hopes rose with the passing hours. Who were our friends on the jury? We had not the slightest idea. Finally, at the end of thirty-six hours the jury reported; it was hopelessly split, six for conviction and six for acquittal. And so they were discharged as a hung jury.

Imagine my great surprise when I learned that it was Mrs. Olson who did the job! Wrecking the prosecutor's plans and upsetting all our calculations, she had from the outset carried on a strong fight for acquittal. She organized the six who voted for us. Her principal aide was a small farmer who, the whole week long, had stared malignantly at me. At one time Mrs. Olson had seven jurors lined up for acquittal, but as the jury walked out to lunch that day, a court official passed word to the seventh, an old and crippled railroad worker, that he would lose his job if he voted "not guilty." So we lost him. We were amazed, and so was the prosecution at the outcome of the trial.

Next day, my wife and I visited Mrs. Olson. She soon cleared up the mystery of her role in the hung jury. She was a firm believer in free speech and held that workers had the right to meet and discuss Communism if they so saw fit. She took seriously the idea that her two boys had died in France fighting for democracy. Besides, at the trial she had gained a new and more favorable conception of Communism.

Mrs. Olson's liberalism came as a great shock to the prosecution. They had not suspected the existence of such an element in the ultrareactionary D.A.R. They never brought my case to trial again. Instead, they picked out C. E. Ruthenberg and convicted him by a more carefully sifted jury. He died as his appeal was going through the upper courts. The rest of the defendants never came to trial. But the state of Michigan kept us all under heavy bail, and it was not until 1933, after being eleven years in the courts, that our cases were finally dropped.

PRIMARY SOURCE 9

The Kellogg-Briand Pact of 1928, eventually signed by sixty-two nations, was hailed by its supporters as the first step in outlawing war. The agreement fell apart in the 1930s, but the pact itself and the movement behind it did reveal a sincere public conviction that the world had to avoid the horrors of another war.

The President of the German Reich, the President of the United States of America, His Majesty the King of the Belgians, the President of the French Republic, His Majesty the King of Great Britain, Ireland and the British Dominions beyond the Seas, Emperor of India, His Majesty the King of Italy, His

Majesty the Emperor of Japan, the President of the Republic of Poland, the President of the Czechoslovak Republic,

Deeply sensible of their solemn duty to promote the welfare of mankind;

Persuaded that the time has come when a frank renunciation of war as an instrument of national policy should be made to the end that the peaceful and friendly relations now existing between their peoples may be perpetuated;

Convinced that all changes in their relations with one another should be sought only by pacific means and be the result of a peaceful and orderly process, and that any signatory Power which shall hereafter seek to promote its national interests by resort to war should be denied the benefits furnished by this Treaty;

Hopeful that, encouraged by their example, all the other nations of the world will join in this humane endeavor and by adhering to the present Treaty as soon as it comes into force bring their peoples within the scope of its beneficent provisions, thus uniting the civilized nations of the world in a common renunciation of war as an instrument of their national policy;

Have decided to conclude a Treaty and for that purpose have appointed as their respective Plenipotentiaries:

[Here are listed the plenipotentiaries]

Who, having communicated to one another their full powers found in good and due form have agreed upon the following articles:

ARTICLE I. The High Contracting Parties solemnly declare in the names of their respective peoples that they condemn recourse to war for the solution of international controversies, and renounce it as an instrument of national policy in their relations with one another.

ARTICLE II. The High Contracting Parties agree that the settlement or solution of all disputes or conflicts of whatever nature or of whatever origin they may be, which may arise among them, shall never be sought except by pacific means.

ARTICLE III. The present Treaty shall be ratified by the High Contracting Parties named in the Preamble in accordance with their respective constitutional requirements, and shall take effect as between them as soon as all their several instruments of ratification shall have been deposited at Washington.

This Treaty shall, when it has come into effect as prescribed in the preceding paragraph, remain open as long as may be necessary for adherence by all the other Powers of the world. Every instrument evidencing the adherence of a Power shall be deposited at Washington and the Treaty shall immediately upon such deposit become effective as between the Power thus adhering and the other Powers parties hereto.

It shall be the duty of the Government of the United States to furnish each

Government named in the Preamble and every Government subsequently adhering to this Treaty with a certified copy of the Treaty and of every instrument of ratification or adherence. It shall also be the duty of the Government of the United States telegraphically to notify such Governments immediately upon the deposit with it of each instrument of ratification or adherence.

PRIMARY SOURCE 10

Franklin D. Roosevelt's well-known First Inaugural Address (March 4, 1933) is best known as the source of his remark "the only thing we have to fear is fear itself." You should note, however, Roosevelt's clear willingness to use the war powers of the presidency to confront the nation's economic crisis. He also uses war as a metaphor to mobilize the populace.

I AM CERTAIN that my fellow Americans expect that on my induction into the Presidency I will address them with a candor and a decision which the present situation of our Nation impels. This is preeminently the time to speak the truth, the whole truth, frankly and boldly. Nor need we shrink from honestly facing conditions in our country today. This great Nation will endure as it has endured, will revive and will prosper. So, first of all, let me assert my firm belief that the only thing we have to fear is fear itself—nameless, unreasoning, unjustified terror which paralyzes needed efforts to convert retreat into advance. In every dark hour of our national life a leadership of frankness and vigor has met with that understanding and support of the people themselves which is essential to victory. I am convinced that you will again give that support to leadership in these critical days.

In such a spirit on my part and on yours we face our common difficulties. They concern, thank God, only material things. Values have shrunken to fantastic levels; taxes have risen; our ability to pay has fallen; government of all kinds is faced by serious curtailment of income; the means of exchange are frozen in the currents of trade; the withered leaves of industrial enterprise lie on every side; farmers find no markets for their produce; the savings of many years in thousands of families are gone.

More important, a host of unemployed citizens face the grim problem of existence, and an equally great number toil with little return. Only a foolish optimist can deny the dark realities of the moment.

Yet our distress comes from no failure or substance. We are stricken by no plague of locusts. Compared with the perils which our forefathers conquered because they believed and were not afraid, we have still much to be thankful for. Nature still offers her bounty and human efforts have multiplied it. Plenty is at our doorstep, but a generous use of it languishes in the very sight of the supply. Primarily this is because rulers of the exchange of mankind's goods have failed through their own stubbornness and their own incompetence, have admitted their failure, and have abdicated. Practices of the unscrupulous money changers stand indicted in the court of public opinion, rejected by the hearts and minds of men.

True they have tried, but their efforts have been cast in the pattern of an outworn tradition. Faced by failure of credit they have proposed only the lending of more money. Stripped of the lure of profit by which to induce our people to follow their leadership, they have resorted to exhortations, pleading tearfully for restored confidence. They know only the rules of a generation of self-seekers. They have no vision, and when there is no vision the people perish.

The money changers have fled from their high seats in the temple of our civilization. We may now restore that temple to the ancient truths. The measure of the restoration lies in the extent to which we apply social values more noble than mere monetary profit.

Happiness lies not in the mere possession of money; it lies in the joy of achievement, in the thrill of creative effort. The joy and moral stimulation of work no longer must be forgotten in the mad chase of evanescent profits. These dark days will be worth all they cost us if they teach us that our true destiny is not to be ministered unto but to minister to ourselves and to our fellow men.

Recognition of the falsity of material wealth as the standard of success goes hand in hand with the abandonment of the false belief that public office and high political position are to be valued only by the standards of pride of place and personal profit; and there must be an end to a conduct in banking and in business which too often has given to a sacred trust the likeness of callous and selfish wrongdoing. Small wonder that confidence languishes, for it thrives only on honesty, on honor, on the sacredness of obligations, on faithful protection, on unselfish performance; without them it cannot live.

Restoration calls, however, not for changes in ethics alone. This Nation asks for action, and action now.

Our greatest primary task is to put people to work. This is no unsolvable problem if we face it wisely and courageously. It can be accomplished in part by direct recruiting by the Government itself, treating the task as we would treat the emergency of a war, but at the same time, through this employment, accomplishing greatly needed projects to stimulate and reorganize the use of our natural resources.

Hand in hand with this we must frankly recognize the overbalance of population in our industrial centers and, by engaging on a national scale in a redistribution, endeavor to provide a better use of the land for those best fitted for the land. The task can be helped by definite efforts to raise the values of agricultural products and with this the power to purchase the output of our cities. It can be helped by preventing realistically the tragedy of the growing loss through foreclosure of our small homes and our farms. It can be helped by insistence that the Federal, State, and local governments act forthwith on the demand that their cost be drastically reduced. It can be helped by the unifying of relief activities which today are often scattered, uneconomical, and unequal. It can be helped by national planning for and supervision of all forms of transportation and of communications and other utilities which have a definitely public character. There are many ways in which it can be helped, but it can never be helped merely by talking about it. We must act and act quickly.

Finally, in our progress toward a resumption of work we require two safeguards against a return of the evils of the old order: there must be a strict supervision of all banking and credits and investments, so that there will be an end to speculation with other people's money; and there must be provision for an adequate but sound currency.

These are the lines of attack. I shall presently urge upon a new Congress, in special session, detailed measures for their fulfillment, and I shall seek the immediate assistance of the several States.

Through this program of action we address ourselves to putting our own national house in order and making income balance outgo. Our international trade relations, though vastly important, are in point of time and necessity secondary to the establishment of a sound national economy. I favor as a practical policy the putting of first things first. I shall spare no effort to restore world trade by international economic readjustment, but the emergency at home cannot wait on that accomplishment.

The basic thought that guides these specific means of national recovery is not narrowly nationalistic. It is the insistence, as a first consideration, upon the interdependence of the various elements in and parts of the United States —a recognition of the old and permanently important manifestation of the American spirit of the pioneer. It is the way to recovery. It is the immediate way. It is the strongest assurance that the recovery will endure.

In the field of world policy I would dedicate this Nation to the policy of the good neighbor—the neighbor who resolutely respects himself and, because he does so, respects the rights of others—the neighbor who respects his obligations and respects the sanctity of his agreements in and with a world of neighbors.

If I read the temper of our people correctly, we now realize as we have never realized before our interdependence on each other; that we cannot merely take but we must give as well; that if we are to go forward, we must move as a trained and loyal army willing to sacrifice for the good of a common discipline, because without such discipline no progress is made, no leadership becomes effective. We are, I know, ready and willing to submit our lives and property to such discipline, because it makes possible a leadership which aims at a larger good. This I propose to offer, pledging that the larger purpose will bind upon us all as a sacred obligation with a unity of duty hitherto evoked only in time of armed strife.

With this pledge taken, I assume unhesitatingly the leadership of this great army of our people dedicated to a disciplined attack upon our common problems.

Action in this image and to this end is feasible under the form of government which we have inherited from our ancestors. Our Constitution is so simple and practical that it is possible always to meet extraordinary needs by changes in emphasis and arrangement without loss of essential form. That is why our constitutional system has proved itself the most superbly enduring political mechanism the modern world has produced. It has met every stress of vast expansion of territory, of foreign wars, of bitter internal strife, of world relations.

It is to be hoped that the normal balance of Executive and legislative authority may be wholly adequate to meet the unprecedented task before us. But it may be that an unprecedented demand and need for undelayed action may call for temporary departure from that normal balance of public procedure.

I am prepared under my constitutional duty to recommend the measures that a stricken Nation in the midst of a stricken world may require. These measures, or such other measures as the Congress may build out of its experience and wisdom, I shall seek, within my constitutional authority, to bring to speedy adoption.

But in the event that the Congress shall fail to take one of these two courses, and in the event that the national emergency is still critical, I shall not evade the clear course of duty that will then confront me. I shall ask the Congress for the one remaining instrument to meet the crisis—broad Executive power to wage a war against the emergency, as great as the power that would be given to me if we were in fact invaded by a foreign foe.

For the trust reposed in me I will return the courage and the devotion that befit the time. I can do no less.

We face the arduous days that lie before us in the warm courage of national unity; with the clear consciousness of seeking old and precious moral values; with the clean satisfaction that comes from the stern performance of duty by old and young alike. We aim at the assurance of a rounded and permanent national life.

We do not distrust the future of essential democracy. The people of the United States have not failed. In their need they have registered a mandate that they want direct, vigorous action. They have asked for discipline and direction under leadership. They have made me the present instrument of their wishes. In the spirit of the gift I take it.

In this dedication of a Nation we humbly ask the blessing of God. May He protect each and every one of us. May He guide me in the days to come.

PRIMARY SOURCE 11

Novelist F. Scott Fitzgerald wrote often and eloquently about the meaning of the "Great War" for his generation. This early chapter from his novel *Tender Is the Night* contains numerous evocations of the war's meaning. Note how quickly the red-haired girl from Tennessee forgets her tears.

DICK turned the corner of the traverse and continued along the trench walking on the duckboard. He came to a periscope, looked through it a moment; then he got up on the step and peered over the parapet. In front of him beneath a dingy sky was Beaumont Hamel; to his left the tragic hill of Thiepval. Dick stared at them through his field glasses, his throat straining with sadness.

He went on along the trench, and found the others waiting for him in the next traverse. He was full of excitement and he wanted to communicate it to them, to make them understand about this, though actually Abe North had seen battle service and he had not.

"This land here cost twenty lives a foot that summer," he said to Rosemary. She looked out obediently at the rather bare green plain with its low trees of six years' growth. If Dick had added that they were now being shelled she would have believed him that afternoon. Her love had reached a point where now at last she was beginning to be unhappy, to be desperate. She didn't know what to do—she wanted to talk to her mother.

"There are lots of people dead since and we'll all be dead soon," said Abe consolingly.

Rosemary waited tensely for Dick to continue.

"See that little stream—we could walk to it in two minutes. It took the British a month to walk to it—a whole empire walking very slowly, dying in front and pushing forward behind. And another empire walked very slowly backward a few inches a day, leaving the dead like a million bloody rugs. No Europeans will ever do that again in this generation."

"Why, they've only just quit over in Turkey," said Abe. "And in Morocco—"

"That's different. This western-front business couldn't be done again, not for a long time. The young men think they could do it but they couldn't. They could fight the first Marne again but not this. This took religion and years of plenty and tremendous sureties and the exact relation that existed between the classes. The Russians and Italians weren't any good on this front. You had to have a whole-souled sentimental equipment going back further than you could remember. You had to remember Christmas, and postcards of the Crown Prince and his fiancée, and little cafés in Valence and beer gardens in Unter den Linden and weddings at the mairie, and going to the Derby, and your grandfather's whiskers."

"General Grant invented this kind of battle at Petersburg in sixty-five."

"No, he didn't—he just invented mass butchery. This kind of battle was invented by Lewis Carroll and Jules Verne and whoever wrote Undine, and country deacons bowling and marraines in Marseilles and girls seduced in the back lanes of Wurtemburg and Westphalia. Why, this was a love battle— there was a century of middle-class love spent here. This was the last love battle."

"You want to hand over this battle to D. H. Lawrence," said Abe.

"All my beautiful lovely safe world blew itself up here with a great gust of high explosive love," Dick mourned persistently. "Isn't that true, Rosemary?"

"I don't know," she answered with a grave face. "You know everything."

They dropped behind the others. Suddenly a shower of earth gobs and pebbles came down on them and Abe yelled from the next traverse:

"The war spirit's getting into me again. I have a hundred years of Ohio love behind me and I'm going to bomb out this trench." His head popped up over the embankment. "You're dead—don't you know the rules? That was a grenade."

Rosemary laughed and Dick picked up a retaliatory handful of stones and then put them down.

"I couldn't kid here," he said rather apologetically. "The silver cord is cut and the golden bowl is broken and all that, but an old romantic like me can't do anything about it."

"I'm romantic too."

They came out of the neat restored trench, and faced a memorial to the Newfoundland dead. Reading the inscription Rosemary burst into sudden tears. Like most women she liked to be told how she should feel, and she liked Dick's telling her which things were ludicrous and which things were sad. But most of all she wanted him to know how she loved him, now that the fact was upsetting everything, now that she was walking over the battle-field in a thrilling dream.

After that they got in their car and started back toward Amiens. A thin warm rain was falling on the new scrubby woods and underbrush and they passed great funeral pyres of sorted duds, shells, bombs, grenades, and equipment, helmets, bayonets, gun stocks and rotten leather, abandoned six years in the ground. And suddenly around a bend the white caps of a great sea of graves. Dick asked the chauffeur to stop.

"There's that girl—and she still has her wreath."

They watched as he got out and went over to the girl, who stood uncertainly by the gate with a wreath in her hand. Her taxi waited. She was a red-haired girl from Tennessee whom they had met on the train this morning, come from Knoxville to lay a memorial on her brother's grave. There were tears of vexation on her face.

"The War Department must have given me the wrong number," she whimpered. "It had another name on it. I been lookin' for it since two o'clock, and there's so many graves."

"Then if I were you I'd just lay it on any grave without looking at the name," Dick advised her.

"You reckon that's what I ought to do?"

"I think that's what he'd have wanted you to do."

It was growing dark and the rain was coming down harder. She left the wreath on the first grave inside the gate, and accepted Dick's suggestion that she dismiss her taxi-cab and ride back to Amiens with them.

Rosemary shed tears again when she heard of the mishap—altogether it had been a watery day, but she felt that she had learned something, though exactly what it was she did not know. Later she remembered all the hours of the afternoon as happy—one of those uneventful times that seem at the moment only a link between past and future pleasure but turn out to have been the pleasure itself.

Amiens was an echoing purple town, still sad with the war, as some railroad stations were:—the Gare du Nord and Waterloo station in London. In the daytime one is deflated by such towns, with their little trolley cars of twenty years ago crossing the great gray cobble-stoned squares in front of the cathedral, and the very weather seems to have a quality of the past, faded weather like that of old photographs. But after dark all that is most satisfactory in French life swims back into the picture—the sprightly tarts, the men arguing with a hundred Voilàs in the cafés, the couples drifting, head to head, toward the satisfactory inexpensiveness of nowhere. Waiting for the train they sat in a big arcade, tall enough to release the smoke and chatter and music upward and obligingly the orchestra launched into "Yes, We Have No Bananas,"—they clapped, because the leader looked so pleased with himself. The Tennessee girl forgot her sorrow and enjoyed herself, even began flirtations of tropical eye-rollings and pawings, with Dick and Abe. They teased her gently.

Then, leaving infinitesimal sections of Wurtemburgers, Prussian Guards, Chasseurs Alpins, Manchester mill hands and old Etonians to pursue their eternal dissolution under the warm rain, they took the train for Paris. They ate sandwiches of mortadel sausage and bel paese cheese made up in the station restaurant, and drank Beaujolais. Nicole was abstracted, biting her lip restlessly and reading over the guide-books to the battle-field that Dick had brought along—indeed, he had made a quick study of the whole affair, simplifying it always until it bore a faint resemblance to one of his own parties.

PRIMARY SOURCE   12

The last selection is from the pen of American poet E. E. Cummings. It comes from a letter to his father that Cummings wrote while serving in the United States Army in 1918. Note the tension between officers and ordinary soldiers that the letter implies.

[Camp Devens]
Dec. 14 '18]

Dear Dad,

The lieutenant-inspector of whose general soldierliness I think I have spoken to you once or twice this morning addressed the men who go on guard today-and-tomorrow. I took down, while he was speaking,certain things which I thought would particularly interest you.

"I have a home in Georgia. My father owns 500 acres and works 15 to 20 niggers. I don't have to be here. I was discharged three times. They can't get rid of me.

"I went to school 3 years.

"I wished they'd sign a bill that every man in uniform would be here five years."

Even more interesting are the following:

"There is a feller up there(at the guardhouse)named Cox(?) he wrote his girl:the first time a guard's back was turned he'd come back to her . . . I got the letter. She didn't . . . I got 2 broken fingers now from Cox(?)and I'll have 2 more.

"You men ought to take a look at what they do to a man at the military prisons,Jay,New York;Leavenworth,Kansas;Fort Angel(?)California. I've been to all of 'em. When a man comes to Fort Jay,the first thing they do is give him a g. d. fine beating. They black his eyes for him. They do that on principle down there. All I ever wore at Jay was a pair of pants and a shirt with the sleeves tore out at the arms,winter and summer,that and my boots leggings and hat. All they do is fight from morning till night there."

Letter #90 in Selected Letters of E. E. Cummings, edited by F. W. Dupee and George Stade. Reprinted by permission of Harcourt Brace Jovanovich, Inc.

He added:"When you men get out of this army you'll be so lonesome for the life you won't know what ails you. Some day you'll hear a military band and the shivers'll go up your spine and you won't know what for,and the next morning you'll wake up in an army bunk and say 'How did I get here?' "—at this point private D. laughed heartily for a whole minute,rocking to and fro with mirth.—"What are you laughing at?" the L.asked.—"I can't help it" was the answer. "I know you can't,I don't mind your laughing,but what are you laughing at?" When private D. responded "at what you said" the laughter became uproarious all over the audience.

I should be pleased to have this letter,which it will be noticed is a verbatim account at first hand,follow the Dial,which it so aptly backs up,to its destination.

Yours for patriotism-of-the-world

7

POSTWAR CULTURE
MOTION PICTURE ANALYSIS

While the 1920s were marked by amusing fads like mah-jongg, marathon dancing, and goldfish swallowing, the decade also witnessed changes that had a lasting impact on American society. Developments in the motion picture industry, for example, revolutionized the field of popular entertainment. During the 1920s, sound was successfully introduced to film, movie stars became national idols, small movie businesses evolved into giant corporations, and Hollywood became the movie capital of the world. By the end of the decade, motion pictures were attracting, out of a total population of just over 120 million, 100 million viewers a week. A uniquely American concept as developed by Hollywood, movies, with their low admission fees, were also a very democratic art. Far from being a passing fad, they rapidly became a key component of a burgeoning popular culture.

While motion pictures always were and remain today primarily a form of mass entertainment, they are also an important subject for historical inquiry. Such inquiry takes place on many levels—levels that can be distinguished by the different prepositions used to describe the relationship between film and history. History *on* film, for example, refers to the ways in which moviemakers use and abuse historical facts and themes in their films. History *in* film, on the other hand, refers to the ways in which motion pictures relate to the society that produces and watches them.

When one studies history *in* film, one uses motion pictures as primary sources capable of reflecting and revealing the cultural values and prejudices of the society to which they are appealing. Quite often, such study involves history *on* film as well. Indeed, distortions of history produced on film often make a motion picture a valuable primary source. D. W. Griffith's 1915 classic, *The Birth of a Nation,* for example, presents a very antiblack and distorted view of Reconstruction. Its portrait of a southern legislature dominated by cigar smoking, whiskey drinking, venal black men and carpetbaggers is an outrageous distortion of historical reality and only one of many such distortions in the film. *Birth of a Nation* does reveal, however, some of the racial stereotypes and historical beliefs that Americans held at this time. A totally unreliable secondary source for Reconstruction, the film is nevertheless an excellent source for understanding American popular attitudes in the early twentieth century. The same is true of the 1939 classic *Gone with the Wind.* Moreover, by comparing the racial stereotypes in the two films, the historian can see if any changes in American racial values occurred during the twenty-five years between them.

Motion pictures are not simply an echo or reinforcement of existing cultural values, however. Often they seek to impart new ideas as well as to reinforce old ones, or to propagandize a whole system of values. In this regard, the relationship of film to history is similar to that of literature, often changing as well as reflecting current values. But historical analysis of film is different and in some ways more complex than an analysis of literature. A film does not have a single author, for example, and an analysis of its contents must therefore include all the individuals and factors involved in its production. And quite often, such an analysis will reveal the existence of specific circumstances that exercise a dominant influence over the film in question.

During the 1930s, for example, the film industry refined and used specific plot "formulas" to maximize commercial success. As a result, almost all American commercial feature films produced during this decade followed set patterns and exhibited stereotypical behavior. Heroes and heroines, for example, had to follow a specific moral code and win, while villains who violated that code lost. Governed by the code, formulas were unable to illustrate sex explicitly on the screen, even though such sex could be blatantly advertised along with the film.

An equally important influence on many films is direct or indirect government intervention, for film is a powerful weapon of mass propaganda. Governments first recognized this fact during World War I and used film as part of their efforts to mobilize populations for a total war effort. The British government made particularly effective use of propaganda and, by its control of the seas and the transatlantic cable, was able to flood the United States with it. According to some scholars, that propaganda played a major role in turning the American people from a neutral to a pro-Allied and anti-German stance. Once the United States entered the war, the Wilson administration organized the Committee on Public Information (CPI) under journalist George Creel, which used film and other media to convince the American people of the righteousness of their struggle. The result was not merely mass mobilization and manipulation for the war effort but also a national hysteria against German-Americans, leftists, and anyone else who questioned the official version of American participation in the war.

During the 1930s, Adolf Hitler and his Nazi cohorts in Germany, most notably Joseph Goebbels, developed the techniques pioneered during World War I and turned film, both documentary and commercial, into an even more effective means of propaganda. Throughout World War II, every major belligerent maintained a large-scale propaganda bureau that devoted major efforts to motion pictures. In the United States, the Office of War Information (OWI) fulfilled this role. Its actual powers were severely circumscribed because the public remembered the lies of World War I and because Congress feared that President Roosevelt might use the agency to further his own political career, but it was able to exert tremendous indirect influence on Hollywood throughout the war.

Propaganda is obvious in the documentary films produced by Hollywood and the government between 1942 and 1945. It is less blatant but just as potent in numerous commercial feature films of this era. Indeed, some scholars argue that *all* films contain propaganda; even when a motion picture, like *Gone with the Wind,* merely reasserts the values of an era, it is reinforcing those values in the public mind and thereby serving a propaganda function.

Film propaganda may affect different audiences in different ways. *The Grapes of Wrath,* a film based on John Steinbeck's novel of that title about the poverty of the dust bowl during the Great Depression, often moved American audiences to tears. When the film was shown in the Soviet Union, Russian audiences were amazed at the number of automobiles owned by those poor Americans! Value changes over time can lead to similar differences in audience reaction, and the propaganda methods and messages that were highly successful in one era can be dismal failures in another. For example, John Wayne's 1968 *The Green Berets,* using racial stereotypes and conventions similar to those that had been so successful in *Sands of Iwo Jima* (1948) and Wayne's other films about World War II, was largely unsuccessful in propagandizing the Vietnam War.

The average viewer does not see the propaganda in commercial feature films or the cultural values that are reflected in them. This is largely due to the fact that the viewer in all likelihood shares those values and is attending the movie for relaxation and entertainment, not for information and education. The student of history, however, cannot afford such a luxury and must analyze films as well as enjoy them.

As we hope you will discover, analysis and entertainment are not mutually exclusive. One can enjoy a good movie and still view it critically provided one knows what to look for and *how* to view it. One of the major purposes of the preceding explanation of history and film, and of the analysis and assignments that follow, is to enable you to view movies critically and use them as primary sources.

Before viewing a film, one should first understand the historical context of the time in which it was produced as well as the specific factors that influenced its production. If the film refers to a past event or time period, one should also be aware of the actual facts involved in that event or time period. In viewing the film, one can then compare the actual events with what is portrayed on the screen, note the differences, and use one's knowledge of the film's historical context in order to explain them. Such knowledge will enable the viewer to note the propaganda in a film and the cultural values involved in the portrayal of different characters and issues. To understand fully such propaganda and cultural values as projected in *Birth of a Nation,* for example, one should have a detailed knowledge of the general racial beliefs and historical interpretations of Reconstruction prevalent in 1915, Griffith's specific beliefs, aims, and methods, and the actual facts of Reconstruction history.

Film historians often place motion pictures in specific categories for purposes of analysis. These categories are known as *genres,* or "formulas," and are determined by common themes, characters, and/or settings (i.e., westerns, comedies, musicals). One of the best genres for exploring the issues discussed above and for using motion pictures as primary sources is the war film. While this genre is defined in different ways by scholars, it is by no means restricted to combat zones and military actions. Rather, the war film deals with civilians as well as soldiers and covers numerous noncombat as well as combat aspects of the war experience.

Our favorite film within this genre is the 1942 classic *Casablanca,* starring Humphrey Bogart and Ingrid Bergman. Below you will find a brief description of the film's historical context as well as examples of what to look for while viewing it. Should your professor decide to use this film in class, the explanation provided will enable you to complete the assignments section of this chapter. Should your professor choose another film, he or she will provide you either with a similar explanation or with sources in which you can find that explanation yourself. The method of analysis will be quite similar and the assignments quite applicable no matter what film is chosen.

CASABLANCA

Casablanca was released in late 1942, just a few weeks after the successful Anglo-American invasion of the French North African colony in which it takes place. Its historical setting is one year earlier, in late 1941, *before* Pearl Harbor and American entry into World War II. At that time the United States was still officially neutral and involved in a great debate between isolationists and internationalists over whether the Axis powers constituted a threat to the country and whether it should enter the war that was already in progress.

By this time in the war, Hitler had already conquered France and most of the rest of continental Europe. He had subsequently annexed northern France (including Paris), while allowing a puppet regime in Vichy under the aged World War I hero Marshal Henri Pétain to rule southern France and the French overseas colonies, including Morocco. Officially, Vichy France became a neutral power in the war; in reality she was subservient to Germany. French citizens who refused to accept this situation joined underground resistance groups and/or the "Free French" forces of General Charles de Gaulle, who had escaped to England after the French military defeat in June 1940. At first, such individuals were few in number.

After France's defeat, England stood alone against Germany and her Italian ally until June of 1941, when Hitler invaded Russia. By December, he seemed to be on the verge of taking Moscow, ending Soviet resistance, and forcing Britain once again to fight alone with virtually no chance of victory. German fortunes would change dramatically in the ensuing year as a result of American entry into the war, successful Soviet counteroffensives in front of Moscow and at Stalingrad, a successful British counteroffensive in Egypt, and the Anglo-American invasion and conquest of North Africa. These facts were known to all audiences watching *Casablanca,* but at the time the movie takes place, Hitler seemed invincible.

The use of historical hindsight for propaganda purposes is evident in many of the film's famous lines, such as "Isolationism is no longer a practical policy" and "I'll bet they're asleep all over America." Historical hindsight is also apparent in the fact that General de Gaulle is portrayed as a popular and powerful figure even though he had virtually no support in French North Africa in late 1941. This overblown portrayal of de Gaulle and his power is, in turn, linked to the extraordinarily large number of European nationalities represented on Rick's (Humphrey Bogart's) staff and the very positive portrayal of their national characteristics and unity of purpose, thereby fulfilling OWI's wartime "advice" that the war be portrayed as an *allied* effort and that America's allies be shown in a positive light.

Cultural values of American society at this time are also projected throughout the film, particularly in the stereotypes of some nationalities ("If he gets a word in, it will be a major Italian victory"), different races (Sam as the loyal, humorous, and subordinate black sidekick), and the female sex ("You'll have to do the thinking for both of us"). They are also apparent in Humphrey Bogart's brilliant portrayal of the characteristic American hero of this era, a figure critics now refer to as the "antihero"; harsh and cynical on the outside to protect himself, but an idealist at heart who responds appropriately in crisis situations.

Propaganda and cultural values are often interwoven in the film, making it extremely difficult at times to distinguish between the two. When the maître d' Carl tells Rick, for example, "I already gave him the best, knowing he's German and would take it anyway," he is emphasizing both a typical American view of Germans and an important political message regarding the dangers of German victory and the need to defeat Hitler. And in the climactic last scene, Rick is not only portraying the self-sacrifice Americans would expect of a hero in wartime but also making clear to viewers the sacrifices still required of all Americans if they hope to win the war. This scene also allowed the film to end in a way that did not violate Hollywood's moral code. *Casablanca* is thus a "classic" film not only in terms of its artistic quality but also in its subtle political messages and cultural stereotypes.

ASSIGNMENTS

1. View *Casablanca* or another movie from this era as instructed by your professor.
2. Briefly describe how one scene in the movie shows projections of American cultural values in this era.
3. Briefly describe how a second scene contains propaganda, whether political or cultural.
4. Briefly describe how a third scene in the movie contains a mixture of cultural values and propaganda.

ADDITIONAL QUESTIONS TO CONSIDER

1. Be prepared to discuss the cultural values and propaganda inherent in the film's portrayal of different nationalities, races, and sexes; its plot; and its version of the stereotypical hero. If you view a war film, what makes it part of this genre, and what does it project as positive and negative characteristics of individuals in wartime? Do these characteristics, the settings, and the issues differ from those one would expect in a movie not concerned with and/or produced during war? Why? If the movie you view is not a war film, what genre does it belong to and what makes it part of that genre?
2. Compare the movie you have viewed with another from this era. What similarities and differences do you notice in terms of character portrayal, plot, positive and negative values, propaganda?
3. Compare the movie you have viewed with one on the same subject produced in a later decade. Again, what similarities and differences do you notice? What generalizations about changing values would you reach from such a comparison?
4. If the movie you view was remade at a later date or used as the basis in some way for a later film (i.e., Woody Allen's *Play It Again Sam* for *Casablanca*), compare the two and be prepared to discuss the changing values they reveal.
5. What specific tools of analysis should the historian bring to motion pictures? What possible problems do you see in using film as a primary source, and what are the limits of film as a source for historical study?

8

FROM DEPRESSION TO GLOBALISM
MEDIA ANALYSIS, HISTORICAL RESEARCH, AND WRITING

The motion pictures discussed in the preceding chapter were but one of a host of post-World War I innovations in the field of communication. Equally if not more important was the commercial development of numerous other prewar inventions, including the radio, the telephone, the phonograph, the automobile, and mass-circulation books and magazines. All these became part of American life after World War I, as well as part of a new media network capable of instantaneous communication throughout the nation and the world.

This network did more than revolutionize the field of communication. It also affected American perceptions, values, and life-styles. With the growth of radio sales, for example, came the growth of commercial stations and networks, mass advertising, and mass spending on consumer items. By 1929, 10 million families owned radios and listened to the hundreds of stations that had come into existence since 1920. On those stations they heard not only news but also sports, entertainment, and millions of dollars worth of advertising encouraging them to buy the new consumer items that were flooding the market. Not surprisingly, sports, entertainment, music, and advertising became major industries during this decade and consumer spending increased enormously, perhaps as much as tenfold for the average American family.

This revolution was by no means limited to the medium of radio. The development of the phonograph—and, later, high-fidelity and stereophonic systems—was equally important in creating the modern music industry and with it a new type of popular culture. Roadside advertising was a byproduct of the commercial development of the automobile. And mass-circulation books and magazines spawned a paperback revolution that included the advent of comic books filled with advertisements as well as new, mass-culture characters.

The media network also showed an extraordinary ability to influence the very nature of the news events it reported. Indeed, it often created those events, as well as national heroes and issues. Charles Lindbergh's enormous popularity after his 1927 solo flight across the Atlantic, for example, was possible not simply because of the invention or commercialization of the airplane but also because of the massive coverage he received in the press, on radio, and in motion pictures. Equally spectacular coverage was given a few years later to the kidnapping and death of his child, coverage that may have severely distorted both the issues and the outcome of the supposed kidnapper's trial.

The fields of sport and entertainment offer equally impressive evidence of media power. Babe Ruth was certainly a great baseball player with or without the media, but he could not have become a national hero without national press coverage or the radio that broadcast baseball games into millions of homes. Without the new motion picture industry and its impact on American values, Rudolph Valentino probably would have remained an obscure dancer. Instead, he became an idol to millions of Americans, and when he unexpectedly died at age thirty-one, more than 25,000 people lined up outside the funeral parlor to view his body. The resulting pandemonium became a "media event" of the first order.

The media also exercised enormous influence on more traditional events and issues. They turned ordinary criminals like Al Capone and John Dillinger into household words and national menaces. Their coverage of the disappearances of airplane pilot Amelia Earhart and evangelist Aimee Semple McPherson prompted national searches. And they transformed a local trial in Tennessee over the teaching of evolution into a national spectacle in which the actual defendant, John Scopes, became the least important consideration in the case.

Politicians quickly realized the power of the new media and began to use it to their advantage. The Washington Naval Conference of 1921–1922 was a huge success partially because Secretary of State Charles Evans Hughes decided to employ media publicity through his highly unorthodox opening speech to mobilize world public opinion in favor of his proposals. Ten years later, Franklin D. Roosevelt electrified the American people both by traveling to the Democratic Convention in an airplane to accept his party's nomination for the presidency and by giving his 1933 presidential Inaugural Address, which was specifically geared to home consumption, via the radio. In the ensuing months, he relied heavily on the radio, through his "fireside chats," to win public support for his proposals and to raise public morale. Simultaneously, his wife Eleanor used media coverage to alter dramatically the role of first lady.

Throughout his presidency, in fact, Roosevelt consistently used the media to elicit popular support and to test out new proposals. In the process, he created numerous national slogans ("nothing to fear but fear itself," "quarantine of aggressor nations," "lend-lease," "arsenal of democracy") and an image of the presidency previously unknown. Three thousand miles away, Adolf Hitler was simultaneously manipulating the media through detailed propaganda to revolutionize German society and thought and to frighten his adversaries into submission with exaggerated displays of his military capacities. Such manipulation of the media could easily boomerang, however. In using the radio, Roosevelt provided his enemies with a powerful weapon of their own. Father Charles Coughlin, for example, might have remained an obscure priest without national radio to carry his message of "social justice" to millions of homes. Furthermore, media coverage often created popular images that were in no way planned and that had negative repercussions later. Secretary of State Frank B. Kellogg, for example, was virtually booted into a Nobel Peace Prize and immortality by media coverage and the consequent public response to his suggestion of a multilateral pact to outlaw war. While neither Kellogg nor any other statesman had illusions about the effectiveness of such a pact, the media lionized Kellogg as a great peacemaker and helped delude the public into thinking war had actually been abolished. According to some historians, the result was a refusal by Western public opinion in the 1930s to recognize the menace posed by the rise of the fascist powers.

Important national leaders also ignored this menace, and in the process they too created a series of powerful if unplanned media images. To present-day Americans, the Munich Conference of 1938 is a picture of pathetic British Prime Minister Neville Chamberlain returning to England, umbrella in hand, waving a piece of paper and promising "peace in our time." Actually, the original Western response to this image was extremely positive; the change in perception occurred six months later, almost overnight, when Hitler violated his pledges and seized the rest of Czechoslovakia.

The post-World War II development of television further strengthened this media network and its power by bringing live images as well as sound into millions of homes. By 1950, close to 4 million households had television sets that were turned on for an average of five hours per day. By 1970, the number of such households had increased to almost 60 million. National leaders now had to be full "media personalities," capable of reflecting a very positive image on screen, and this image became much more important than the content of their proposals. As in earlier years, these leaders both manipulated the media and found themselves victimized by unintended consequences of their manipulation. In 1947, for example, President Harry Truman sold his "Truman Doctrine" to the American Congress and people by following a senator's advice to "scare hell" out of the public, only to find his overblown anticommunist rhetoric being used against him a few years later by Senator Joe McCarthy. McCarthy, in turn, was soon destroyed by the very media he had used to achieve his popularity when, in the televised army-McCarthy hearings, he projected the image of an unkempt bully. In his famous "Checkers" speech of 1952, Richard Nixon was able to use television to save his political career; eight years later, however, his poor television image in comparison to John F. Kennedy's may have cost him a presidential election.

As these examples show, the media network that developed after World War I has had enormous power. It has created events, changed them, and tremendously influenced public perception of them. It has manipulated people and has been manipulated by them. It has projected planned and desired images that later became undesirable, and it has projected images that no one planned or desired but that nevertheless had an important impact on future events. In view of such power, no analysis of events over the last sixty-five years would be complete without the inclusion of media influence. Your written assignment involves careful examination of the media's influence on one specific event during this time period.

ASSIGNMENTS

1. Using either the information provided in your textbook and class or specific instructions from your professor, choose one event or issue from the years 1920–1960 that the media reported.
2. Making use of the skills discussed in Chapter 1, go to the library and prepare a bibliography of appropriate works to be consulted for a research paper on both the event or issue and the media coverage. Read these works and take notes accordingly.
3. Making use of the skills discussed in the preceding chapters, research, outline and write a three- to five-page, typewritten, double-spaced paper (750 to 1,250 words) that explains both what happened and how media coverage affected the event itself and/or how people perceived it.
4. As an alternative assignment, research and write a 3 to 5-page paper on the use one American president made of the media for a specific purpose or issue.

ADDITIONAL QUESTIONS TO CONSIDER

1. Historians often argue over whether people's perceptions of reality are more important than what actually happened. Which side of this argument does the information you uncovered for your paper tend to support?
2. Some people see a conspiracy in the media's distortion of events. Does the information you found for your paper support such a conclusion? If not, what factors account for such distortion?

3. During the 1960s, Canadian scholar Marshall McLuhan concluded in an oft-quoted phrase that "the medium is the message." Do you agree? Why?

4. On the same day, watch a television news show, listen to a radio news broadcast of equal length, and read the front page of your daily newspaper. For each of the three, note the amount of time and space given to each news item. Then compare the news items and the time or space each medium gave to each item. Were the items the same? Were the relative time and space given the same? Which medium gave you the most information? Which gave you the information in the most entertaining manner? If there was a disparity in the "facts" presented for the same piece of news, which medium would you believe? Why?

5. It is conceivable that for future generations, a minor event not even reported in today's news will be considered more significant than all the events that were reported. Given this fact as well as what you have discovered in your research, what are the strengths and limitations of media-reported events as historical sources?

9

GENERATIONAL CHANGE AND CONFLICT IN RECENT AMERICAN HISTORY
SOURCES IN ORAL HISTORY

In 1961, John Fitzgerald Kennedy, the youngest man ever elected president, succeeded Dwight David Eisenhower, who was up to that point the oldest man ever to occupy the White House. Kennedy told those assembled at his inauguration and millions of others watching on television that "the torch has been passed to a new generation of Americans—born in this century, tempered by war, disciplined by a cold and bitter peace, proud of our ancient heritage. . . ."

Kennedy's rhetoric had a point he may not have intended, for his election signaled the beginning of one of the most dramatic and long-lasting shifts in political generations to take place in the history of American presidential elections. Prior to 1961, the largest age difference between an incumbent president and his successor had been the fifteen years between Andrew Jackson and Martin Van Buren in 1836. Kennedy was twenty-seven years younger than Eisenhower, and his generation would dominate presidential politics into the 1980s. All presidents since 1961 were born in an eighteen-year period, running from Lyndon Johnson's birth in 1908 to Jimmy Carter's in 1924. Even Ronald Reagan, the oldest man ever to hold the presidency, was born during these years (1911). Hence what had in 1961 been the youngest generation to hold the presidency is now the oldest, and it has held that office for a quarter of a century.

Like those of individuals, the lifelong perceptions of entire generations are often shaped by dramatic events that occurred when they were relatively young. For the Kennedy generation, those events were clearly the Great Depression and World War II, and numerous historians have noted the extraordinary persistence of our recent presidents and their advisers in applying the historical "lessons" they learned in the 1930s and '40s to the '60s, '70s, and '80s.

Yet much of the political agenda of the period from 1960 to 1980 was determined by young, often anonymous Americans with very different ideas who were determined to have their say in the nation's destiny. While John Kennedy was making plans for his inaugural, for example, four young black freshmen at North Carolina Technical and Agricultural College decided to go to the segregated lunch counter at the Woolworth's department store in downtown Greensboro and request service. This action on the part of Joseph McNeill, Ezell Blair, Jr., Franklin McCain, and David Richmond inspired what came to be called "sit-ins" all over the South. By September 1961, the Southern Regional Council reported that more than 70,000 blacks and whites, most of them students, had joined sit-ins to protest unjust racial practices.

Not only black youths moved into the political arena in the 1960s; American Indians and Mexican-Americans became politically active as well. Indians banished the Dartmouth College "Indian" mascot, seized Alcatraz Island, and offered to buy it from the U.S. government for $24 in beads and cloth. At a demonstration at Plymouth Rock in 1970, a young Mohawk commented, "That damn rock, I'd like to blow it up. It was the start of everything bad that has happened to the American Indian." Mexican-Americans demanded bilingual education, protested caricatures in advertising like the "Frito Bandito," and promoted the idea of "La Raza."

Nor was youth protest restricted to ethnic minorities. Young men and women of all backgrounds became politically active in a variety of causes ranging from war protest to free speech. Additionally, other youth dropped out of society and joined the counterculture. The slogan "Don't trust anyone over thirty" gained wide currency among disaffected youth, and pundits and politicians alike began to worry over what was called "the generation gap." As Tom Hayden, one of the founders of Students for a Democratic Society put it in a virtual caricature of Kennedy's inaugural address, "We are the people of this generation, bred in at least modest comfort, housed now in universities, looking uncomfortably to the world we inherit." Or as Sarah Davidson recalled, "We were certain that we belonged to a generation that was special. We did not need or care about history because we had sprung from nowhere. . . . We had glimpsed a new world where nothing would be the same and we had packed our bags."

The conflict between generations has long been an acknowledged force in history. Some scholars argue that the U.S. Constitution, for example, reflected the views of the young men of the American Revolution who were imbued with continental visions of what the United States might be. Encyclopedias of social science accept the notion that political revolutions are the work of young adults. Yet the duration and intensity of youth protest in the 1960s leave open the question of whether it was normal generational conflict or not.

Demographic analysis reveals that there was at least one aberrant fact that partly explains the conflict of the sixties: the protestors were part of the largest generation ever in American history. From 1800 onward, the long-term trend in the American birthrate had been downward; in fact, there had not been a decade since in which the birthrate rose, even infinitesimally, until 1940–1950, when it catapulted upwards by *35 percent.* From 1950 to 1957, the birthrate rose another *15 percent.* Beginning in 1957 this "baby boom" collapsed and the American birthrate plunged, reaching zero population growth (i.e., only the number of births the U.S. population would need to reproduce itself) and declining to 1.8 children per woman in 1980.

What the size of the baby boom generation tells us historically is not yet clear, but certainly the shared experience of that generation will profoundly influence the nation's history once the torch that the Kennedy generation received in 1960 is passed on once more. How different are the values of the baby boom generation compared to those of earlier generations of Americans? What are some of the ways in which this question can be answered?

One relatively new type of source that might be tapped to answer this question is oral history. Actually, oral history is probably the oldest form of history known to the human race; thousands of years before the development of printing presses or even written language, tribal storytellers verbalized the history of their people for succeeding generations. As Alex Haley discovered in researching *Roots,* the history of his own family, this tradition of oral history is still valuable and very much alive in Africa as well as other portions of the globe.

Over the last fifty years, however, a new type of oral history has emerged, one that uses the oral tradition as a primary rather than a secondary source. Beginning in the Great Depression with the Federal Writer's Project, interviewers have asked ordinary Americans to talk about their lives. With the passage of time, specific techniques and practices have developed for conducting and using such oral history interviews.

Based on the use of recent technology such as the portable tape recorder, these interviews constitute a relatively new and important type of primary source. They are in some ways similar to a traditional and still popular source, the memoir or autobiography. But whereas that written source has for most of its existence been the almost exclusive preserve of a nation's elite, oral histories have no such limits. Interviews are indeed often conducted with the leaders of society, but many oral historians prefer to interview everyday, anonymous Americans as a way of discovering what the mass of people were thinking and doing during an era under investigation. As you will see, such interviews can also be an effective way of discovering the shared experiences and values of a generation and the ways in which those experiences and values make that generation different from its predecessors.

In *Hard Times,* his classic oral history of the 1930s, Studs Terkel has Diane, a young journalist, comment on the Depression:

> Every time I've encountered the Depression, it has been used as a barrier and a club. It's been a countercommunication. Older people use it to explain to me that I can't understand anything: I didn't live through the Depression. They never say to me: We can't understand you because we didn't live through the leisure society. All attempts at communication are totally blocked. All of a sudden there's a generation gap. It's a frightening thing.
>
> What they're saying is: For twenty years I've starved and I've worked hard. You must fight. It's very Calvinistic. Work, suffer, have twenty lashes a day, and you can have a bowl of bean soup.
>
> I've never understood a society of want. We don't have a society of want —not on a general level. We have a society of total surplus: unwanted goods and unwanted people.

Diane's remarks provide a good introduction to the oral history selections reproduced below since she suggests that different generations perceive history differently. Thus oral history should be a good vehicle for exploring generational differences; this is, at least, an idea for you to ponder as you read these oral history excerpts.

We selected the ten excerpts from five representative works in oral history partly to provide you with a brief acquaintance with the growing literature in that field but also to reflect two distinct generations of American historical experience. The first five selections are from Americans who were young adults during the Second World War; the next five are from young adults of the Vietnam era. A careful reading of these excerpts should provide you with some ideas about the experience and values of the two generations as well as some insights into the history of the 1940s and 1960s.

ASSIGNMENTS

1. Read each of the oral history excerpts carefully. Take notes as it seems appropriate to you, including within them data provided on key events of the

1940s and 1960s and individual as well as shared experiences, reactions, and beliefs.

2. Using these oral history excerpts and your notes, write a two- to three-page (250- to 750-word) essay describing what distinguished the 1960s baby boom generation from its predecessor.

3. As an alternative assignment, write an essay on the topic "The Generation Gap of the 1960s: Fact or Fiction?" Within that essay, comment on the experiences and beliefs that you believe do and/or do not distinguish this generation from its predecessors.

ADDITIONAL QUESTIONS TO CONSIDER

1. Using the reference section of the library, particularly publications that deal with demographic analysis, can you identify broad behavior and thought patterns common to the generation born between 1900 and 1924? What would a comparison between that generation and the one born between 1945 and 1957 show in the areas of voting, education level, real income, home ownership, employment, racial attitudes, and religious beliefs?

2. Does lumping the beliefs of millions of Americans under those of a single generation distort the historical record? If so, why and how? If not, why not? How representative of their entire generation are the ten people interviewed?

3. Since all of the oral histories sampled here were done after 1975, might it be argued that they themselves represent changing perspectives on the nation's past? For example, does Studs Terkel's choice of the title *The Good War* represent his generation's judgment on the "bad" wars which followed 1945?

4. How do the beliefs of the people interviewed compare to your beliefs and those of your generation? How do you account for the differences?

ORAL HISTORIES OF THE 1960s

One of the nation's best known pioneers in oral history is Chicago-based radio commentator Studs Terkel. These two selections are taken from *"The Good War": An Oral History of World War Two*, published by Pantheon Books in 1984.[1]

EXCERPT 1

From Anthony Scariano, whose World War II experience was with the OSS, a precursor of the CIA.

Our boys, most of us, were somewhat liberal. We were Italian Americans who were recruited from the working-class areas of the big cities: New York,

[1]Reprinted by permission of Pantheon Books, a division of Random House, Inc., from *"The Good War": An Oral History of World War Two* by Studs Terkel; pp. 103 and 122. Copyright © 1984 by Studs Terkel.

Chicago, Cleveland, Boston, all over. We weren't interned like the Japanese, but we felt, as Italians, we had to prove ourselves. We weren't very political, but we'd sit around the fire in our villa and argue about the war. Would it mean a better America? Would it mean an end to injustice? We were just learning about the Holocaust. We really believed in this war . . . The boys really believed that a better world would come.

EXCERPT 2

From Dellie Hahne, a military wife, whose comments echo the wartime movement of women into the work force.

There was a letter column in which some woman wrote to her husband overseas: "This is an exact picture of our dashboard. Do we need a quart of oil?" Showing how dependent we were upon our men. Those of us who read it said, This is pure and simple bullshit. 'Cause if you don't know if you need a quart of oil, drive the damn thing to the station and have the man show you and you'll learn if you need a quart of oil. But they still wanted women to be dependent, helpless.

I think a lot of women said, Screw that noise. 'Cause they had a taste of freedom, they had a taste of making their own money, a taste of spending their own money, making their own decisions. I think the beginning of the women's movement had its seeds right there in World War Two.

Black-Americans experienced "The Good War" differently than their white counterparts. The two selections which follow are drawn from Mary Penick Motley's *The Invisible Soldier: The Experience of the Black Soldier in World War II.*[2]

EXCERPT 3

From Lieutenant Lacey Wilson who spent the war in the Aleutians after experiencing a number of incidents of racial violence during training.

"Stateside I encountered every possible racial insult. The one I shall always remember was not in a direct form of a put-down but it was the most disgusting of them all. At a train station in Texas I had to walk down an alley to the back of an eatery to get something to eat. Yet there were white MPs with German prisoners of war inside enjoying each other's company over a steak dinner. It sickened me so I could not eat a bite after ordering. I was a citizen soldier in the uniform of my country and I had to go through an alley to the back door while some of Hitler's storm troopers lapped up the hospitality of my country. . . .

"Black soldiers of World War II showed more courage just surviving, as well as fighting back by all means possible, in southern and in northern camps, than young people today can possibly imagine. Hell we fought the 'man,' the system, and the Axis powers. . . .

EXCERPT 4

From Staff Sergeant David Cason, Jr., from Michigan who, as a recent high school graduate in 1943, described himself as a "super-patriot."

"By now my friend and I had no false ideas about the white man's army so it became a game of seeing just how much we could avoid doing. We found out one of the most effective little gimmicks was to take a clip board, pad, and pencil and go up to the headquarters area and just walk around. No one ever bothered to ask us what we were doing up there. If our IQs said we were pretty smart cookies you can be assured we put every bit of our brain power together in the art of evading, dodging, and lying if caught. However we were very careful to make sure the 'great white father' was unaware that we were goofing off three-quarters of the time. The other quarter 'they' didn't consider worth bothering about, besides they didn't quite dig us. I mean our IQs as stated in the files made us some kind of freaks to them. . . .

War time upheavals both in the 1940s and in the 1960s produced floods of refugees out of the war zones. Many of these refugees sought shelter in the United States. Some of their experience is recaptured in Joan Morrison and Charlotte Fox Zabusky, *American Mosaic: The Immigrant Experience in the Words of Those Who Lived It. American Mosaic* is the source for Excerpts 5 and 6.[3]

EXCERPT 5

From Serge Nicholas, a Russian refugee from the war in Manchuria who arrived in the United States in 1938.

My experiences in the army were not exactly happy, but they were the making of me. The army was a University of Life for me. It was an environment where from early morning till late at night, I had to speak the language and take orders in English. I *had* to communicate. I had been living in the Russian ghetto, and if it hadn't been for the war I might not ever have had any reason to leave. It's so easy for the immigrant to become part of that community. This

---

[3]Reprinted from Joan Morrison and Charlotte Fox Zabusky, *American Mosaic: The Immigrant Experience in the Words of Those Who Lived It*, pp. 187 and 426. Reprinted by permission of E. P. Dutton.

is a big obstacle. You pick up a Russian newspaper or your neighbor speaks the same language—so you don't advance. You are just in the past and the whole world goes by at a very rapid rate. It becomes too comfortable. It takes a force, a push, an unusual event, to get you out of it. The army did it for me.

EXCERPT 6

From Hoa Tran, who came from South Vietnam to Columbus, Ohio in 1975.

. . . I decided to go to college. I'm studying accounting. Some Vietnamese friend told me it's very easy to find job if I graduate from this college. You get very good education. Top income will be after I graduate. I think that I will have a permanent job.

There are things I'm unhappy about, but I push them aside. I don't think about that. But that's my personal philosophy. I have friends who are very discouraged, very unhappy. They had high positions; now they're delivering milk, working in factory. When I told my friend I'm working as waiter, he said, "But what about your head? You're used to working with your head." I laughed.

The United States' military involvement in Vietnam had consequences for American society that historians are just beginning to understand. One area for study is clearly the experiences of the thousands of American fighting men who served in that long and unpopular war. Excerpts 7 and 8 are taken from Mark Baker, *Nam: The Vietnam War in the Words of the Men and Women Who Fought There.* Baker does not identify his informants so these two excerpts are presented without biographical data.[4]

EXCERPT 7

My second year in Nam I got into the Air Wing. All I . . . did was smoke pot and ride gunner on helicopters. But they were beginning to send Marines back, and they were trying to push me back to the States again. I wasn't having any of that. I had to go up in front of a full bird colonel and lie to him about why I had to stay in Vietnam. Here I am, an Italian boy from Brooklyn, New York. I told the colonel that I took some money from loan sharks back home and I'm in trouble, they're going to kill me and hurt my family. As the colonel can see, if he checks my records, I've been saving my money and I ain't been on R&R—which luckily was true. He fell for it. What does he know? He's from Fishbite Falls somewheres, right? He let me stay.

I was going to stay a third year, but they gave me a year early-out and made me go back home. Some guys they had to lock up because they wouldn't leave Vietnam. A lot of guys wanted to die there. I mean, I wanted to die there. . . .

EXCERPT 8

I went home straight from California to O'Hare Airport in Chicago. I got home about three in the morning. Everybody in the house got up and said hello. Then they all went back to sleep. At 8:30 when my father left for work, he woke me up to say, "Listen, now that you're home, when are you going to get a job?"

I packed up and left. I haven't been home since.

As with World War II, the experience of black soldiers in Vietnam was unlike that of white soldiers although the United States army had been integrated by the 1960s and black soldiers met less systematic discrimination. Excerpts 9 and 10 are from Wallace Terry, *Bloods: An Oral History of the Vietnam War by Black Veterans.*[5]

EXCERPT 9

From Specialist 4 Charles Strong, of a South Carolina migrant background, who served one year as a machine gunner in Vietnam.

When I was in Vietnam, it was not important to me where I died. Now it is very important to me. I made a promise in 'Nam that I would never risk my life or limb to protect anybody else's property. I will protect my own. So this country is not going to tell me to go out again to stop the spread of communism. In Germany we were buying beef for the GIs that came from Communist countries. They telling us to fight the spread of Communism, but they be helping the Communist economy. I don't walk around blind anymore. If another war breaks out and they want me to go, I'd rather die. I'll fight anyone here in America. But if they come and get me to send to some other country, I'm going to have my gun ready for them.

EXCERPT 10

From Norman Alexander McDaniel who spent more than six years as a captive of the North Vietnamese.

My personal feeling is that black people have problems and still have problems in America. But I never told them [his captors] that, because I had no

[5]From Wallace Terry, *Bloods: An Oral History of the Vietnam War by Black Veterans.* Reprinted by permission of Random House, Inc. Copyright © 1984 by Wallace Terry.

intention of helping them to defeat us. We deal with our problems within our own country. Some people just do not live up to the great ideals our country stands for. And some blacks don't take advantage of the privileges and opportunities we have. Although black people are kind of behind the power curtain, we have just as much claim to this country as any white man. America is the black man's best hope.

10
CONTEMPORARY AMERICA
GENERAL INTERPRETATION
AND HISTORIOGRAPHY

During the 1960s and early 1970s, Americans participated in an intense and bitter debate over the Vietnam War. Today that debate continues, although in different form. For when American citizens argue over proper U.S. foreign policy in the contemporary world, they often cite the historical "lessons" of Vietnam, and those lessons are as numerous and contradictory as the foreign policy alternatives that are espoused. To those who favor military intervention in Central America, for example, the key lessons of the Vietnam War are that the United States suffered a devastating defeat because it applied inappropriate strategies and was weakened by a divided populace, and that these problems can and should be eliminated in future conflicts if American security is to be preserved. To those who oppose intervention in Central America, however, the key lessons of Vietnam are that the United States cannot stop third world nationalist revolutions, that it has no business or interest in trying to do so, and that any such effort will only result in disaster. Because each side appeals to basic American principles to support its point of view, this debate contains echoes of the earlier debate over U.S. overseas expansion and participation in World War I.

As the debate illustrates vividly, history involves more than simply what happened in the past. Historians also attempt to understand why

152

events took place, what those events meant during their time, and what they mean today. And while discovering what happened is fairly easy and straightforward, answering these other questions will often lead to debate and disagreement among all citizens, not only historians. This is because individuals view the past from their own perspectives in time and place, and these perspectives are constantly shifting with events and values. As a result, different groups and different generations approach from different vantage points the questions of why events took place and what they mean; they thus draw very different conclusions.

As you studied in the last chapter, these differing vantage points often divide generations in their views of the past. For the generation that came of age during the 1930s and '40s, the most important "lessons" of history involve the dangers of economic depression and the appearance of dictators bent on world conquest; for the generation that came of age during the 1960s and '70s, on the other hand, the greatest danger seems to lie in presidents who abuse and are corrupted by power in the name of a crusade against communism. Differing vantage points also divide individuals within a generation who draw different lessons from the past. President Lyndon Johnson and Senator J. William Fulbright, for example, drew very different historical lessons in their argument over Vietnam; similarly, Republicans and Democrats draw upon very different historical lessons when they disagree over contemporary American foreign policy.

Historians also disagree in their assessments of why events took place and what they mean, for they are as subject as any other individuals to the differing perspectives resulting from different experiences in time and place. Such disagreements concern not historical *facts* but the meaning and *interpretation* of those facts. Analysis of such differences and changes in historical interpretation is part of *historiography,* the study of the writing and writers of history.

In addition to disagreeing over the causes, consequences, and meaning of specific events, historians also disagree over the general conclusions that should be drawn regarding the entire sweep of American history. More than is the case with individual events, such disagreements divide historians by generations and generational perspectives. It is no accident, for example, that the generation which lived through the Great Depression tended to interpret the American past largely in economic terms. Nor is it accidental that many members of the next generation of historians, having experienced the ideological excesses of the Cold War and McCarthyism, rejected economic analyses in favor of a new emphasis on moral and/or psychological factors.

This chapter is designed to introduce you to these broad interpretations of the past and, in the process, to help you reach some conclusions of your own about American history and your place in it. At the end of this chapter you will find a historiographical essay that explains the general conclusions reached by different historians regarding the central themes of American history. As you read this essay and study these differing interpretations, you should realize that each interpretation is closely related to the era in which it was written. You should also realize that these interpretations are not to be approached simply on the basis of "right" vs. "wrong," but rather on the basis of why they made sense during their time and which one, either individually or in combination with others, best accounts today for the *totality* of the American experience.

Since you are part of a new generation in American history, none of these interpretations may appear totally satisfactory to you. None of the historians discussed grew up in your environment, and none of them can view the past and present the way you do. As the historian Carl Becker pointed out many years ago, each of us is our own historian, interpreting the past in light of our own experiences with the present as well as our knowledge about the past and acting accordingly. It is therefore only proper that your last assignment involve interpreting the American past in a way that is meaningful for you.

ASSIGNMENTS

1. Read the historiographical essay and excerpts provided at the end of this chapter, along with any information on conflicting interpretations that your textbook may provide.
2. After completing this reading, think about your own past and choose a public event that occurred during your lifetime and that you presently believe to be the most significant event in your lifetime for the study and understanding of American history.
3. Using the appropriate skills discussed in different chapters of this volume, write a two- to five-page (500- to 1,500-word) essay in which you

   a. explain this event
   b. place it within the context of a broad issue or issues running through all of American history since 1876
   c. trace and interpret one of those issues in such a way as to show that it is a major theme in American history. You may select one of the themes used by other historians and discussed in the historiographical essay, or you may select another one of your own choosing.

For example, if you were the same age as your instructors in this course, you might very well pick the Army-McCarthy hearings of 1954, or McCarthyism in general. You would explain and interpret this phenomenon, and would point out that it is a fairly recent example of a series of strong themes throughout American history, the most obvious of which is anticommunism. You would argue that McCarthyism is also a classic example of at least two other broader and deeper themes in the American past: (1) intolerance for dissent and those whom the majority calls deviant and (2) a search for internal scapegoats when events appear to threaten the nation. You would then choose one of these themes and trace it from the attacks on blacks and immigrants in the late nineteenth century, through the anti-German crusade of World War I, the "red scare" of 1919, the fundamentalist attack on the teaching of evolution during the 1920s, and the internment of Japanese-Americans during World War II. Finally, you would reach a set of conclusions that incorporated your data in such a way as to offer a general interpretation of the American past.

ADDITIONAL QUESTIONS TO CONSIDER

1. Why do you believe the event you chose is the most significant in your lifetime for the study of American history? What possible future events could lead you to choose a different event?
2. How does your interpretation relate to the previous historical interpretations discussed below? If you chose one of those interpretations, what events in your lifetime make that interpretation relevant and meaningful to you? If you chose a different one, why? In other words, analyze yourself and your environment in order to explain why you view the American past as you do.
3. What interpretations of the American past did you hold when this course began? To what extent have those interpretations changed and why?
4. Compare your event and interpretation with those chosen and developed by other students in the class. Does a pattern emerge? If so, why? If not, which events and interpretations appear most valid to you, and why?

GENERAL INTERPRETATIONS OF AMERICAN HISTORY

Three major interpretations dominated historical writing in the United States from the nineteenth century through World War II: the nationalist or "Whig" approach of George Bancroft; the frontier thesis of Frederick Jackson Turner; and the economic class-conflict analysis of Charles Beard. Each of these is discussed below, and excerpts from each are presented. Then several approaches and syntheses that have arisen since World War II are presented; a concluding section comments upon these interpretations.

GEORGE BANCROFT AND THE NATIONALIST INTERPRETATION

The nationalist or "Whig" approach perceives the United States as the cradle and laboratory of world progressive values. It interprets American history as the evolution and triumph of those values—most notably democracy and individual liberty—over the forces of tyranny and special privilege. All the great popular movements and individuals in American history, it maintains, are linked by this common ideological thread, and their triumph has ensured the preservation and victory of human rights both within the United States and around the world.

George Bancroft, one of the earliest American historians, was also one of the first to use this approach. During his long and productive life (1800–1891), he not only wrote American history but also participated in its making as a high-ranking Democrat (secretary of the Navy and ambassador to London and Berlin); his historical perspective subsequently tended to associate the triumphs of democracy with the triumphs of the Democratic party. Nevertheless, he was a superb historian and is remembered today as the "father" of American history.

Bancroft's approach clearly reflected the values of the era in which he lived. Ever since the Puritans landed in Massachusetts in the early seventeenth century, Americans had tended to see themselves as a unique, "chosen" people with a world mission and to equate their own historical experiences with those of the Old Testament Israelites. After the American Revolution, this view was secularized and nationalized, becoming synonymous with American patriotism. According to this vision, the United States was a unique and divinely inspired nation whose birth and development were the keys to an unfolding millenium of human freedom and progress. In such a vision, all events in American history were, by definition, part of God's plan, and the entire emerging pattern held vast significance for all peoples.

Despite its age, Bancroft's interpretation remains one of the most popular and accepted explanations of the American past. In its most common form, it links the Jacksonian Democrats of the 1830s, the antislavery North during the Civil War, the progressives during the early twentieth century, the New Deal during the Great Depression, and the American role in the two world wars and the Cold War with the original principles of the American Revolution. The resulting vision of triumphant liberty and democracy as exemplified by the United States can still be found in almost all political speeches, in many textbooks, and, too, in the writings, both historical and political, of Bancroft's descendant Arthur Schlesinger, Jr.

The following excerpts, which illustrate this approach to American history, are taken from Bancroft's multivolume *History of the United States of America*.

The United States of America constitute an essential portion of a great political system, embracing all the civilized nations of the earth. At a period when the force of moral opinion is rapidly increasing, they have the precedence in the practice and the defence of the equal rights of man. The sovereignty of the people is here a conceded axiom, and the laws, established upon that basis, are cherished with faithful patriotism. While the nations of Europe aspire after change, our constitution engages the fond admiration of the people, by which it has been established. Prosperity follows the execution of even justice; invention is quickened by the freedom of competition; and labor rewarded with sure and unexampled returns. Domestic peace is maintained without the aid of a military establishment; public sentiment permits the existence of but few standing troops, and those only along the seaboard and on the frontiers.

A gallant navy protects our commerce, which spreads its banners on every sea, and extends its enterprise to every clime. Our diplomatic relations connect us on terms of equality and honest friendship with the chief powers of the world, while we avoid entangling participation in their intrigues, their passions, and their ways. Our national resources are developed by an earnest culture of the arts of peace. Every man may enjoy the fruits of his industry; every mind is free to publish its convictions. Our government, by its organizations, is necessarily identified with the interests of the people, and relies exclusively on their attachment for its durability and support. Even the enemies of the state, if there are any among us, have liberty to express their opinions undisturbed; and are safely tolerated where reason is left free to combat their errors. Nor is the constitution a dead letter, unalterably fixed: it has the capacity for improvement, adopting whatever changes time and the public will may require, and safe from decay so long as that will retains its energy. New states are forming in the wilderness; canals, intersecting our plains and crossing our highlands, open numerous channels to internal commerce; manufactures prosper along our watercourses; the use of steam on our rivers and railroads annihilates distance by the acceleration of speed. Our wealth and population, already giving us a place in the first rank of nations, are so rapidly cumulative that the former is increased fourfold, and the latter is doubled, in every period of twenty-two or twenty-three years. There is no national debt, the government is economical, and the public treasury full. Religion, neither persecuted nor paid by the state, is sustained by the regard for public morals and the earnestness of an enlightened faith. Intelligence is diffused with unparalleled universality; a free press teems with the choicest productions of all nations and ages. There are more daily journals in the United States than in the world beside. A public document of general interest is, within a month, reproduced in at least a million of copies, and is brought within the reach of every freeman in the country. An immense concourse of emigrants of the most various lineage is perpetually crowding to our shores, and the principles of liberty, uniting all interests by the operation of equal laws, blend the discordant elements into harmonious union. Other governments are convulsed by the innovations and reforms of neighboring states; our constitution, fixed in the affections of the people, from whose choice it has sprung, neutralizes the influence of foreign principles, and fearlessly opens an asylum to the virtuous, the unfortunate, and the oppressed of every nation.

And yet it is but little more than two centuries since the oldest of our states received its first permanent colony. Before that time the whole territory was an unproductive waste. Throughout its wide extent the arts had not erected a monument. Its only inhabitants were a few scattered tribes of feeble barbarians, destitute of commerce and of political connection. The axe and the ploughshare were unknown. The soil, which had been gathering fertility from the repose of ages, was lavishing its strength in magnificant but useless vegetation. In the view of civilization the immense domain was a solitude.

It is the object of the present work to explain how the change in the condition of our land has been brought about; and, as the fortunes of a nation are not under the control of blind destiny, to follow the steps by which a favoring Providence, calling our institutions into being, has conducted the country to its present happiness and glory.

1834.

The foregoing words, written nearly a half-century ago, are suffered to remain, because intervening years have justified their expression of confidence in the progress of our republic. The seed of disunion has perished; and universal freedom, reciprocal benefits, and cherished traditions bind its many states in the closest union.

1882.

FREDERICK JACKSON TURNER AND THE FRONTIER INTERPRETATION

In 1893, a young historian named Frederick Jackson Turner suggested that the frontier held the key to understanding America's national character and history. Signifying a constantly moving line that separated the edge of white settlement from the wilderness, this frontier had long been one of the most distinguishing characteristics of the United States. According to Turner, it was also the birthplace of the most important American values, characteristics, ideas, movements, and people. Democracy, individualism, nationalism, practicality, and ingenuity, for example, were all traits that arose out of the frontier experience. Furthermore, with each successive movement of that frontier, these traits were constantly reaffirmed until they became key components of the American psyche. The most important aspects of American history and life, Turner concluded, could be understood only in reference to the unprecedented existence of this fluid frontier.

It is no accident that Turner wrote his thesis during a decade that, ironically, witnessed the declaration of the end of the frontier by the Bureau of the Census as well as severe economic depression and domestic turmoil and the beginnings of American overseas imperialism. For Turner and for many Americans, these events were closely linked and only reinforced an age-old American belief in the necessity for a frontier to ensure domestic tranquillity and certain values. According to recent historians, Turner's thesis thus stands as a primary source for the 1890s, an explanation of American imperialism, and a secondary interpretation of the American past.

This interpretation—the frontier thesis—was the first to emphasize material factors of the environment over ideas and to see development of the United States in American rather than European terms. Despite the fact that careful historical study has cast doubt upon the validity of many of its assertions, Turner's thesis remains today a major school of interpretation and the focal point for much historical discussion. It has also become a key component of the national mythology, as is clearly seen by the continuing American love affair with the cowboy.

The following excerpts are taken from Turner's famous 1893 essay "The Significance of the Frontier in American History," reprinted in *The Annual Report of the American Historical Association for the Year 1893.*

Up to our own day American history has been in a large degree the history of the colonization of the Great West. The existence of an area of free land, its continuous recession, and the advance of American settlement westward, explain American development.

. . . American social development has been continually beginning over again on the frontier. This perennial rebirth, this fluidity of American life, this expansion westward with its new opportunities, its continuous touch with the simplicity of primitive society, furnish the forces dominating American character. The true point of view in the history of this nation is not the Atlantic coast, it is the great West.

. . . Our early history is the study of European germs developing in an American environment. Too exclusive attention has been paid by institutional students to the Germanic origins, too little to the American factors. The frontier is the line of most rapid and effective Americanization. The wilderness masters the colonist. . . . Little by little he transforms the wilderness, but the outcome is not the old Europe. . . . here is a new product that is American. . . . each frontier leaves its traces behind, and when it becomes a settled area the region still partakes of the frontier characteristics. Thus the advance of the frontier has meant a steady movement away from the influence of Europe, a steady growth of independence on American lines. And to study this advance . . . is to study the really American part of our history.

. . . the frontier promoted the formation of a composite nationality for the American people. . . . In the crucible of the frontier the immigrants were Americanized, liberated, and fused into a mixed race, English in neither nationality or characteristics. . . .

In another way the advance of the frontier decreased our dependence on England. . . . Before long the frontier created a demand for merchants. As it retreated from the coast it became less and less possible for England to bring her supplies directly to the consumer's wharfs, and carry away staple crops, and staple crops began to give way to diversified agriculture for a time. The effect of this phase of the frontier action upon the northern section is perceived when we realize how the advance of the frontier aroused seaboard cities. . . .

The legislation which most developed the powers of the National Government, and played the largest part in its activity, was conditioned on the frontier. Writers have discussed the subjects of tariff, land, and internal improvements, as subsidiary to the slavery question. But when American history comes to be rightly viewed it will be seen that the slavery question is an incident. . . . The growth of nationalism and the evolution of American political institutions were dependent on the advance of the frontier. . . .

The public domain has been a force of profound importance in the nationalization and development of the Government. . . . Administratively the frontier called out some of the highest and most vitalizing activities of the General Government. . . . As frontier States accrued to the Union the national power grew. . . .

It is safe to say that the legislation with regard to land, tariff and internal improvements . . . was conditioned on frontier ideas and needs. But it was not merely in legislative action that the frontier worked against the sectionalism of the coast. The economic and social characteristics of the frontier worked against sectionalism.

It was this nationalizing tendency of the West that transformed the democracy of Jefferson into the national republicanism of Monroe and the democracy of Andrew Jackson. The West . . . , shut off by the Middle States and the mountains from the coast sections, had a solidarity of its own with national tendencies. On the tide of the Father of Waters, North and South met and mingled into a nation. The fierce struggle of the sections over slavery on the western frontier does not diminish the truth of this statement; it proves the truth of it. Slavery was a sectional trait that would not down, but in the West it could not remain sectional. . . .

But the most important effect of the frontier has been in the promotion of democracy here and in Europe. . . . the frontier is productive of individualism. Complex society is precipitated by the wilderness into a kind of primitive organization based on the family. The tendency is anti-social. It produces antipathy to control, and particularly to any direct control. . . . frontier individualism has from the beginning promoted democracy.

The frontier states that came into the Union in the first quarter of a century of its existence came in with democratic suffrage provisions, and had reactive effects of the highest importance upon the older States whose peoples

were being attracted there. An extension of the franchise became essential.
. . . The rise of democracy as an effective force in the nation came in with
western preponderance under Jackson and William Henry Harrison, and it
meant the triumph of the frontier with all its good and with all its evil elements. . . .

So long as free land exists, the opportunity for a competency exists,
and economic power secures political power, but the democracy born of free
land, strong in selfishness and individualism, intolerant of administrative
experience and education, and pressing beyond its proper bounds, has its
dangers as well as its benefits. Individualism in America has allowed a
laxity in regard to governmental affairs which has rendered the spoils system and all the manifest evil that follow from the lack of a highly developed
civic spirit. In this connection may be noted also the influence of frontier
conditions in permitting lax business honor, inflated paper currency and
wild-cat banking. . . .

From the conditions of frontier life came intellectual traits of profound
importance. . . . to the frontier the American intellect owes its striking characteristics. That coarseness and strength combined with acuteness and inquisi-
tiveness; that practical, inventive turn of mind, quick to find expedients; that
masterful grasp of material things, lacking in the artistic but powerful to effect
great ends; that restless, nervous energy; that dominant individualism, working for good and for evil, and withal that buoyancy and exuberance which
comes with freedom—these are traits of the frontier, or traits called out elsewhere because of the existence of the frontier. Since the days when the fleet
of Columbus sailed into the waters of the New World, America has been
another name for opportunity, and the people of the United States have taken
their tone from the incessant expansion which has not only been open but has
even been forced upon them. He would be a rash prophet who should assert
that the expansive character of American life has now entirely ceased. Movement has been its dominant fact, and, unless this training has no effect upon
a people, the American energy will continually demand a wider field for its
exercise. But never again will such gifts of free land offer themselves. For a
moment, at the frontier, the bonds of custom are broken and unrestraint is
triumphant. There is not *tabula rasa.* The stubborn American environment is
there with its imperious summons to accept its conditions; the inherited ways
of doing things were also there; and yet in spite of environment, and in spite
of custom, each frontier did indeed furnish a new field of opportunity, a gate
of escape from the bondage of the past; and freshness, and confidence, and
scorn of older society, impatience of its restraints and its ideas, and indifference to its lessons, have accompanied the frontier. What the Mediterranean
Sea was to the Greeks, breaking the bond of custom, offering new experiences,

calling out new institutions and activities, that, and more, the ever retreating frontier has been to the United States directly, and to the nations of Europe more remotely. And now, four centuries from the discovery of America, at the end of a hundred years of life under the Constitution, the frontier has gone, and with its going has closed the first period of American history.

CHARLES BEARD AND THE ECONOMIC INTERPRETATION

In 1913 Charles Beard, a young historian from Columbia University, shocked the historical profession with the publication of *An Economic Interpretation of the Constitution.* Attacking the then accepted notion that the Constitution had been written by a group of brilliant, disinterested patriots, Beard interpreted the document as a conservative, counterrevolutionary effort by individuals with specific economic and class interests at stake.

Beard's work began a thirty-eight-year process of reinterpreting much of America's past. A large number of historians after Beard argued that American history could be understood only by examining the underlying economic forces at work and the social classes those forces had produced. They saw the struggle among these forces and classes—most notably between agrarians and commercial/industrial capitalists in the eighteenth and nineteenth centuries—as the basic causal factor in all the major struggles and events of the American past. The Revolution, Constitution, Federalist-Republican controversy, Jacksonian era, and Civil War were thus, in actuality, all class struggles between these two groups, with the northern victory in 1865 marking the final triumph of an industrial order in the United States and the beginnings of conflict between the industrial classes —most notably capital and labor—that has dominated American history ever since.

Class conflict had been a key component in the Marxist view of history long before Beard and his students began writing, but it was only in the early twentieth century, when the progressive and New Deal movements and the Great Depression emphasized the evils of unregulated capitalism, that a modified form of this approach to history became popular in the United States. Interestingly, public acceptance of this approach was in no way equated with an acceptance of the Marxist view of history. Rather, the class conflict historians and their followers used this analysis to call for a peaceful reform, rather than a violent eradication, of American capitalism. In this sense, their interpretations fit in perfectly with the reformist spirit of the progressive movement and the New Deal, even though their analyses pointed to the need for more drastic change.

Beard himself was the most prolific and brilliant historian within this group, and his numerous works dominated American historiography for much of this century. Although recent scholarship has questioned many of his conclusions and methods, numerous historians still adhere to his general approach to the study of American history.

Reprinted below is the concluding section of Beard's 1913 *An Economic Interpretation of the Constitution,* followed by excerpts from his introduction to the 1935 edition of that volume. In this introduction, Beard explained the origins of his economic approach and the political environment in which his 1913 study was written while replying to some of his critics.

Conclusions

At the close of this long and arid survey—partaking of the nature of catalogue—it seems worth while to bring together the important conclusions for political science which the data presented appear to warrant.

The movement for the Constitution of the United States was originated and carried through principally by four groups of personalty interests which had been adversely affected under the Articles of Confederation: money, public securities, manufactures, and trade and shipping.

The first firm steps toward the formation of the Constitution were taken by a small and active group of men immediately interested through their personal possessions in the outcome of their labors.

No popular vote was taken directly or indirectly on the proposition to call the Convention which drafted the Constitution.

A large propertyless mass was, under the prevailing suffrage qualifications, excluded at the outset from participation (through representatives) in the work of framing the Constitution.

The members of the Philadelphia Convention which drafted the Constitution were, with a few exceptions, immediately, directly, and personally interested in, and derived economic advantages from, the establishment of the new system.

The Constitution was essentially an economic document based upon the concept that the fundamental private rights of property are anterior to government and morally beyond the reach of popular majorities.

The major portion of the members of the Convention are on record as recognizing the claim of property to a special and defensive position in the Constitution.

In the ratification of the Constitution, about three-fourths of the adult males failed to vote on the question, having abstained from the elections at which delegates to the state conventions were chosen, either on account of their indifference or their disfranchisement by property qualifications.

The Constitution was ratified by a vote of probably not more than one-sixth of the adult males.

It is questionable whether a majority of the voters participating in the elections for the state conventions in New York, Massachusetts, New Hampshire, Virginia, and South Carolina, actually approved the ratification of the Constitution.

The leaders who supported the Constitution in the ratifying conventions represented the same economic groups as the members of the Philadelphia Convention; and in a large number of instances they were also directly and personally interested in the outcome of their efforts.

In the ratification, it became manifest that the line of cleavage for and against the Constitution was between substantial personalty interests on the one hand and the small farming and debtor interests on the other.

The Constitution was not created by "the whole people" as the jurists have said; neither was it created by "the states" as Southern nullifiers long contended; but it was the work of a consolidated group whose interests knew no state boundaries and were truly national in their scope.

Introduction to the 1935 Edition

THIS volume was first issued in 1913 during the tumult of discussion that accompanied the advent of the Progressive party, the split in Republican ranks, and the conflict over the popular election of United States Senators, workmen's compensation, and other social legislation. At that time Theodore Roosevelt had raised fundamental questions under the head of "the New Nationalism" and proposed to make the Federal Government adequate to the exigencies created by railways, the consolidation of industries, the closure of free land on the frontier, and the new position of labor in American economy. In the course of developing his conceptions, Mr. Roosevelt drew into consideration the place of the judiciary in the American system. While expressing high regard for that branch of government, he proposed to place limitations on its authority. He contended that "by the abuse of the power to declare laws unconstitutional the courts have become a law-making instead of a law-enforcing agency." As a check upon judicial proclivities, he proposed a scheme for "the recall of judicial decisions." This project he justified by the assertion that "when a court decides a constitutional question, when it decides what the people as a whole can or cannot do, the people should have the right to recall that decision when they think it wrong." Owing to such declarations, and to the counter-declarations, the "climate of opinion" was profoundly disturbed when *An Economic Interpretation of the Constitution* originally appeared.

Yet in no sense was the volume a work of the occasion, written with reference to immediate controversies. Doubtless I was, in common with all other students, influenced more or less by "the spirit of the times," but I had in mind no thought of forwarding the interests of the Progressive party or of its conservative critics and opponents. I had taken up the study of the Constitution many years before the publication of my work, while a profound calm rested on the sea of constitutional opinion. In that study I had occasion to read voluminous writings by the Fathers, and I was struck by the emphasis which so many of them placed upon economic interests as forces in politics and in the formulation of laws and constitutions. In particular I was impressed by the philosophy of politics set forth by James Madison in Number X of the *Federalist,* which seemed to furnish a clue to practical operations connected with the formation of the Constitution—operations in which Madison himself took a leading part.

[Beard was referring here particularly to Madison's idea that economic interests shaped politics. Madison wrote in *Federalist* Number X: "The diversity in the faculties of men, from which the rights of property originate, is not less an insuperable obstacle to a uniformity of interests. The protection of these faculties is the first object of government. From the protection of different and unequal faculties of acquiring property, the possession of different degrees and kinds of property immediately results; and from the influence of these on the sentiments and views of the respective proprietors, ensues a division of society into different interests and parties. . . . The most common and durable source of factions has been the various and unequal distribution of property. Those who hold and those who are without property have ever formed distinct interests in society. Those who are creditors, and those who are debtors, fall under a like discrimination. A landed interest, a manufacturing interest, a mercantile interest, a moneyed interest, with many lesser interests, grow up of necessity in civilized nations and divide them into different classes, actuated by different sentiments and views. The regulation of these various and interfering interests forms the principal task of modern legislation, and involves the spirit of party and faction in the necessary and ordinary operations of the government."]

. . .

One thing . . . my masters taught me, and that was to go behind the pages of history written by my contemporaries and read "the sources." In applying this method, I read the letters, papers, and documents pertaining to the Constitution written by the men who took part in framing and adopting it. And to my surprise I found that many Fathers of the Republic regarded the conflict over the Constitution as springing essentially out of conflicts of economic interests, which had a certain geographical or sectional distribution. This discovery, coming at a time when such conceptions of history were neglected by writers on history, gave me "the shock of my life." And since this aspect of the Constitution had been so long disregarded, I sought to redress the balance by emphasis, "naturally" perhaps. At all events I called my volume "an economic interpretation of the Constitution." I did not call it "the" economic interpretation, or "the only" interpretation possible to thought. Nor did I pretend that it was "the history" of the formation and adoption of the Constitution. The reader was warned in advance of the theory and the emphasis. No attempt was made to take him off his guard by some plausible formula of completeness and comprehensiveness. I simply sought to bring back into the mental picture of the Constitution those realistic features of economic conflict, stress, and strain, which my masters had, for some reason, left out of it, or thrust far into the background as incidental rather than fundamental. In the minds of some, the term "Marxian," . . . means an epithet; and in the minds of others, praise. With neither of these views have I the least concern. For myself I can say that I have never believed that "all history" can or must be "explained" in economic terms, or any other terms. He who really "explains" history must have the attributes ascribed by the theologians to God. It can be "explained," no doubt, to the satisfaction of certain mentalities at certain times, but such explanations are not universally accepted and approved. I confess to have hoped in my youth to find "the causes of things," but I never thought that I had found them. Yet it has seemed to me, and does now, that in the great transformations in society, such as was brought about by the formation and adoption of the Constitution, economic "forces" are primordial or fundamental, and come nearer "explaining" events than any other "forces." Where the configurations and pressures of economic interests are brought into an immediate relation to the event or series of events under consideration, an economic interpretation is effected. Yet, as I said in 1913, on page 18, "It may be that some larger world process is working through each series of historical events; but ultimate causes lie beyond our horizon." If anywhere I have said or written that "all history" can be "explained" in economic terms, I was then suffering from an aberration of the mind.

Nor can I accept as a historical fact . . . that the economic interpretation of history or my volume on the Constitution had its origin in "Marxian theories." As I point out in Chapter I of my *Economic Basis of Politics,* the germinal idea of class and group conflicts in history appeared in the writings of Aristotle, long before the Christian era, and was known to great writers on politics during the middle ages and modern times. It was expounded by James Madison, in Number X of the *Federalist,* written in defense of the Constitution of the United States, long before Karl Marx was born. Marx seized upon the idea, applied it with rigor, and based predictions upon it, but he did not originate it. Fathers of the American Constitution were well aware of the idea, operated on the hypothesis that it had at least a considerable validity, and expressed it in numerous writings. Whether conflicting economic interests bulk large in contemporary debates over protective tariffs, foreign trade, transportation, industry, commerce, labor, agriculture, and the nature of the

Constitution itself, each of our contemporaries may decide on the basis of his experience and knowledge.

Two other *caveats* should be entered. It has been lightly assumed by superficial critics, if not readers of the volume, that I have "accused the members of the Convention of working merely for their own pockets." The falsity of this charge can be seen by reference to page 73 of the original text still standing. There I say clearly: "The only point considered here is: Did they [the members] represent distinct groups whose economic interests they understood and felt in concrete, definite form through their own personal experience with identical property rights, or were they working merely under the guidance of abstract principles of political science?"

It has also been lightly assumed that this volume pretends to show that the form of government established and powers conferred were "determined" in every detail by the conflict of economic interests. Such pretension was never in my mind; nor do I think that it is explicit or implicit in the pages which follow. I have never been able to discover all-pervading determinism in history. In that field of study I find, what Machiavelli found, *virtù, fortuna,* and *necessitá,* although the boundaries between them cannot be sharply delimited. There is determinism, necessity, in the world of political affairs; and it bears a relation to economic interests; otherwise Congress might vote $25,000 a year in present values to every family in the United States, and the Soviet Government might make every Russian rich; but this is not saying that every event, every institution, every personal decision is "determined" by discoverable "causes."

Nevertheless, whoever leaves economic pressures out of history or out of the discussion of public questions is in mortal peril of substituting mythology for reality and confusing issues instead of clarifying them. It was largely by recognizing the power of economic interests in the field of politics and making skillful use of them that the Fathers of the American Constitution placed themselves among the great practicing statesmen of all ages and gave instructions to succeeding generations in the art of government. By the assiduous study of their works and by displaying their courage and their insight into the economic interests underlying all constitutional formalities, men and women of our generation may guarantee the perpetuity of government under law, as distinguished from the arbitrament of force. It is for us, recipients of their heritage, to inquire constantly and persistently, when theories of national power or states' rights are propounded: "What interests are behind them and to whose advantage will changes or the maintenance of old forms accrue?" By refusing to do this we become victims of history—clay in the hands of its makers.

CHARLES A. BEARD.

RECENT INTERPRETATIONS

The interpretations of Bancroft, Turner, and Beard dominated historical writing in the United States through World War II. Beginning with the 1950s, however, a new generation of historians began to reexamine the American past.

Many of these historians used a revised and updated nationalist approach. While accepting portions of the Turner and Beard analyses, they viewed ideas as more important than material factors and returned to the evolution of liberty and democracy as the key theme in American history. Some, like Arthur Schlesinger, Jr., adopted a Bancroft-like stress on the importance of the Democratic party in this evolution. Others, however, maintained that too much emphasis was still being placed on conflict in the American past.

Labeled "consensus historians," these individuals argued that the truly distinguishing characteristic of American history was the lack of real conflict over broad social goals. Louis Hartz noted in *The Liberal Tradition in America* (1955) that the United States, with no feudal past and thus no true class consciousness, had never developed any conservative or radical alternatives to the prevailing middle-class, liberal ideology. Because of this basic ideological agreement, Americans had throughout their history shown an extraordinary willingness to work out their differences within the existing political structure and to accept compromise.

Historians like Daniel Boorstin, in *The Genius of American Politics* (1953), celebrated these results. Others like David Potter, in *People of Plenty* (1954), placed them within a modified frontier framework by arguing that the key to understanding most American characteristics, including this lack of serious conflict, was the existence of unprecedented material abundance throughout American history. A few historians even combined the consensus findings with a modified Beardian approach, but their conclusions were far less optimistic than those of Boorstin and Potter.

Richard Hofstadter, in many ways the most prominent historian of this era, belongs to this latter group. Using psychology and other tools of the social sciences, Hofstadter pointed out in a series of pivotal works that the American consensus had led to some fundamental problems. Hofstadter maintained that most American reform movements had been primarily motivated not by any desire for meaningful change but by the need to work out mass neuroses that had arisen because of society's refusal to come to grips with the very real changes caused by economic and class factors. As a result, these movements had accomplished very little, had often degenerated into witch-hunts, and—in the process—had revealed prominent negative characteristics. Hofstadter chose two of these as titles for two of his major works: *Anti-Intellectualism in American Life* (1963) and *The Paranoid Style in American Politics* (1965).

During the early 1960s, William Appleman Williams also pointed out severe weaknesses in the American consensus, but he relied more heavily on Turner and Beard and much less on psychological factors than had Hofstadter. In *The Contours of American History* (1961), Williams argued that the consensus had been maintained only by using expansion onto the frontier as a means of escaping the challenges and contradictions posed to American liberalism by the economic and class realities of American history. The frontier was of pivotal importance in the American past, but not in the positive way Turner had seen it. To the contrary, it was a critical component of what Williams referred to as *The Great Evasion* (1964) of American history. Using this analysis in much the same way as Beard's followers had used his approach, Williams's students reinterpreted much of American history during the 1960s.

Each of these post-World War II interpretations was closely linked to the events of that era. Consensus history, for example, reflected an intellectual rejection of Marxist-originated class conflict and economic determinism—a rejection that fit in perfectly with the Cold War against the Soviet Union. The acceptance of psychological interpretations, in turn, offered an alternative analytic framework to Marxism as well as a way to lump communism with the other "dangerous" and "irrational" popular movements of fascism and McCarthyism. With the Vietnam War and the domestic turmoil of the 1960s, however, many Americans began to question the basic tenets of the Cold War and the American consensus theory. The result was the development of a new analysis of American history that also served as a radical critique of American actions and values in the 1960s.

Yet, none of these post-World War II interpretations was completely new. Each contained elements of the three original interpretations of American history as well as new insights, and they thereby illustrated, once again, the continuity that exists in historical interpretations. Furthermore, *all* interpretations of the American past, from Bancroft through Williams, have shared a key belief in the uniqueness of the American experience. There are signs that this basic assumption may be the next to be questioned by American historians in the 1980s.

ABOUT THE AUTHORS

Mark A. Stoler was born in New York City in 1945. He received his B.A. from the City College of New York in 1966, and his M.A. and Ph.D. in history from the University of Wisconsin in 1967 and 1971. Specializing in U.S. diplomatic and military history, he has authored *The Politics of the Second Front* (Greenwood, 1977) and a series of articles dealing with World War II strategy, diplomacy, and historiography, the Vietnam war, and the teaching of U.S. history. He has been a member of the History Department at the University of Vermont since 1970, and in 1984 he received the University's Outstanding Faculty award. He has also been a lecturer at the University of Wisconsin—Milwaukee, a visiting professor in the Strategy Department of the Naval War College in Newport, Rhode Island, and a Fulbright lecturer at the University of Haifa in Israel.

Marshall True has degrees from Bates College (B.A.) and the University of Virginia (M.A., Ph.D.) and has been teaching American history for twenty years. A specialist in the cultural and social history of the nineteenth century, Professor True recently edited and compiled, with William A. Doyle, *Vermont and the New Nation,* a collection of documents illustrating the national context of Vermont's founding. He also edits the journal *Vermont History* and is working on a biography of nineteenth-century scholar and soldier Ethan Allen Hitchcock. At the University of Vermont since 1967, Marshall True lives in East Fairfield with Charon True, an attorney, and is the father of four children: daughters Julia and Katherine, and twin sons Adam and Steven.

A NOTE ON THE TYPE

The text of this book was composed in Melior, a typeface designed by Hermann Zapf and issued in 1952. Born in Nürnberg, Germany, in 1918, Zapf has been a strong influence in printing since 1939. Melior, like Times Roman, another popular twentieth-century typeface, was created specifically for use in newspaper composition.